MATILDA COXE STEVENSON

MATILDA COXE STEVENSON

Pioneering Anthropologist

By Darlis A. Miller

UNIVERSITY OF OKLAHOMA PRESS : NORMAN

Library of Congress Cataloging-in-Publication Data

Miller, Darlis A., 1939–
    Matilda Coxe Stevenson : pioneering anthropologist / by Darlis A. Miller.
        p.   cm.
    Includes bibliographical references and index.
    ISBN 978-0-8061-3832-9 (hardcover) ISBN 978-0-8061-9311-3 (paper)
    1. Stevenson, Matilda Coxe, 1850–1915. 2. Indianists—Southwest, New—Bio-
graphy. 3. Women Indianists—Southwest, New—Biography. 4. Pueblo Indians—
Social life and customs. 5. Southwest, New—Social life and customs. I. Title.

    E57.S74M56 2007
    301.092—dc22
    [B]

                                                                      2007010404

The paper in this book meets the guidelines for permanence and durability of
the Committee on Production Guidelines for Book Longevity of the Council on
Library Resources. ∞

For August, Dean, Ann D., Sylvia,
Frank, Ann C., Ellen, and Marilyn

Contents

Illustrations

Zia women and girls pounding clay for new camp floor
Matilda Coxe Stevenson in her later years

Maps

Foreword

The history of anthropological research at Zuni Pueblo is, in many ways, a microcosm of the history of American anthropology. It may be inevitable, A. Thomas Kirsch often pointed out, that histories and biographies should create the illusion that anthropology consists of "great men" and "great women" or "great books," or both. Such a view, he was quick to add, is a distortion, as the overwhelming majority of anthropologists have neither been great men or great women, nor have they produced great books. Matilda Coxe Stevenson was a pioneer, and her "The Zuni Indians" (1904) is a "classic" Southwestern ethnology, but Matilda Coxe Stevenson would not be on a list of anthropology's "greats." She was and continues to be marginalized, and yet margins are where the action is.

Margins are sometimes threatening and dangerous, as they touch upon lines and boundaries. Margins are often revealing and exciting, as they draw on the insight and imagination of others. Margins are also betwixt and between, places of risk and failure. Matilda Coxe Stevenson lived on the margins between cultures and on the edges of the emerging discipline of anthropology. She was a woman in a man's world in the Southwest and in Washington, D.C., and she lived on margins that still exist.

When Matilda Coxe Stevenson arrived at Zuni Pueblo in fall 1879 with a Smithsonian Institution–sponsored expedition led by her husband, Colonel James Stevenson, anthropology was only emerging as a discipline. The Stevensons went to the Southwest to gather collections and to engage in other "ethnologic work."

The ethnologists of Tilly's time were not equipped as we are to examine the assumptions we bring with us and the "situated" nature of anthropological inquiry. Anthropology has become increasingly self-conscious regarding the political, epistemological, and biographical contexts in which fieldwork is undertaken. Consequently, when we go to Tilly's work for answers to our questions, we find that her answers—for all their nineteenth-century scientific rigor and concern for accuracy—were shaped by very different (unstated and unexamined) questions. Nevertheless, as Darlis Miller's biography makes clear, Tilly's openness and reflexivity in describing the circumstances of her fieldwork afford us the opportunity to reflect upon the ethics and consequences of interpersonal relationships in cross-cultural understanding and to consider again the questions to which she sought answers.

For some, then, the beginnings of the discipline of anthropology are linked to the development of a particular theoretical perspective and research agenda. Others, however, would date the beginning of anthropology to E. B. Tylor's appointment as reader in anthropology at Oxford in 1884, the year he visited Zuni, met Jim and Tilly Stevenson, and afterward praised the Stevensons' husband-wife approach to their studies, in which "really half of the work of investigation . . . fall[s] to her," especially what can be "learned through the women of the tribe." Before Jim's death in 1888, Tilly's publications included "The Religious Life of the Zuni Child" (1887), and much of her work was with and about women.

Tilly was Jim's constant companion as they collected materials for the Smithsonian Institution at the Rio Grande pueblos, at Zuni, and at the Hopi villages in northeastern Arizona. The Stevensons often visited the trader Thomas V. Keam at his trading post east of the Hopi mesas, where Jim purchased collections of pottery and other artifacts, and the couple enjoyed Keam's hospitality. During

October and November 1885, the Stevensons made collections in the villages on First and Second Mesa and at Oraibi, where a confrontation led to an infamous image of Tilly in the *Illustrated Police News* showing her forcing her way into a Hopi kiva. That event has overshadowed Tilly's unsurpassed documentation of a Navajo Nightway ceremony that took place near Keams Canyon in early October 1885. Authorship of "Ceremonial of Hasjelti Dailjis and Mythical Sand Painting of the Navajo Indians" (1891) was attributed (by Tilly) to James Stevenson. Naakaiisneez (Tall Mexican, known as John Navajo) was acknowledged for his assistance with translation and recording the ritual and narratives associated with it—an uncommon acknowledgment in early ethnographic writing.

In 1890 Tilly became the first and only professional woman permanently employed as a staff ethnologist by the Bureau of Ethnology, a position she held until her death on June 24, 1915. Much of Darlis Miller's biography explores insightfully the contexts and events of Tilly's struggle to accomplish her work as a woman in a world dominated by men, both in Washington, D.C., and in the Southwest.

Nearly a century has passed since Tilly conducted her last research in the Southwest. Triloki Nath Pandey might have included himself when he wrote in 1972, "Few if any other tribal groups have been studied by as many gifted observers and professional anthropologists as the Zuni Indians." He went on to list Stevenson and Cushing and many who followed, including some of the great men and women of anthropology: A. L. Kroeber, Elsie Clews Parsons, Ruth Benedict, Ruth Bunzel, and more recent field-workers. If we add to this list those who studied the Zuni from afar—in libraries, especially in France, rather than in the field—the list is even larger, including Emile Durkheim and Marcel Mauss, Claude Levi-Strauss, Lucien Sebag, and others. Of recent works on Zuni, Dennis Tedlock's *Finding the Center: The Art of the Zuni Storyteller* (1972) and Barbara Tedlock's *The Beautiful and the Dangerous: Dialogue with Zuni Indians* (1992) reveal a shift from the "participant observer" of Tilly's time to "collaboration," and on to the "observation of participation," a self-consciousness characteristic of modern anthropology.

As a discipline concerned with cross-cultural understanding, as well as an understanding of ourselves, anthropology continues to struggle with the situated nature of its theory, methods, and biographies of the individual anthropologists. Tilly Stevenson had little reason to reflect on her work and her role as an ethnologist or as a woman in Zuni Pueblo. However, as Darlis Miller makes clear, Tilly reveals more of herself than histories of anthropology have ever suggested, and, in doing so, she continues to be relevant and of far more than "marginal" interest. What we have in this biography of Matilda Coxe Stevenson is a work that is sensitive and humane as well as erudite and insightful. At points, Tilly might be chagrined by what history has left of her story; at the same time I suspect she would feel affirmed by what Darlis Miller has written.

Louis A. Hieb

Preface

Matilda Coxe Stevenson (1849–1915) helped to define the contours of anthropological research in the United States during the late nineteenth and early twentieth centuries. The first woman anthropologist to work in the American Southwest, she also was the only professional woman employed as a staff scientist in the Bureau of American Ethnology. She belonged to a generation of pioneer women anthropologists whose achievements and contributions to the discipline are often overlooked. An indefatigable field researcher, Stevenson devoted her life to the study of Pueblo Indian culture and society. Given the state of the development of anthropology in the late nineteenth century, her work was truly remarkable.

During her lifetime, Stevenson published two ethnographies, "The Sia" (1894), the first ethnography of a Rio Grande Pueblo, and her magnum opus, "The Zuni Indians: Their Mythology, Esoteric Fraternities, and Ceremonies" (1904), still considered the most important work on the Zuni Indians. Among her shorter publications are "The Religious Life of the Zuni Child" (1887), "Zuni Ancestral Gods and Masks" (1898), "Zuni Games" (1903), "Ethnobotany of the Zuni Indians" (1915), three brief reports on the Tewa, and two works published posthumously, "The Taos Blue Lake Ceremony" and "Dress and Adornment of the Pueblo Indians." At the time of her death, she had completed a four-hundred-page manuscript on the Tewa Indians, which has since dropped out of sight—lost to public knowledge and erased from Stevenson's record. Because she had a penchant for accuracy, insisting that her data be verified by three Indians (none knowing that the others had talked to her), her work has stood the test of time. Through these publications, she contributed to a better understanding of Pueblo cultures and helped to undermine prevailing racist stereo-types by showing that Indians were rational human beings with rich traditions and valid religions.

As a woman in a profession dominated by men, Stevenson struggled all of her life against male biases that limited women's recognition and advancement in scientific circles, and like other professional women, she also had to contend with the constraints that society imposed on ambitious women. Her struggles to obtain equal treatment within the all-male Bureau of American Ethnol-ogy are documented in her professional papers, housed in the National Anthropological Archives (NAA). This correspondence, starting in 1890, when she first obtained a permanent staff position in the bureau, and ending with her death in 1915, also provides insight into field techniques used by early-day ethnologists. Although modern-day researchers disavow many of her intrusive and aggres-sive maneuvers to obtain data, she nonetheless embraced a surprising number of practices valued by today's anthropologists—giving voice to native peoples in her publications, acknowledging their con-tributions, and situating herself in the telling of their stories.

The only known cache of Stevenson's personal papers are also located at the NAA. These are less complete than her profes-sional papers, disappointingly so when one attempts to reconstruct her childhood, her school years, and her courtship and marriage to James Stevenson. Still, sufficient documents have been located to provide insight into these early years. Born into an upper-middle-class family on May 12, 1849, she spent most of her formative years in Washington, D.C., where she developed an unconventional interest in the sciences. Her parents, well known in the capital's social circles, supported and nurtured her educational interests. She married James Stevenson, executive officer of Ferdinand V. Hayden's Geological Survey of the Territories, in 1872, and her life thereafter was forever changed. Ideally suited to each other, they developed a strong emotional bond that sustained Tilly (as Matilda was known to family and friends) long after Jim died in 1888.

Tilly accompanied her husband on at least three of Hayden's surveys, experiencing the hardships of western travel, sharing his enthusiasm for the West, and encountering American Indians for the first time. When Hayden's survey ended in 1879, Jim became John Wesley Powell's executive officer of the newly created Bureau of Ethnology (later Bureau of American Ethnology [BAE]). From then until his death, the Stevensons conducted ethnological research in the American Southwest, thus becoming the first husband-wife team in anthropology. Until the end of her life, Tilly credited her husband with having taught her the methods of ethnologic research.

Matilda Coxe Stevenson has been described in the literature as a "formidable woman"—overbearing, officious, strong willed, outspoken, humorless. Anecdotes to back these assessments have been handed down by scholars and critics since her death in 1915, and such assessments now seem irrefutable. The anecdotes invariably highlight perceived flaws in her character, and have been used to detract from her research and contributions to anthropology. In the course of writing this book, I have found evidence that raises questions about, and often refutes, this anecdotal history. One story claims, for example, that when Tilly lived in the Smithsonian's red-stone castle, visitors "were met on occasion with (varying with the version) a whiskey bottle, a book or a chamber pot hurled down the stairs from her tower apartment."[1] It is highly unlikely, however, that Stevenson ever lived in the castle. A 1993 history of the Smithsonian building states that only a "handful of men in the nineteenth century" had living quarters there, and that after Joseph Henry (the first secretary of the Smithsonian) died in 1878, "no new lodgers seem to have been taken in."[2] Claims also have been made, largely based on hearsay evidence, that Stevenson became an alcoholic (or was verging on alcoholism) as she grew older.[3] In 1913, however, the head of the BAE, Frederick W. Hodge, investigated a similar charge of drunkenness that a combative neighbor lodged against her, and found no truth in the allegation.

Still, there was something about Stevenson's personality that aroused opposition, sometimes outright hostility, especially among male scientists who seemingly resented her encroachment into their domain. To be successful in a man's world, Stevenson had to be strong willed, determined, resolute in the face of opposition. Anthropological fieldwork also demanded that its practitioners, male and female alike, be sturdy and tenacious people, capable of spending long periods away from familiar surroundings, often in demanding and alien environments. In her dealings with associates and other professionals, Tilly could be assertive, sharp tongued, opinionated, and sometimes arrogant. But, as Eliza McFeely points out, "It is unlikely that [Stevenson] was any more imperious or difficult than many other anthropologists."[4]

Although negative assessments of Stevenson's personality have been given full coverage in the literature, Tilly's many good points— a softer side to her character, as it were—have not been adequately publicized. I have uncovered a wealth of material to support a more positive image of this pioneering ethnologist. For example, she forged strong and enduring friendships with colleagues, members of the Women's Anthropological Society, acquaintances she met along the way, and Indian peoples with whom she studied. Many viewed her as a warmhearted and generous friend. In researching Stevenson's story, I found her to be an intelligent, strong-willed, courageous, energetic, and talented field researcher, one with a subtle sense of humor, an intense love for her husband and family, and a passion for her work. She also was a fighter who demanded to be treated equally with her male colleagues and who, by example and deeds, fostered equality for all professional women.

In the course of writing this book, I have benefited from the knowledge, advice, and kindness of many scholars. First, I would like to thank Richard W. Etulain, Professor Emeritus of History, University of New Mexico, for initially suggesting that I write this biography, and for his constant support during the long process of bringing it to fruition. My thanks also to Charles E. Rankin, Associate Director, University of Oklahoma Press, whose enthusiasm for the project never wavered.

I am deeply indebted to Nancy J. Parezo, first for the scholarship and energy that went into *Hidden Scholars: Women Anthropologists and the Native American Southwest* (University of New Mexico Press, 1993), a thought-provoking examination of the lives and careers of many pioneer women anthropologists, and second for sharing her materials on Matilda Coxe Stevenson during the early stages of my research. Her generosity was very much appreciated. Special heartfelt thanks go to the anthropologists and historians who read parts or all of the manuscript; their critical remarks have made this a much better biography than it might otherwise have been: Richard W. Etulain, E. Richard Hart, Louis A. Hieb, Joan M. Jensen, and Terry Reynolds. I also want to thank Lou Hieb for sharing his considerable knowledge about early-day anthropologists who worked with the Hopis, Navajos, and Zunis, and Terry Reynolds for delightful lunch conversations after she had read each of the chapters.

I am indebted to several scholars in the Washington, D.C. area, especially to my dear friend Linda Lear, who provided inspiration, moral support, and good food and spirits during research trips to the National Anthropological Archives (NAA). For assistance at the NAA and for answering later inquiries, I would like to thank Paula Fleming, Jeannie Sklar, Susan McElrath, Vyrtis Thomas, Sarah Rice, and Daisy Njoku. Also my thanks to Ruth Selig, National Museum of Natural History; Bill Cox, Smithsonian Institution Archives; Michael Rhode, National Museum of Health and Medicine; and Mike Musick, National Archives, for their assistance in locating sources.

I am indebted to the following for providing copies of documents and answering questions: Diane Bird, Laboratory of Anthropology, Santa Fe, New Mexico; Lee H. Whittlesey and Tara Cross, Yellowstone National Park; Valerie Lutz, American Philosophical Society; Emily Balmages, Bancroft Library; Eunice J. Schlichting,

Putnam Museum, Davenport, Iowa; Richard J. Hourahan, Rye Historical Society, Rye, New York; Ronnie Peacock, University of Northern Colorado; Thomas J. Devon, Longview, Texas; and the staffs at the New Mexico State Records Center and Archives, the Fray Angélico Chávez History Library, and Museum of New Mexico Photo Archives. Special thanks also to historians Kevin Fernland, Catherine Lavender, and Donald Worster, for sharing their knowledge about topics important to this biography; to Rosemary Zumwalt and Desley Deacon, for answering questions about Elsie Clews Parsons; and to Joan Mark, for answering questions about Alice Fletcher.

From the beginning of my career as a historian, I have relied upon the goodwill and services of librarians and staff members at the New Mexico State University Library. To them I say a thousand thanks. I am especially indebted to Jivonna Stewart and her coworkers in Interlibrary Loan for courageously wading through and filling all of my requests. I am also grateful to my colleagues, past and present, at New Mexico State University for camaraderie and stimulating discussions.

Finally, I would like to thank my extended family for their love, support, and good company (this book is dedicated to them): August Miller, Dean Miller, Ann DeBusschere, Sylvia Walker, Frank Menke, Ann Cullen, Ellen Taliaferro, and Marilyn Lindquist.

MATILDA COXE STEVENSON

CHAPTER 1

The Early Years

Matilda Coxe Evans was born in Texas just three and one-half years after it had been annexed to the United States. To most Americans, this sprawling, largely unknown territory was foreign and mysterious—part of the great "frontier." Yet Tilly's parents, Alexander Hamilton Evans and Maria Matilda Coxe Evans, had chosen to leave the relative comforts of their home in Washington, D.C., in 1846 or early 1847, to move to the east Texas town of San Augustine. We can only speculate about their motives. Foremost in Alexander's mind must have been the glowing reports of economic opportunities awaiting an industrious man in a region known as the gateway to Texas. But the move also indicates an adventurous spirit on the part of Tilly's parents, a willingness to cast off family ties to start life anew out west. This sense of adventure, accompanied by a strong curiosity about new people and places, may well have been the Evanses' greatest legacy to their eldest daughter, the future ethnologist Matilda Coxe Stevenson.

San Augustine already had acquired the trappings of civilization by the time the Evans family arrived. Established in 1832, thirty miles west of the Sabine River on the road leading to San Antonio, the town quickly became a business center that catered to surrounding farm families. Among its many fine houses was the two-and-one-half-story residence of James Pinckney Henderson, the first governor of the state of Texas. During the 1840s, when the population of the town and nearby countryside may have reached four thousand, two schools of higher learning—the University of San Augustine and Wesleyan Male and Female College—operated there, although each was short-lived. Contributing to the town's cultural and social life were an active thespian society, a Masonic lodge, and a handful of churches. These developments, along with "the high cultural level of many of its citizens," led historian William Ransom Hogan to conclude, "San Augustine of that day must provide a notable exception to any attempt to characterize . . . Texas as devoid of the best in the civilization of the period."[1]

Maria Coxe of New Jersey and Alexander Evans of Virginia had wed in Washington's St. John's Episcopal Church, situated across from the White House, in February 1844. Their first child, Robert Dale Evans, was born later that same year, but died shortly before his third birthday, after the family had moved west. While living in Texas, Maria gave birth to three more children: Richard in 1847, Matilda (Tilly) on May 12, 1849, and Elizabeth (Betty) in 1851. Tilly's paternal grandmother, Elizabeth, also lived with the family during these years.[2]

Coming from upper-middle-class families, Maria and Alexander Evans readily entered into San Augustine's social and economic life. Most of their nearest neighbors were southerners, approximately their same age, with young children who also had been born in Texas. Living next door, however, were the English emigrants Henry and Elizabeth Sansom and their infant daughter Fanny. The Reverend Sansom had established the first Episcopal church in town in 1848, and the Evanses were among the parish's first communicants. So, too, was Frances C. Henderson, wife of former governor Henderson, whose persistent requests for a resident Episcopal clergyman had led to Sansom's arrival.[3]

Tilly's father, a lawyer and journalist by profession, became editor of San Augustine's only newspaper, the *Redlander*, in 1848. Although the journal had wide circulation in east Texas, Evans must have struggled to make ends meet, for in the late 1840s the prosperity of the town began to decline.[4] In hopes of gaining new patronage, Evans penned a letter in December 1853 to his friend the legendary Sam Houston, leader of the Texas Revolution, the first elected governor of the Texas Republic, and now a U.S. senator, seeking his support in landing a contract to print congressional laws for east Texas. By this date, Tilly's mother had returned to Washington, probably with the children, where she gave birth to her third daughter, Nina, in November 1853.[5] Although Tilly was only four years old when she left Texas, the family's memories of those years must have enlivened many of its later conversations and left imprinted on her young mind a romantic image of the West, then seen as a land of promise and untold challenges.

Life in the capital during the 1850s, the time of Tilly's childhood, was vividly described by Virginia Clay-Clopton, wife of U.S. Senator Clement C. Clay of Alabama, in her published memoirs. The city claimed a population of fifty-two thousand, many of whom worked in government offices or as domestics in wealthier people's homes. Pennsylvania Avenue, the senator's wife recalled, was "but sparsely and irregularly built up. The greatest contrast in architecture existed, hovels often all but touching the mansions of the rich." Cornerstones for the Washington Monument and the Smithsonian Institution had been laid in the previous decade; construction on both structures continued into the fifties. Clay-Clopton also remembered the gaiety of the city when she first arrived (1853): "[The hospitality] of the capital was synonymous with an unceasing, an augmenting round of dinners and dances, receptions and balls." Even so, she also observed the widening social division between northerners and southerners as the nation drew closer to civil war. Late in 1856 she wrote in a letter to her father-in-law, "Everything is excitement and confusion. . . . Southern blood is at boiling temperature all over the city." The saddest day in her life, she later avowed, was January 21, 1861, when she watched from the Senate gallery as her husband and other southern senators left the Senate chambers.[6]

In this milieu the Evanses attempted to carry on a normal family life. When Tilly's father returned to the capital, he continued to make a living as a lawyer and journalist. According to an obituary published upon his death in 1893, he "practiced extensively before the United States Supreme Court and Court of Claims" in antebellum Washington, and also became a well-known newspaper man, serving as head of the Associated Press. The article pictured Evans as a "prominent figure" in the city's "intellectual, social, and business circles."[7]

The decade of the fifties witnessed an expansion of the Evans household. In 1855 Maria gave birth to their fifth surviving child, George-Anna (Georgie) Evans; two years later a nephew, Robley D. Evans of Virginia, came to live with the family to take advantage of the Washington schools. Young Evans, whose father had died when he was ten years old, later entered the Naval Academy in 1860, and went on to become one of the most prominent men in the navy, rising to the rank of rear admiral and commanding the Asiatic fleet. In his memoirs, written several years after his aunt and uncle had died, Evans recalled with warmth the time he spent in their house: "I found this new home a real home, and from my uncle and aunt I received all the loving-kindness and attention that I could have had from my own parents; they treated me as one of their own children, except that they were never as severe with my small faults as they were with theirs." He went on to say, "To my dear aunt I owe a deep debt of gratitude for her unfailing love and sympathy."[8]

This brief glimpse of the senior Evanses suggests that Tilly grew up in a happy, closely knit family, the parents guiding the children's behavior and providing for their education. Tilly must have learned at an early age to respect certain conventional standards of polite society. In later years, she valued her association with "cultured" men and women and took pride in her own home for its "culture and refinement." To a friend, she recalled that her parents, "so well known in Washington," had been "highly respected not only for their intellectual attainments and culture, but for their lovely characters" as well.[9] Yet, offsetting this streak of conservatism was a strong element of independence, which allowed Tilly to move beyond the roles of wife, mother, and social hostess typically assigned to women of her class.

Tradition holds that Tilly Evans's first formal education came from governesses at private schools in Washington. The federal census for 1860 shows only that she and her three oldest siblings had attended school during the year. Surely all the Evans children received encouragement in their studies from their parents, especially from their father, who was friends with Washington's leading politicians and scientists. He no doubt deserves credit for sparking Tilly's interest in the sciences. Years later, writing to congratulate family-friend Charles D. Walcott on his appointment as the secretary of the Smithsonian, she avowed, "I first knew the Smithsonian when a very young child, accompanying my father in his visits to Prof. [Joseph] Henry [the first secretary of the Smithsonian], and I learned to love the place, next to dear Prof. Henry himself."[10]

It is likely also that Tilly accompanied her father on trips to the Capitol, located not far from the Evans residence at 509 E Street.[11] Her cousin Robley Evans later recalled that after moving to Washington, he spent much of his spare time roaming the halls of Congress, where he met many of his uncle's friends, including Congressman John A. Logan of Illinois, later a U.S. senator and vice-presidential candidate. Tilly's father was well known on Capitol Hill. In 1857 he was tapped by Lewis Cass, secretary of state in James Buchanan's administration, to carry dispatches to England. And for two years, 1859–1860, he worked as chief clerk for the Committee on Claims in the House of Representatives.[12]

It is uncertain what impact the coming sectional war had on Tilly and her family. Did Tilly's father feel a continuing loyalty to his native state? Was the family divided in its sympathies? Robley Evans, a cadet at Annapolis when the war broke out, remained loyal to the Union, but his younger brother fought for the Confederacy. Cadet Evans, on leave in the fall of 1862, spent time in Washington at his uncle's house, now abandoned by the family and under a housekeeper's charge. Perhaps early on the senior Evans had removed his wife and children from the city to keep them out of harm's way.[13]

Other residents who remained in Washington recognized the city's precarious position. When war broke out in April 1861, the capital was only lightly defended, and rumors abounded of an impending secessionist attack. An atmosphere of gloom and pessimism seemed to hang over the city. Mary Henry, the daughter of Joseph Henry, who lived with the rest of her family in lodgings on the second floor of the Smithsonian building, captured some of these feelings in her diary. On July 16, 1861, just days before Union troops were defeated at the Battle of Bull Run, she wrote, "We went up into the high tower to see the troops pass over into Virginia. . . . It was sad very sad to see them go. I could not feel patriotic." Mary also wrote of the city's vulnerability to occupation by Confederate forces. She recorded on July 22:

> All day long bodies of stragling [Union] troops have been coming into the city & the streets lined with men seated upon the side walks in the pelting rain. Their officers many of them killed, their companys broken up they did not seem to know where to go. Our Army has been completely routed could the Southerners have attacked the city on Sunday night it might very readily have been taken.[14]

It remains unclear where the Evans family went immediately after leaving the capital. Old-time Texas residents later recalled that Alexander H. Evans fled Washington to join the Confederate army.[15] But in her sixties, Tilly remembered that her father had moved the family to Philadelphia in 1861 or 1862 to take advantage of its better schools. The Evanses possibly found refuge among Maria Evans's relatives, who may still have lived in the area. Maria's mother had been born in Philadelphia, and her father had been a judge on the Pennsylvania bench. In later years, Maria's sister Theodosia also made her home in the city.[16]

Despite the uncertainties of the family's situation in the early days of the war, we know that Tilly Evans enrolled in a private school sometime after moving to Philadelphia. Still, the city was not the secure haven that the senior Evans may have envisioned. In June of 1863, Confederate forces under General Robert E. Lee invaded Pennsylvania. Twelve-year-old Tilly surely was aware of the city's wartime preparations and dislocations. News of advancing Confederate troops led to a flurry of activity in this urban center of more than a half million people: men flocked to recruiting stations, bankers prepared to send away their valuables, and others made ready to leave town. A diarist recorded, "Philadelphia is not considered safe, and a thousand excited rumors are filling the air!"[17]

Tilly would soon learn that on June 26, Confederate troops had appeared in Gettysburg, more than one hundred miles west of Philadelphia. A young Gettysburg schoolgirl, Matilda (Tillie) Pierce, only a year older than Tilly Evans, had gaped at the enemy cavalrymen as they entered the town and galloped down the street in front of her house. "What a horrible sight," she later recalled. "Clad almost in rags, covered with dust, riding wildly, pell-mell down the hill toward our home! Shouting, yelling most unearthly, cursing, brandishing their revolvers and firing right and left." Thereafter, Tillie Pierce witnessed much of the carnage that took place in the three-day Battle of Gettysburg (July 1–3), which left the countryside littered with dead and mangled bodies.[18]

When news of the Union's victory over General Lee reached Philadelphia on July 4, residents staged celebrations throughout the city—setting off fireworks and joining in other jubilant demonstrations. They also observed the arrival of the first contingent of some ten thousand Gettysburg casualties. Philadelphia, in fact, served as the major Union hospital center for the war's duration; more than 150,000 soldiers and sailors were treated for their wounds and other illnesses in the city's military and civilian hospitals.[19] As luck would have it, one of these soldiers was Tilly Evans's future husband, James Stevenson, who, three months prior to Gettysburg, had sought help for an eye problem in a West Philadelphia facility.[20]

Because no one in Tilly's family apparently kept a diary during these turbulent years, we have no way of knowing whether its members were adversely affected by her father's southern birth. Historian Gary B. Nash points out that prior to the outbreak of war, Philadelphia was "almost as much a southern as a northern city." On a single block of one fashionable street lived families from Virginia, South Carolina, Mississippi, and other slave states.[21]

After the firing on Fort Sumter, Unionists in Pennsylvania seemingly demanded of everyone a show of allegiance to the U.S. flag, often attacking or intimidating southern sympathizers and destroying their property. In this charged atmosphere, a prudent gentleman maintained a "judicious silence" or proclaimed himself a staunch Unionist. Even though antiwar sentiment grew as time went by, and peace meetings were held openly in Philadelphia and elsewhere, after Gettysburg, Union men showed even less tolerance of dissenting viewpoints than they had before the battle. It must have been particularly trying for the many Pennsylvania families (like the Evanses) who had relatives living in the South.[22]

During these unsettled times, Tilly Evans enrolled in one of the most prominent schools in Philadelphia. She and other young girls, such as Tillie Pierce, benefited from the tremendous growth of female academies and seminaries (the terms were interchangeable) that occurred in the United States between 1830 and 1860. The founders of these schools, often women or ministers, wanted to provide a secondary education that would prepare young women for their roles as wives and mothers. With well-developed minds, so the reasoning went, women would impart virtue and proper values to husbands and children. Typically the schools offered more than the ornamentals (music, painting, and drawing), which some eighteenth-century educators stressed as a means of improving chances for matrimony.[23] In the mid-nineteenth century, Pennsylvania female academies offered instruction in a variety of subjects, including the sciences (often astronomy, chemistry, botany, and geology), mathematics, history, geography, reading, composition, and languages, as well as ethics and religion. No doubt the curriculum depended on the size of the teaching staff. Some Pennsylvania schools were one-teacher affairs, with the founder teaching all the subjects; others had staffs of four or more teachers.[24]

Tilly Evans attended Miss Anable's English, French, and German school, located at 1350 Pine Street. Established in 1848, the school continued to prosper into the 1880s.[25] Anna M. Anable, a middle-aged single woman, ran the establishment with the assistance of her younger sister Fanny and possibly one or more other teachers.

In later years, Tilly kept up a sporadic correspondence with Anna Anable, who retained an affectionate memory of young Tilly. Writing to her former student in March 1877, Anable exclaimed, "Your kind heartfelt letter of the 9th inst. was very welcome, showing, as it did, that years had not changed the warm heart of the delicate child of ten years ago."[26]

When the Evanses returned to Washington, D.C., about 1868, they found the capital considerably changed. The population of the District of Columbia had leaped from 75,000 residents in 1860 to at least 120,000 six years later. More than 30,000 of the new city dwellers were black southern men and women who came during and after the war and lived in makeshift settlements that had rapidly turned into slums. Also new to the city were families from the North, Midwest, and West, some of the men coming as officeholders, others as opportunists hoping to make fortunes off government contracts. The more affluent dominated the city's social life, replacing the many southerners who had fled the capital as war approached.[27]

The city was as badly illuminated after the war, however, as it had been in former days, and most of its streets remained unpaved. Pennsylvania Avenue, once a cobbled thoroughfare, was now filled with ruts and potholes because of the heavy wartime traffic. The avenue, in fact, remained as unimpressive as it had been in the 1850s. "The south side of the Avenue," one historian writes, "from 15th Street to the Capitol was occupied by cheap saloons, gambling houses and pawn shops."[28]

But the Evans family soon witnessed an all-out drive by politicians and businessmen to turn Washington "into a capital city worthy of the United States," a move brought about in part by talk of moving the national capital to St. Louis. By the close of 1873, the board of public works reported that the district now had 58.5 miles of wooden pavement (which deteriorated rapidly in Washington's weather), 28.5 miles of concrete pavement, and 93 miles of cobble, macadam, and gravel roads. A few hundred miles of sidewalks and sewers had been installed, as well as three thousand gas lamps, and more than sixty thousand trees had been planted. Pleased with these costly improvements (which bankrupted the board of public works), President Ulysses S. Grant avowed in his message to Congress on December 3, 1873, "The city of Washington is rapidly assuming the appearance of a capital of which the nation may be well proud. . . . Each citizen visiting the capital feels a pride in its growing beauty."[29]

Once back in Washington, Alexander Evans reestablished his law practice and soon became one of the city's leading patent attorneys. The Evans household in 1870 consisted of Alexander, Maria, four of their children (ranging in ages from fifteen to twenty-three), and two black domestic servants. In February, Tilly's nineteen-year-old sister Betty had married twenty-six-year-old Augustus G. Kellogg, a lieutenant commander in the U.S. Navy. The newly married couple lived next door to the Evanses, sharing the residence with Lieutenant Commander Robley D. Evans and William Evans, probably Robley's younger brother. Both William and Tilly's brother Richard are listed in the 1870 census as lawyers.[30]

According to tradition, after leaving Philadelphia, Tilly Evans continued her studies with her father (possibly studying law) and with the chemist William M. Mew, soon to begin a twenty-nine-year career in the chemical laboratory attached to the Army Medical Museum, located for many of these years in the old Ford's Theater.[31] Joseph Henry had taken a keen interest in Mew as a young man and supervised his chemical studies in the laboratory of the Smithsonian. It may have been through her father's connection with Professor Henry that Tilly made the acquaintance of the chemist, known as Dr. Mew after 1882, when he received an honorary degree of Doctor of Medicine from Columbian University (now George Washington University).[32]

Tilly's parents no doubt encouraged their eldest daughter's intellectual curiosity. Clearly, she was eager for opportunities that went beyond the domestic roles of wife and mother, then thought to be the proper calling for young women. She had developed an unconventional interest in the sciences, and apparently aspired to become a mineralogist. But to succeed would require her to overcome formidable barriers, including the widely held perceptions that women were incapable of thinking scientifically and that their proper focus was on home and family. Then, too, few employment opportunities were available for middle-class Euro-American women outside the home.[33]

The handful of women who became scientists in colonial and early republican times often acquired their knowledge of science (as Tilly Evans did) from their fathers, other relatives, or friends. In the early nineteenth century, some women expanded their education by attending lectures, visiting museums, or reading the new textbooks designed to popularize science, especially among women readers. For example, Almira Hart Lincoln, the sister of Emma Hart Willard (founder of Troy Female Seminary in New York State), grew wealthy publishing textbooks in botany, chemistry, natural philosophy, and geology. Young Tilly may have studied from one of Lincoln's books, or perhaps she gained inspiration from a text similar to Jane Kilby Welsh's *Familiar Lessons in Mineralogy and Geology*, published in the mid-1830s. At any rate, in Tilly's youth, women had few opportunities to obtain advanced knowledge in colleges or universities, most of which remained male bastions until the 1870s and 1880s.[34]

Ambitious, energetic, undoubtedly self-confident, and with a curiosity about life, Tilly Evans's plans to become a mineralogist were altered when, a year or so after the family resettled in the capital, she made the acquaintance of, and later married, James Stevenson, the executive officer of Ferdinand V. Hayden's Geological Survey of the Territories. At the time the young couple met, Jim (as he was known) was an experienced explorer, a self-taught geologist, and a seasoned ethnologist. Born in Maysville, Kentucky, on December 24, 1840, Stevenson had hired on at age sixteen as Hayden's assistant on Lieutenant Gouverneur Kemble Warren's 1856 expedition to the Yellowstone River country. Hayden, who was to become one of the nation's most prominent geologists, had made his first fossil-collecting trip into the Badlands of Dakota three years earlier. Stevenson again teamed up with him on Captain William F. Raynold's 1859–60 expedition to the upper reaches of the Missouri. During these years, Jim spent an unknown number of winters among the Blackfoot and Dakota Indians, leading to his lifelong interest in ethnology. At the outbreak of the Civil War, he enlisted as a private in the Eighteenth New York Infantry and rose to the rank of second lieutenant, although later he was given the courtesy title of colonel. At war's end, he rejoined Hayden on his western explorations and became, in the words of historian Richard A. Bartlett, his "right-hand man."[35]

The couple may have been introduced by their mutual friend, Congressman John A. Logan, an ardent supporter of Hayden's work, or by one of the many scientists who frequented the Smithsonian. Whatever the case, Jim was a perfect match for young Tilly. Although he was older by nine years, they shared common interests in mineralogy and in the American West. The tales he told of his western adventures must have stimulated her imagination—perhaps even raised the expectation of sharing similar ventures in the future. Gracious, modest, and affable, with appropriate social and political connections, Jim would be most acceptable to Tilly's parents and would move easily in their circle of friends.[36]

Like other young women of her era, Tilly no doubt looked for intimacy and companionship in marriage. Indeed, social historian Carl Degler states that marriages in the nineteenth century usually were "based upon affection and mutual respect between the partners." Only one letter remains from their days of courtship, but it suggests their compatibility. Jim's affectionate message to Tilly, written on December 30, 1871, four months before their marriage, was accompanied by the gift of a penholder, which, he explained, was "to pay the forfeit of Philopena" (a penalty of love or friendship). Anticipating further travels with Hayden, Jim closed his letter with these words: "[The penholder] will, I trust[,] facilitate you in communicating your gentle thoughts when the donor, unfortunately, chances to be far away." And so they were married, on the evening of April 18, 1872, just weeks before Jim departed on another of Hayden's expeditions. What lay ahead for the couple, Tilly had no way of knowing, but the allure of the West would cast as strong a spell upon her as it had upon her husband.[37]

CHAPTER 2

The Hayden Survey

In a letter dated August 22, 1872, Tilly Stevenson penned these words to her absent spouse: "My dearest[,] my joy was beyond expressing in words. I felt as if a great light had suddenly broke upon me; that after a long long night day had dawned in all its loveliness. I thought my heart would burst from so much joy. You were *well* and had succeeded."[1] Earlier, on July 29, Jim—along with Nathaniel P. Langford—made the first successful ascent in recorded history of the Grand Teton, a feat many experienced mountaineers had declared was impossible. Only after he returned to Virginia City, Montana, to pick up supplies for the Hayden survey was he able to telegraph news of his success to Tilly, which she received the night before she wrote these poignant words.[2]

The Stevensons left few letters and no diaries that would help enlighten us about their early years together. But this "love letter," written fewer than five months after their wedding, testifies to the intensity of Tilly's feelings for her husband. She must have become Jim's partner and helpmate right from the start, entering wholeheartedly into his work, sharing his interests, and welcoming his associates and friends into their home.[3]

Like other Euro-Americans of their generation, the couple became caught up in the nation's great expansion westward following the Civil War. For many, the West represented the future, a place of new beginnings and opportunities where anyone with persistence could succeed. Eastern newspapers kept readers apprized of western developments and whetted their appetites for more information about the region. Congress focused its attention on the West also, wrestling with such critical issues as public land laws, Indian policy, statehood for western territories, and land grants to railroads, all of which received coverage in the press. And with completion of the first western railroads, starting in 1869 when the Union Pacific met the Central Pacific at Promontory, Utah, vast new areas were opened to settlement and exploitation.[4]

To provide more accurate information about this land, Congress financed four great scientific surveys, which crisscrossed the West from 1867 until 1879, mapping immense stretches of the interior and compiling inventories of its natural resources. Hayden's survey became the largest, best funded, and best known, receiving more publicity perhaps than the other three combined—mainly because he was a master at promoting his own accomplishments. Still, the surveys headed by Clarence King, George M. Wheeler, and John Wesley Powell, like Hayden's, contributed enormously to the knowledge of the American West.[5]

For nearly seven years following their marriage, the Stevensons' lives revolved around Hayden's Geological Survey of the Territories. They must have lived apart for a good part of each summer, for Jim's growing responsibilities as Hayden's executive officer kept him in the field overseeing and outfitting teams of scientists that explored huge chunks of the interior. Still, during these years, Tilly herself acquired firsthand knowledge of western travel (its difficulties and esthetic pleasures) when she accompanied Jim on at least three expeditions. On one occasion, she encountered American Indians for the first time, an experience that must have piqued her curiosity about their ways of life, and presaged her long career as an ethnologist. Also during the Hayden years, the Stevensons developed a relationship that allowed them to work together successfully as the first husband-wife team in anthropology.

Jim Stevenson played two vital roles in Hayden's success—the first as a crack administrator of day-to-day field operations, and the second as a lobbyist on Capitol Hill. Typically, once Hayden secured funding for the season's work, Jim took charge of the spring rendezvous, a gathering of the scientists at a predetermined location before they headed out to explore. He usually preceded the men to collect supplies; organize equipment, horses, and mules; and coordinate subsequent travel plans. Once the survey got under way, he served as quartermaster, keeping everyone supplied with rations and whatever else might be needed.[6] Early on, Hayden testified to Stevenson's value to the survey. In a letter to Secretary of the Interior Jacob D. Cox dated October 15, 1869, Hayden avowed, "My principal assistant, Mr. James Stevenson . . . has rendered me indispensable services throughout the entire trip."[7]

More effusive praise came from the pen of Hiram M. Chittenden, historian of Yellowstone National Park, remembered now primarily for his history of the fur trade. In his Yellowstone book, published in 1895, Chittenden wrote: "It rarely happens that a master is so far indebted to a servant for his success, as was true of the relation of Dr. Hayden and James Stevenson. Stevenson's great talent lay in the organization and management of men. . . . His extraordinary influence with Congressmen was a vital element in [the survey's] early growth."[8]

Indeed, Hayden's success in the field rested on the size of his annual appropriation from Congress. As Richard A. Bartlett put it, over the years he became increasingly "adept at wringing money from tight-fisted congressmen," but he also relied on the persuasive talents of Stevenson. Jim became friends with a number of legislators, including men with whom he and Tilly would socialize: Henry L. Dawes of Massachusetts, John A. Logan of Illinois, and Henry M. Teller of Colorado. Among the many who recognized Jim's special talents for lobbying was Henry W. Elliott, private secretary to Joseph Henry; Elliott accompanied Hayden's survey as artist during three successive seasons (1869–71). In a letter to Hayden dated August 23, 1875, Elliott declared: "Jim has a peculiar natural adaptability for certain diplomatic service which is indispensable and which is possessed by none in your whole party as by him, with the partial exception of [Frederick] Endlich who is the strongest advocate you have after Jim." G. Brown Goode, director of the U.S. National Museum, later remarked that Jim Stevenson's cordial relations with congressmen extended to members of both parties, all of whom "had faith in his integrity."[9] These same diplomatic skills would permit Jim and Tilly, who followed his example, to win the confidence of Pueblo Indians, among whom they would later work as ethnologists.

In the months preceding their wedding, Jim had lobbied on Capitol Hill for passage of the Yellowstone Park Act, introduced in Congress on December 18, 1871. The entire nation seemingly had become entranced with the wonders of the Yellowstone, thanks in large part to the publicity given to Hayden's exploration of the region the previous summer.[10] Tilly's family undoubtedly caught her future husband's enthusiasm and avidly watched as the bill made its way through Congress.

The Hayden Survey in 1871 had made the first scientific exploration of the area that now includes Yellowstone National Park and Grand Teton National Park, at the time "a virtual terra incognita." Several of Hayden's crew had accompanied him on previous trips, including Jim Stevenson, Cyrus Thomas (John A. Logan's former brother-in-law), Henry W. Elliott, and the photographer William Henry Jackson. A guest of the survey was Thomas Moran, one of the most renowned landscape artists of the nineteenth century. New members were William B. Logan (Logan's nephew) and Robert Adams, Jr., who thenceforth joined Hayden every summer through 1875. Adams later practiced law in Philadelphia, became a U.S. congressman, and proved to be a staunch friend of Tilly Stevenson's during one of the most difficult periods in her professional career.[11]

Although wives of Hayden's survey members are rarely, if ever, mentioned in official reports, they nonetheless often played important roles on the geological surveys, helping in a variety of ways to advance their husbands' careers. Occasionally we catch glimpses of these women in newspapers, diaries, reminiscences, and private letters. William Henry Jackson records in his autobiography, for example, that on the 1871 trip his wife, Mollie, accompanied him by train as far as Ogden, Utah, the jumping-off place for the Yellowstone expedition. Most of Hayden's crew camped for a few days outside of town at a spot sometimes called "Camp Stevenson," but the Jacksons stayed in an Ogden hotel. "It was her first trip into the Rocky Mountain section," Jackson later recalled, "and it made a pleasant little holiday for both of us." Not only did Mollie provide companionship during the journey, but, when the survey headed north from Camp Stevenson, she returned to Omaha to supervise Jackson's photography shop during his absence.[12]

Hayden's party set out on horseback from Ogden on June 10. After crossing through Utah, Idaho, and southern Montana, they reached the valley of the Yellowstone on July 17. They spent thirty-eight days exploring the heart of the Yellowstone region, collecting geological, botanical, and natural history specimens, studying land formations, and charting geysers and hot springs. The landscape truly astonished them; especially enthralling were Yellowstone Falls and the Grand Canyon, where artists Elliott and Moran stopped to sketch and paint, and Jackson took photographs.[13]

When the men reached Yellowstone Lake ("one of the most beautiful scenes I have ever beheld," Hayden later wrote), the men assembled a twelve-foot-long boat, which Jim christened "the Annie" as a tribute to Anne Dawes, daughter of Congressman Dawes (a firm supporter of Hayden's expeditions) and the sister of survey member Chester Dawes. On the morning of July 29, Stevenson and Elliott set sail to explore the nearest island. Elliott subsequently bestowed Jim's name on the island, and Hayden, in recognition of his assistant's contributions to the survey, also attached his name to a 10,852-foot peak southeast of the lake. These place names—"Stevenson's Island" and "Mount Stevenson"—are still in use today.[14] Eventually the expedition made its way to Evanston, Wyoming, on the Union Pacific Railroad, where on October 1, the survey disbanded.[15]

Once Jim returned to Washington at the end of the 1871 expedition, he and Tilly must have spent as much time together as possible before the April wedding. For the past year, whenever Jim was in town he resided at 915 L Street NW, close to the Evans family residence on 10th Street. Early in their relationship, Tilly would have introduced him to members of her household, which seemed always to include a stray relative or two. Sometime in 1872, the Evanses moved to 912 M Street NW, where the senior Evans and his son Richard had their office as patent attorneys. Also residing in the family home were Tilly's married sister Betty, Betty's husband Lieutenant Commander A. G. Kellogg, and Tilly's cousin William Evans.[16]

Hayden had returned from Yellowstone with an enormous number of images created by the survey's artists and photographer. He had three hundred of Jackson's exposures immediately made into prints, and used them to publicize the wonders they had seen. Both he and Jim worked tirelessly in lobbying for the park bill, which Congress approved without a dissenting vote and President Ulysses S. Grant signed into law on March 1, 1872. According to Hayden's biographer, Mike Foster, "A favorable climate for the idea of a national park already existed, and there can be no doubt the pervasive imaging of the West, so effectively orchestrated by Hayden, played a large part in creating that favorable climate." Most historians agree that Hayden's efforts were crucial in getting the bill approved.[17] Jim Stevenson's work on behalf of the park, however, is usually overlooked. Yet after Jim's untimely death in 1888, a handful of Washington scientists, including John Wesley Powell and William H. Holmes, agreed that he had been "instrumental" in setting aside the Yellowstone as the nation's first national park.[18]

Because of the publicity surrounding the Yellowstone expedition, Hayden became an instant celebrity, heralded as "the greatest explorer of the American West." A dazzled Congress rewarded him with an unprecedented appropriation of $75,000 to continue his Yellowstone survey during the summer of 1872.[19] Tilly possibly accompanied Jim to this year's rendezvous site at Ogden, even though none of the written documents mention her presence.

At least four other women, however, traveled with Hayden's survey, at least for part of the summer. Misfortune involving three of them focused historical attention on their presence. Newlywed Emma Hayden, who rode the train west with her husband, fell from a wagon sometime after reaching Ogden, injuring herself so severely she did not attempt to go farther.[20] Mary Blackmore also traveled to Ogden with her husband, William, an English entrepreneur and Hayden's guest on the survey. The Blackmores then continued by stagecoach to Fort Ellis, Montana, whence one division of the survey (under Hayden's command) would enter the Yellowstone. Travelers considered this grueling stage ride of nearly 430 miles to be "almost unendurable" because of the heat, dust, and crowded condition of the stage, as well as "the loss of sleep for three or four nights and days."[21] For Mary, the trip proved fatal. She became quite ill as the stage neared Bozeman (three miles east of the fort), where she died on July 18. Mount Blackmore, twenty-five miles south of Bozeman in the Gallatin Range, is named in her memory.[22]

Jenny Leigh, the Shoshone wife of one of Hayden's employees, the Englishman Richard "Beaver Dick" Leigh, made the most arduous trip of the four women. Years earlier, at age sixteen, Jenny had married Beaver Dick, a guide and trapper who spent most of his adult life in the northern Rockies. In 1872 he hired on to lead the way for Hayden's second division (under Jim Stevenson's control), which explored the Snake and Teton River areas west of the Teton Range, before hooking up with Hayden's party at Fire Hole Basin in the heart of Yellowstone Park. Jenny and her four children accompanied Beaver Dick for the entire trip, the Leighs erecting a teepee close to the main encampment at each stop along the way. Sadly, late in 1876, smallpox decimated the family; Jenny and all of her children, which now numbered six, including a newborn, died from the disease. Leigh and Jenny lakes, at the base of the Grand Tetons, are named for the guide and his wife.[23]

Finally, Annie P. Cope, along with her daughter Julia, accompanied her husband, the paleontologist Edward D. Cope, on the train ride to Fort Bridger in southwestern Wyoming, where he was to initiate a paleontological study of the Green River Basin as part of Hayden's survey. Annie and Julia apparently lived at the military post while Edward was in the field. In September, ill with fever, he returned to Fort Bridger, where his wife cared for him. On the twentieth of that month, she wrote to tell Hayden that her husband was unable even to sit up in bed. Two days later, the feverish paleontologist again had Annie write to Hayden describing some of the fossils he had discovered. Cope was still recuperating at the fort on October 13, when he wrote to his mother-in-law, "Thy daughter, my excellent wife, has shown the talents of her family for nursing. She has attended me faithfully and saved me much suffering and no doubt much time."[24] Although their husbands' achievements have been heralded in history books, these women's support behind the scenes mostly has gone unrecorded, though not necessarily unappreciated by the men.

A major highlight of the 1872 season, and one that received wide publicity in the press, was James Stevenson and Nathaniel P. Langford's successful ascent of the highest summit in the Teton Range. Langford, the newly appointed superintendent of Yellowstone National Park, had joined Jim's party at Fort Hall, Idaho, as a guest of the survey. In an article published the following year in *Scribner's Monthly*, Langford gave an exciting account of this historic climb. Twelve climbers had attempted the ascent; only Stevenson and Langford reached the top, but not without a mishap that almost cost Jim his life. Jim, who usually ranged ahead of the others, lost his footing while trying to reach a higher ridge; this left him dangling with his face to the wall of the mountain, "his entire weight coming upon his hands." By repeated kicks with the toe of his boot into the ice and snow that partially covered the wall, he gained a new foothold, enabling him "to spring on one side to a narrow bench of rock, where he was safe."[25]

In subsequent years, Langford spent portions of each winter in Washington, where he frequently talked to Tilly and Jim "in the presence of friends" concerning the two men's achievement. Langford later recalled, "[Mrs. Stevenson] was proud of her husband's part in it."[26] Tilly's pride surfaces in the letter she wrote to Jim after she first learned of his success. This letter is important for other reasons as well. First, it shows a softer side to Matilda Coxe Stevenson than usually is depicted in descriptions of her by a later generation of scholars and critics. Second, it helps validate Charles D. Walcott's statement, in a letter of condolence to Tilly at the time of Jim's death, that her friends all knew that "a strong bond . . . united you and Mr. Stevenson."[27]

In her August 22 letter to Jim, Tilly poured out her feelings, expressing her concern for his safety and her newfound love. "Well, my darling brave good husband," she wrote, "this [letter] may have to wait some time at Ft. Hall for you. I have no idea when you will be there but I could not resist writing immediately to tell you of my joy to know you are well, and how proud and happy I feel at your success." She continued: "I would consider it a great privilege to be near, and kiss your noble brow, and those hands that I know have done such hard work. And then I would forget the homage due the successful explorer, and rest in your arms and kiss the lips of my own dear James." She closed by saying, "Darling I am eternally your fondly devoted Tilly, your proud happy wife."[28]

Tilly's missive to Jim was typical of the love letters that middle- to upper-middle-class couples wrote to each other in the nineteenth century. Victorian passion often found expression in such intimate correspondence. Moreover, as scholar Karen Lystra observes, "within the circle of romantic love, [nineteenth-century] men and women shared their interior lives with such intensity that many felt as if they had merged part of their inner being," surely an emotion that the Stevensons experienced.[29]

When Hayden shifted the survey to Colorado the spring of 1873, Tilly accompanied Jim for part of the season, probably traveling with him to Denver via the recently completed Kansas Pacific Railroad. The town and its hinterland stood on the brink of a new economic boom, brought about in part by improved transportation facilities, new discoveries of precious metals, and better methods of processing the ores. By the time the Stevensons arrived in May,

Denver's population already must have exceeded by several thousand the 4,759 people living there in 1870.[30]

Visitors to the mile-high town often wrote approvingly of its growth and appearance. In 1867, the Frenchman Louis Simonin found Denver to be "well built," its houses "attractive, constructed of brick, stone or wood." Another visitor, Isabella Bird, the adventurous Englishwoman who toured the Rocky Mountain region of Colorado on horseback during the fall and early winter of 1873, described Denver as "a busy place, the *entrepot* and distributing point for an immense district, with good shops, some factories, fair hotels, and the usual deformities and refinements of civilization."[31] The Stevensons would have found comfortable lodging in one of the local hotels, such as the American House, Dyer's Hotel, or Ford's Hotel, and good meals at Ford's or Delmonico's restaurants on Larimer Street. The Front Range of the Rockies, with snow clinging to the tallest peaks, must have looked resplendent in the spring sunshine.

Soon after reaching Denver, Jim established the survey's headquarters about four miles outside of town at Miers Fisher's ranch along Clear Creek, where the scientists and camp employees gradually assembled. The narrow-gauge tracks of the Colorado Central Railroad passed nearby and continued up Clear Creek Canyon, connecting Denver with the mining towns of Black Hawk, Central City, and Nevadaville.[32] William H. Jackson used this line to travel the short distance between Denver and headquarters. Luckily for historians, he kept a diary that spring and summer, providing details of camp life, commentary on his fellow survey members, and insights into the rigors of surveying among the towering peaks of the Rockies. He also documented some aspects of Tilly's travels with Jim.[33]

Hayden divided the survey that summer into six parties, three assigned to survey separate districts along the eastern portion of the Rockies, and three—including Jim's quartermaster party and Jackson's photographic party—to traverse the entire area to be explored.[34] On May 24, the day he left headquarters, Jackson wrote in his diary, "Beautifully clear day and the mountains came out very distinctly." For the next month or so, Jackson's small crew zigzagged along a route that took them to Long's Peak, north of Denver, then south along the Front Range to the vicinity of Pikes Peak. On June 10, Jim and Tilly met up with Jackson in Black Hawk, bringing with them on the Colorado Central a large bundle of mail for the explorers. That same day, the Stevensons rode out to Jackson's camp, remained for dinner, and then returned to town, where Jackson joined them in the evening for tea, apparently at their lodgings in a local hostelry. Later that month, Jim and Tilly traveled to Denver, at which time Tilly probably left the survey for the East Coast.[35] Jim spent the rest of that summer in the mountains delivering supplies to Hayden's various survey parties.

When Jim returned to Washington later that year, he joined Tilly at their residence at 933 H Street NW. Their house was situated less than a half mile south of Tilly's parents' house on M Street, and about the same distance north of the survey's headquarters on the corner of Eleventh Street and Pennsylvania Avenue.[36] Jim would spend the winter and following spring conferring with other scientists in Hayden's offices, attending to official correspondence, planning for the next season's expedition, and sharing lobbying duties with Hayden on Capitol Hill. Tilly no doubt took as much pride as Jim in the accolades that foreign scientists bestowed on Hayden's survey. In May 1873, for example, the British Assyriologist Sir Henry Rawlinson (who deciphered cuneiform) spoke highly of Hayden and Stevenson's work in an address before the Royal Geographical Society of London. Two years later, Archibald Geikie, head of the Scottish branch of the British Geological Survey, expressed similar sentiments in an essay published in *Nature*.[37]

Hayden's survey returned to Colorado for the 1874 season, getting a late start because of congressional delays in approving its appropriation. Tilly probably accompanied Jim to Denver when he returned there on July 11 to coordinate plans for the summer's expedition. Other survey members gradually assembled at the rendezvous site on Clear Creek outside of Denver; Hayden arrived on the 18th, after one of his divisions had already taken to the field.[38]

Besides overseeing the quartermaster unit, Jim had a special mission that season: to guide the artist Thomas Moran to the Mount of the Holy Cross. This peak, a little more than fourteen thousand feet in elevation and approximately 150 miles west of Denver, featured deep crevices that looked like a cross when filled with snow. In 1873 Hayden's men had been the first in recorded history to reach its summit, and Jackson, from Notch Mountain across the ravine, captured its image with a camera. Jackson's photographs thrilled the American public and inspired Moran's journey west to sketch the snowy cross.[39]

Jim Stevenson and Moran had become close friends during the 1871 survey of Yellowstone. Almost certainly the artist visited the Stevensons when he traveled to Washington from his studio in Newark, New Jersey.[40] Moran's letter to his wife, dated August 10, 1874, gives us one of the few glimpses we have of Tilly in Colorado during this year's survey. On Saturday, August 8, the small Stevenson–Moran party left Denver, the men on horseback, Tilly probably in a carriage. Late in the afternoon, after traveling a distance of twelve miles, they reached the village of Morrison and spent the evening at "the house of a man named Morrison, whose daughter, a widow about 16 years old, played the piano & sang for us. . . . Mrs. Stevenson, being in Denver, accompanied us as far as Morrisons and then went back."[41]

On August 21, after fourteen days of travel, Moran and Stevenson reached a point on Notch Mountain that gave them a spectacular view of the phenomenon they had come to see. From the sketch he drew on the spot, Moran later painted a five-by-seven-foot canvas of the Holy Cross, which won high praise from the nation's art critics. Retracing their route, the party returned to Denver on August 30.[42]

Tilly may have spent the entire summer in Colorado, traveling with Jim whenever possible and taking in local attractions at other times. In September or early October, they traveled south together on the Denver and Rio Grande Railroad to the new resort town of Colorado Springs, where, on October 3, they met up with two divisions of the survey, one headed by Hayden, the other by Jackson. The photographer's party had just completed a sweep through southwestern Colorado, visiting Los Pinos Agency for the Ute Indians and then continuing southwest to the Mancos River area, where they located the ancient Indian ruins and cliff dwellings of the Mesa Verde region.[43]

By mid-October the Stevensons had returned to Denver, and would soon entrain for the East Coast. Tilly probably had her first significant encounter with American Indians before she left Colorado. Jackson notes in his diary entry for October 13, "Stevenson got a carriage & with a '*guid*' [*sic*] went 7 m[iles] above town" to a large Ute encampment. He fails to name the other occupants of the carriage, but he implies that Tilly went along. After taking four negatives, Jackson states, he then had dinner with the Stevensons.[44]

Both the Ute and Arapaho Indians (traditional enemies) had been frequent visitors to Denver following the 1859–61 Colorado gold rush period.[45] By 1874, however, the federal government had forced the Arapahos out of Colorado, and induced the Utes to relinquish part of their traditional homeland, restricting them to lands west of the 107th meridian of longitude (several miles west of the Continental Divide), but excluding them from the mineral-rich San Juan Mountain region of southwestern Colorado.[46] Since 1871, however, the government had operated a Ute agency in Denver to accommodate tribal members who made the annual fall hunting trip to the area to shoot buffalo. One of their favorite camping spots was on Cherry Creek, where Jackson took his photographs in 1874. From this location, the Utes frequently traveled into town to sell hides and purchase supplies in the local stores.[47]

The Ute encampment that Tilly visited in October was that of Chief Quinkent's people, one of three bands making up the Northern Utes. Quinkent (known to non-Indians as Douglass) was among the most popular of the Northern Ute leaders and had a large following. Whether Tilly and Jim visited this encampment prior to October 13 cannot be determined, but most likely they did, since the Utes often remained in the area for several weeks.[48] Among the Utes, according to anthropologist Nancy Parezo, Tilly "made her first tentative ethnographic study." Tilly would later credit her husband for teaching her "the rudiments of ethnographic technique."[49]

Jim Stevenson temporarily left the Hayden survey after the 1874 season to pursue a private business venture. In a letter dated March

8, 1875, Robert Adams, now a practicing attorney in Philadelphia, informed Hayden that Jim seemed "to be quite settled in his new business," and then he added, "you must miss him very much in many ways."[50] Indeed, in his fall report to Secretary of the Interior Zachariah Chandler, Hayden grumbled: "The various changes which have occurred in the personnel of the party during the past year has thrown an immense amount of executive labor on me, which has exhausted my strength, and consumed my time to such an extent that I have not been able to give the necessary attention and study to my portion of the [1874] report." About a year after his departure, however, Jim returned to the survey, which, according to his friend Henry W. Elliott, was "his first and best love."[51] He would serve as Hayden's executive officer during the final three years of the survey, its demise brought about in 1879 by the creation of the U.S. Geological Survey, under the direction of Clarence King.

Tilly's last journey with Hayden's survey came during the summer of 1878, when she accompanied Jim for at least part of the season. The four divisions of this year's expedition would concentrate on the mountainous regions of northwestern Wyoming, with one division given the task of making "a specially-detailed geological and geographical survey of the Yellowstone National Park." In mid-July, the scientists rendezvoused in Cheyenne, their departure from Washington again delayed because of congressional tardiness in passing an appropriation bill.[52]

After reaching Cheyenne on July 19, Jim found lodging at the Railroad House, where other survey members already had gathered. Several days later, as reported in the *Cheyenne Daily Leader*, he left town for Ogden, from which point he would go to Bozeman, "thence into Yellowstone Park with supplies for the expedition."[53]

Only as the survey ended its operations in Wyoming did the press also mention Tilly. On October 16, the day after Hayden left Cheyenne to return to Washington, the Cheyenne newspaper reported, "Capt. James Stevenson, of the Hayden survey, who, with Mrs. Stevenson have been stopping at the Railroad house [*sic*] several days, expect[s] to leave for Washington on Friday." Their departure was delayed, however—perhaps because of difficulties in settling business accounts or because of snowstorms, which had plagued the region for several days. In a private letter, Jim had noted on September 26, "The snow is deep here [Cheyenne] and the thermometer below zero—Stormed for the past 4 days."[54] The Stevensons finally left Cheyenne on October 27, stopping over in Omaha so that Jim could arrange to have railroad passes validated for survey members. On November 8, he sent a terse telegram to Hayden (who may have been in Philadelphia), announcing his arrival in Washington.[55]

Hayden's scientists would spend the next several months analyzing specimens and compiling reports. Jim turned to Tilly for help in drafting his treatise on the large collection of "geyser phenomena" that he had assembled while in Wyoming. "Emphatically a man of deeds, not of words" (as John W. Powell once put it), Jim felt more comfortable in the field than behind a desk, and consequently completed only a few manuscripts in his lifetime. After his marriage, he apparently handed his notes over to Tilly, gladly accepting her help in preparing the papers that would carry only his name.[56]

Jim continued handling administrative details for Hayden, until by congressional law the survey went out of existence on June 30, 1879. The end of Hayden's U.S. Geological and Geographical Survey of the Territories (the survey's official name since 1873) marked a turning point in Tilly Stevenson's life.[57] During the Hayden years, she had become a seasoned traveler, conditioned to the unexpected difficulties of rail transportation. Her treks to the West no doubt appealed to her sense of adventure and reinforced her desire to do important work. She acquired skills in writing up her husband's field notes, and had ample opportunity to observe how he handled administrative chores, interacted with other scientists, and approached American Indians, all of which helped prepare her for her future work. The one experience that would have the most lasting effect was her visit to the Utes, for she was to spend the rest of her life recording the lifeways of Indians. For the next seven years, she served her apprenticeship as an ethnologist under the careful guidance of her more experienced husband, the newly appointed executive officer of John Wesley Powell's Bureau of Ethnology.

CHAPTER 3

Becoming an Anthropologist

arly in August 1879, Tilly and Jim Stevenson, along with Frank Hamilton Cushing and John K. Hillers, arrived by train in Las Vegas, New Mexico, the current terminus of the Atchison, Topeka and Santa Fe Railroad. Here they remained for several days to collect the supplies, wagons, and mules necessary for their overland trek and eventual stay at their chief destination, Zuni Pueblo, located in the dry upland plateau region of west-central New Mexico. In the months that followed, Tilly immersed herself in the business of her husband, sent west by John Wesley Powell, director of the newly organized Bureau of Ethnology, as head of the bureau's first collecting and research expedition to the Southwest.[1] Working beside her husband, she must have discovered a special affinity for ethnographic fieldwork. This awareness, plus her enormous vitality, sense of adventure, and inquisitive mind, as well as Jim's tutelage and support, started Matilda Coxe Stevenson on the path to becoming one of the nation's premier ethnologists.

Tilly Stevenson first conducted fieldwork in New Mexico at a time when anthropologists were largely self taught, and the "science of man" was beginning to emerge as a professional discipline. Powell played a vital role in organizing the systematic study of North

America's indigenous societies. During his travels west as head of the Geographical and Geological Survey of the Rocky Mountain Region, Powell had spent a good deal of time collecting vocabularies and studying the lifestyles of Indian peoples. A visit to the Hopi and Zuni pueblos in 1870 presaged his later decision to send scientific expeditions to the region.[2]

In lobbying for the bill that consolidated the four western surveys into a single institution, the U.S. Geological Survey (1879), Powell persuaded Congress to include a provision that allotted $20,000 to complete the reports of his former survey, mainly the monograph series *Contributions to North American Ethnology*, under the direction of the Smithsonian Institution. Spencer F. Baird, who had succeeded Joseph Henry as secretary of the Smithsonian upon the latter's death the previous year, immediately appointed Powell to carry out this work. In subsequent weeks, with no clear mandate from Congress, he began to organize his new empire, the Bureau of Ethnology.[3]

At the time Powell formulated plans for the bureau, he was guided by the theories of Lewis Henry Morgan, the nation's most prominent anthropologist in the 1870s and, according to historian Donald Worster, Powell's "intellectual father." In *Ancient Society*, published only two years before the bureau's creation, Morgan presented his now-famous three-stage cultural evolutionary scheme. All societies, he posited, advanced through savagery and barbarism to civilization, with Euro-Americans having reached the high end of the scale, American Indians someplace beneath them. He urged the scientific community to study all American Indian peoples now before their traditional lifestyles disappeared. Morgan's book so captivated Powell that he stayed up late to read it, and he later made sure that ethnologists on his staff had their own copies.[4]

The Stevensons, as well as other bureau employees, carried this evolutionary mindset with them when they went into the field. And they shared Morgan's sense of urgency to gather as much information as possible about Indian cultures before they became extinct. With railroads inching their way into the Southwest, it seemed only a matter of time before outside influences changed indigenous societies beyond recognition. Over the years, no anthropologist

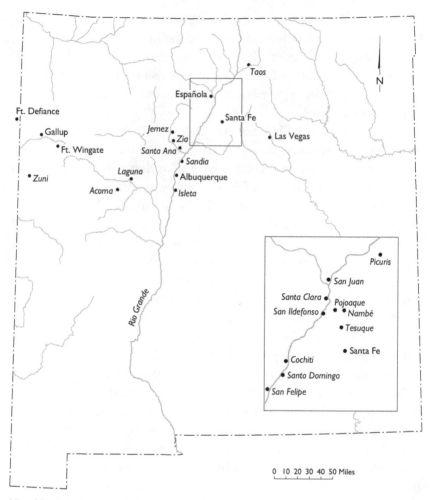

New Mexico Towns and Pueblos

exhibited greater devotion to this "salvage ethnology" than Matilda Coxe Stevenson.[5]

Before leaving Washington, Jim received Powell's written orders, which read in part: "You are hereby placed in charge of the party organized to make ethnological and archaeological explorations in south-western New Mexico and contiguous territory. Mr. J. K. Hillers has been instructed to report to you as photographer and Mr. F. H. Cushing of the Smithsonian Institution will assist you in making collections and in other ethnologic work."[6] Powell ignored the role Tilly was to play in the coming months, but he later stated that she had accompanied the expedition as a "volunteer coadjutor in ethnology."[7]

Jim traveled to New Mexico with letters of introduction from General William T. Sherman, commander-in-chief of the army; General Montgomery C. Meigs, quartermaster general; Spencer F. Baird; and William K. Rogers, private secretary to President Rutherford B. Hayes. The letters expressed similar sentiments—that Stevenson, an eminently qualified scientist, had been commissioned by the Smithsonian Institution to conduct investigations in ethnology and natural history. The writers requested that government officials in the Southwest assist him in carrying out his work. The army, in fact, rendered valuable service to the expedition, furnishing tents for quarters and wagons and mules for transportation, and allowing Jim to purchase supplies at cost at western military posts. Jim also received support from Commissioner of Indian Affairs Ezra A. Hayt, who instructed U.S. Indian agents in Colorado and New Mexico "to render him aid and cooperation in the discharge of his duties."[8]

Late in August, the expedition left Las Vegas in wagons and on muleback, traveling over an old stage route to Santa Fe. Tilly and her companions spent the first night at the village of San José, located on the Pecos River, where a dance was held in their honor. They bivouacked the second night among the ruins of the abandoned Pecos Pueblo and Catholic mission, situated farther up the Pecos. As the sun was setting the following day, they caught their first sight of Santa Fe, the territorial capital of New Mexico.[9]

During the week or more they spent in the capital, Colonel Edward Hatch, commanding the District of New Mexico, assisted them in gathering additional supplies. He also instructed officers throughout the district to collect "Indian relics" and other "curiosities" from their neighborhoods and ship them to Santa Fe in care of Jim Stevenson.[10] When not packing supplies, Tilly and the others bartered for pottery that Indians brought in from nearby pueblos, and also made a quick trip to Tesuque Pueblo, just north of Santa Fe, to purchase more "specimens."[11]

The expedition left Santa Fe for Zuni with one six-mule wagon, one four-mule wagon, and an army "ambulance" (a two- or four-wheeled vehicle drawn by mules). Twenty-two-year-old Cushing rode astride a mule the entire distance of roughly 190 miles. They were accompanied by Hispanic drivers and a Hispanic cook, one of whom probably served as interpreter once they reached Zuni.[12] After ten days on the road, being "constantly exposed to the burning sun of New Mexico" (as Tilly later recalled), the travelers reached Fort Wingate, about forty miles north of Zuni. Colonel George P. Buell, the fort's commanding officer, greeted them warmly and extended further aid over the next several weeks. Writing from Fort Wingate on September 16, Jim informed Powell that he already had made "arrangements with a gentleman to have a large collection made for us at the Navajo settlement & at the Moquis [Hopis]."[13]

The "gentleman" Jim referred to was undoubtedly Thomas V. Keam, former interpreter and special agent for the Navajos and the owner of two Indian trading posts, one just south of Fort Defiance (a day's ride north of Fort Wingate), and the other located in what was known as Keams Canyon, thirteen miles east of First Mesa, where three of the Hopi villages were situated. Keam was a frequent visitor to Fort Wingate, and was to become good friends with the Stevensons in the months and years to follow.[14]

Jim Stevenson's party, enlarged by a handful of "ladies and gentlemen" from the fort (including Mrs. Buell), arrived at Zuni on September 19.[15] Tilly now had her first glimpse of the village she would come to know intimately in the course of her fieldwork. The visitors soon pitched a camp of six white government tents in the corral of the Presbyterian mission a quarter of a mile north of the pueblo. Cushing recalled that the governor of Zuni (Patricio Pino, or Ba:lawahdiwa, his Zuni name) came to the camp that evening with a small delegation and, after eating sparingly of food set before him, asked if the visitors wished anything. Before departing, he invited them to join him the next day to feast on peaches and melons.[16]

The Stevensons witnessed that night, and indeed throughout their stay in Zuni, the good manners and hospitality for which the Zunis have been known since they first encountered American fur trappers in the 1820s. To cite one well-known example, George C. Yount's party, traveling east from the Colorado River early in 1827, reached the village "more dead than alive." "These kind and humane people," Yount later recalled, fed them nourishing meals and nursed many of them back to health. The same hospitality was extended to U.S. soldiers in 1846 when they arrived at Zuni "hungry and cold" shortly after the United States took possession of New Mexico. Housed with individual families, they consumed meals of mutton stew, flavored with vegetables, and wafer-thin bread. One soldier noted in his diary, "It was the best dinner I had ever sat down to," adding that the Zunis "have the reputation of being the most hospitable people in the world, which I believe they merit in every respect."[17]

Over the years, the Zunis cooperated with the U.S. Army in many ways, providing guides in the 1850s, for example, for topographical engineers searching for the best railroad route across the Southwest. Early on they recognized the economic benefits to be derived from this cooperation. They received substantial sums of money—about $4,000 in 1856—for selling corn to feed military horses and mules at Fort Defiance, and they also provided forage to army detachments that visited the pueblo. According to historian C. Gregory Crampton, army personnel were the most influential American visitors to Zuni from the Mexican War period [1846–48] through the early 1870s.[18]

Contacts between Zunis and Euro-Americans increased greatly in following years, especially after the Atlantic and Pacific Railroad was built north of Zuni in 1881. When the Stevensons arrived at the pueblo two years earlier, they encountered a handful of outsiders who had taken up residence on Zuni land: the Presbyterian missionaries and teachers Taylor and Mary Ealy with their two little girls and assistant Jennie Hammaker, and Douglas D. Graham, a trader who recently had established a store near the village.[19]

At the time the Stevensons entered the Southwest, the Zunis had an estimated population of fifteen hundred, making this pueblo the largest of the nineteen located in New Mexico.[20] In Tilly's first publication about the Zunis (1881), she described the pueblo as resembling "a great beehive, with the houses piled one upon another in a succession of terraces, the roof of one forming the floor or yard of the next above, and so on, until in some cases five tiers of dwellings are successively erected." She depicted the Zunis as peaceful agriculturalists, raising sheep, goats, horses, burros, and a few cattle, as well as wheat, corn, beans, pumpkins, gourds, melons, and peaches on farms and orchards located from five to twenty miles from the pueblo.[21] During the spring and summer, most Zunis lived in outlying settlements near the fields, returning to the main village after the harvest. Closer to home, the Zunis tended "waffle gardens" (so named because of their construction into small squares and rectangles), where they raised chiles, onions, melons, and herbs.[22]

A day or two after arriving in Zuni, Jim met with village officials to tell them the object of his visit. Cushing later described this meeting in colorful detail: "We told them, as well as we could through our Mexican interpreter, that we were from Washington . . . that their father was anxious to see how they lived, and to get some of their beautiful articles to show his white children; therefore he had sent us there with many fine things to trade." Jim closed the meeting "by giving the multitude a liberal feast of coffee and sugar." Tilly also recalled that the Zunis promised Mr. Stevenson "every possible aid," a promise they "sacredly kept."[23]

Jim rented a large room in the governor's house for the photographer, and secured through the courtesy of Taylor Ealy two rear rooms in the mission to use as a trading establishment. While Tilly and Jim kept busy bartering for objects that the Indians brought in, Hillers and Cushing wandered through the pueblo, the former taking photographs and the latter "measuring, sketching, and note-taking." Ealy documented some aspects of this burst of activity. In a diary entry for September 23, he noted, "Mr. and Mrs. Stevenson bought a great amount of pottery." And in a letter dated the following day, he wrote, "All or many of the old pieces of pottery are being bought up, to be sent to Washington; every nook and corner of the Pueblo are being photographed."[24]

For Spencer Baird, the secretary of the Smithsonian, the chief mission of Jim Stevenson's expedition was to collect Indian artifacts; he believed, like many of his associates, that the study of material culture was crucial for understanding non-Western societies. In justifying the emphasis he placed on collecting over other ethnological research, he raised the specter of European collectors pirating away these national treasures. Powell also saw the importance of collecting material culture, though he came to resent Baird's "heavy hand" in overseeing bureau expenditures and attempting to shape its research plans. In his third annual report, Powell urged that "the work of collecting should be prosecuted energetically" before objects were carried away by "visitors and speculators."[25]

During this trip to Zuni, the Stevensons (sometimes with Cushing's aid) collected more than two thousand objects. Earthenware articles, both ancient and modern, made up the largest part of the collection—water vases, canteens, paint pots, ladles, water jugs, eating bowls, spoons, salt and pepper boxes, bread bowls, cups, cooking pots, and so on. To illustrate "the domestic life and art" of the Zunis, they also collected stone axes, hammers, metates, pestles, baskets, toys, foods, medicines, dyes, and clothing.[26]

In letters to Washington, Jim kept Powell informed of the expedition's progress. Writing from Fort Wingate on October 12, he enthusiastically announced, "Our success has been beyond our expectations. I brought from Zuni yesterday two large wagon loads—loaded up to the bows—comprising the most curious & choice specimens ever gathered from this country, & I send the wagons back early in the morning for another large load. . . . I have already filled 42 large boxes, many of them as large as [desks at the Smithsonian]." He had completed a catalogue of the materials collected to date (undoubtedly with Tilly's help) and acquired the Zuni name for each object.[27]

In exchange for Zuni artifacts, the Stevensons offered calico cloth, lamps, candles, soap, tobacco, dentalium shells, and sleigh bells; they also traded lumber and possibly window glass for the labor that Zunis performed. The villagers especially wanted lumber, since they sawed none themselves. Earlier that summer, Taylor Ealy had informed the Pueblo Indian agent in Santa Fe that "almost daily they come to me to buy lumber," but, because of its high cost, he was unable to sell them any. So the Stevensons filled a need. "Each

Indian who aided in making boxes for packing the Government collection," Tilly later recalled, "received enough lumber to make a door, the Indians being taught to make the doors and hang them."[28]

The Zunis already had entered the American marketplace by the time the Stevensons arrived, and some now preferred to receive money rather than trade goods. The standard price was $1.00 per day for labor. Ealy had paid this amount the previous year, mostly in trade goods, to the Indians who helped dig his well and build his house. The Zunis accepted two yards of red flannel or seven yards of muslin for a day's work. They also bargained with Ealy, asking $5.00 to collect the mail at the Fort Wingate post office and $36 to travel to Billy Crane's, a stage station near the post, to collect three wagonloads of lumber.[29]

Approximately three weeks after arriving at Zuni, the Stevensons and Hillers returned to Fort Wingate, leaving Cushing behind to pack Indian artifacts in crates and continue his observations of Zuni culture.[30] Jim sent Hillers on ahead to photograph the six thousand Navajos expected to gather for the distribution of annuity goods at Fort Defiance, site of the Navajo Agency in eastern Arizona. He followed a few days later, planning to stop at the agency before continuing to the Hopi villages, some eighty miles farther to the west. He met up with Keam at Defiance, and shortly after was to write a letter to the Commissioner of Indian Affairs in support of Keam's efforts to be named Indian agent to the Hopis. Tilly, however, did not accompany Jim on this part of the field trip. In his October 12 letter, Jim wrote, "Mrs. S. is here at Wingate with Mrs. Buell, the Commandants wife[.] Genl. Hatch . . . insisted on her coming here, where she will remain till I am ready to come home."[31]

The quantity of goods that Keam secured for Jim Stevenson that fall is unknown, but it must have been substantial. Before starting on the trip to Fort Defiance, Jim informed bureau officials that a wagonload of material had already been collected for him from the Hopis and Navajos. As a result of this expedition, at least thirteen hundred items were obtained from the two tribes and later accessioned into the Smithsonian. The major part of this collection consisted of clay pottery—water vases, water jugs, cups,

Northeast Arizona

eating bowls, and cooking vessels—but it also included baskets, toys, clothing, hair and dress ornaments, and stone fetishes.[32]

Early in November the Stevensons returned to Zuni—in a raging wind and sandstorm. At first they lived in government tents pitched on the mission grounds, but moved into the Ealys' parlor about the time that snow fell and the nights grew colder. They remained at Zuni approximately two weeks before departing for Fort Wingate and eventually making their way to Washington, D.C.[33]

During their stay in Zuni, the Stevensons took special note of the daily activities going on about them, including a seemingly endless round of religious rites and ceremonies. When they first arrived in the pueblo, families were returning from outlying farming villages with produce, the women soon busily husking corn and preparing grain, peaches, and pumpkins for drying. Almost nightly they could hear Indians singing and beating a drum in preparation for a forthcoming dance.[34] Tilly also accompanied Jim to meetings of various secret organizations (usually forbidden to outsiders) and observed parts of the great Sha'lako festival. In preparation for the Sha'lako, which occurs annually in November or early December, the Zunis slaughtered oxen "by the dozen, sheep by the hundred." The women baked large amounts of loaf bread in outdoor ovens and watched over "huge vats of mutton stew, fired with red chili," simmering on indoor hearths. Swarms of visitors arrived—Navajos, Hopis, and Indians from the Rio Grande pueblos, all eager to witness the colorful dances and partake of the liberal feasts prepared by their hosts.[35]

The Stevensons also established rapport with important Zuni personages, thus laying the groundwork for the success of their future ethnological studies. They met the former governor Pedro Pino (Patricio Pino's father), one of the few elders who spoke Spanish, and who so impressed Tilly that she wrote in 1881, "Though holding no official position his fluency in speaking Spanish, together with his mature judgment and good sense, commands for him a high seat in the councils of his people."[36]

During this trip, Tilly began a long-lasting friendship with We'wha, a Zuni *lhamana,* "a man who combined the work and social roles of men and women" and dressed in women's clothes. We'wha was thirty years old (the same age as Tilly), a skillful potter and weaver, and a respected member of the pueblo. She knew the Ealys, apparently helped Mary Ealy with housework, and may have assisted Mrs. Ealy and Jennie Hammaker in the classroom. She also had begun to learn English.[37] Later, Tilly would write a humorous account of her attempt to introduce soap into the pueblo by teaching We'wha to wash clothes. In this anecdote, she identified We'wha as a male, though elsewhere the ethnologist employed the female pronoun in referring to her friend.

[The writer] selected as a pupil a man who had adopted woman's dress and who was known to be the strongest, most active, and most progressive Indian in the tribe; but he was averse to the work, and at first refused to wash. He looked on in silence for a time while the writer worked. Never having had any experience in that work herself, she soon had most of the water from the tub on the floor and was drenched to the skin. The pupil exclaimed: "You do not understand that which you would teach. You do not understand as much as the missionary's wife; she keeps the water in the tub and does not make a river on the floor. Let me take your place."[38]

Before returning to Fort Wingate early in October, Tilly had commissioned We'wha to make some "little things," possibly for her private collection. But Cushing informed Jim in a letter dated October 15 that, despite his prodding, We'wha had failed to complete the assignment.[39] In the draft of a second letter to Jim, Cushing explained that We'wha had told Miss Hammaker "that the preparations for the winter festivities—meaning [weaving] blankets, grinding corn, etc.—will so occupy her that she cannot make [the objects]." Almost as an afterthought, he added, "I trust, however, to the persuasive powers of Mrs. Stevenson—which are very great—for bringing this obstinate woman to terms."[40]

Over the years, Tilly acquired a reputation for being aggressive and domineering in her efforts to document the lifestyles of Pueblo Indians. Totally dedicated to the task of "saving" Indian culture for posterity, she never questioned the morality of her actions, never once asked whether Indians had the right to deny her access to their sacred knowledge. In her single-minded devotion to science, she sometimes upset Indians with her intrusive behavior. On this expedition, however, Cushing seemingly recognized Tilly's special talent for eliciting cooperation without necessarily giving offense— despite his own prickly relationship with her. Genuinely interested in Indian people, she found much to admire in their religion and lifestyles; her sincerity won the respect and subsequent cooperation of many Indian priests and elders, and helped her establish cordial relations with numerous Indian families.[41]

Still, like other pioneer ethnologists, both Tilly and Cushing at times antagonized their Indian hosts. Cushing often used bluff and aggression to gain access to ceremonial chambers and to overcome opposition to his note-taking and sketching.[42] By her own admission, Tilly resorted to subterfuge on occasion to obtain information. The Zunis "were so opposed to having their masks and rituals 'carried away on paper,'" she later wrote, "that it was deemed prudent to make but few ceremonial pictures with the camera, and the altars and masks were sketched in color by the writer without the knowledge of the people." She also met stiff resistance when she attempted to enter a ceremonial room during the night ceremonies of the Council of the Gods. As she described it years later, one man protested more persistently than the others, "declaring that no American shall enter." But a rain priest intervened, and Tilly achieved her goal. "The Kia'kwemosi, hearing the disturbance, [left] the ceremonial chamber by the side entrance, and, reproving the man in severe words for intruding upon forbidden ground, escorts the guests [the Stevensons] to the chamber and seats them by the altar."[43]

From the beginning of the 1879 expedition, relations between Cushing and the Stevensons were strained. Part of the trouble stemmed from Cushing's unclear status. As an assistant curator at the National Museum, he had received verbal orders from Spencer Baird to go west with James Stevenson, find a suitable tribe among the Pueblo Indians, and learn all he could about them. Yet, clearly, Cushing was expected to defer to Jim as head of the expedition. For the most part, the young ethnologist did, but not without complaining in letter after letter to Baird of Jim's alleged insensitivity and failure to treat him as an equal partner. No doubt he felt competition with both Stevensons to establish his identity as an ethnologist. His sense of being mistreated was not unusual, however; historian J. Kirkpatrick Flack believes that "unrelenting antipathies were the rule not the exception" among natural scientists in the late nineteenth century.[44]

At times, Cushing seemed almost apologetic in registering complaints against a man universally recognized as a superior executive officer, conceding in an unsent letter to Baird, dated October 15, that Jim was "an able and most excellent *business* manager, and, I think, as kind an executive officer as ever went into [the] field." In a following letter, Cushing wrote of Stevenson's habit of stopping by his quarters to inquire about his well-being. But although he described Jim as a "most thoroughly good natured" officer, he continued to complain, alleging, for example, that Jim failed to leave adequate supplies for him when the expedition left for the Hopi villages and again when it departed for Washington. That Cushing soon gained a reputation as "an inveterate complainer" helps to place his remarks in perspective. Even John Wesley Powell, one of Cushing's most staunch mentors, acknowledged his difficult personality in a letter to the Reverend Edward Everett Hale of Boston (1883): "I appreciate with you Mr. Cushing's unfortunate temperament. He fancies he has enemies where none exist."[45]

Still, Cushing attributed most of his difficulties with the Stevensons to Tilly, who, in the words of a Cushing scholar, "would be his lifelong rival as an expert on Zuni." Cushing apparently believed that Tilly controlled most of her husband's decisions, a highly unlikely supposition. That Tilly Stevenson was an unconventional woman surely accounts for much of Cushing's rancor toward her. Neither a mother nor a wife who stayed home while her husband took care of the world's business, she failed to comply with Victorian expectations of proper feminine behavior. She was determined to carve out a career for herself as an ethnologist, and the very traits that would allow her to succeed—ambition, drive, confidence, stubbornness— indeed traits that many nineteenth-century men admired in themselves and in other professionals, seem to have aroused in Cushing a deep-seated animosity.[46]

Tilly, on her part, had little patience for Cushing's youthful exuberance, which, early in the expedition, led him to take side trips away from the main caravan, evidently without notifying Jim. Nor did she approve of Cushing's move into the expedition's rented room about a week after arriving in Zuni or his subsequent adoption of Indian dress and immersion into Zuni daily affairs. Years later she expressed her feelings about Cushing on the back of a photograph picturing him in a costume that he had made out of Zuni materials: "Frank Hamilton Cushing in his fantastic dress worn while among the Zuni Indians. This man was the biggest fool and charlatan I ever knew." Tilly's propensity to speak her mind, apparent in this inscription, must also have contributed to the friction between the two ethnologists.[47]

Prior to their departure for Washington, the Stevensons secured a trio of objects from the old Spanish mission in Zuni, an action that would involve them in a controversy that continues to engage modern scholars. The building had fallen into disrepair, the Zunis having long ago abandoned the Catholic church. Jim's bold statement that he obtained from the ruins "in the dead hour of night" two four-foot-high images (statues of the archangels Saint Michael and Saint Gabriel) and part of the altar has led some writers, including Cushing, to conclude that he looted the church. In "Outline of Zuni Creation Myths" (1896), Cushing noted that "a party of Americans who accompanied" him to Zuni "desecrated the beautiful antique shrine of the church" when it carried away the images. Cushing's friend Adolph F. Bandelier, who visited Zuni in 1883, expressed a similar sentiment, recording in his diary that the church had been "plundered by the Washington party in the most shameless manner." Modern researchers often discount Tilly's claim that a council of religious and civil officers decided that "it would be well to have these objects go with the other Zuni material to the 'great house' (National Museum) in Washington, where they would be preserved." But a notation in Taylor Ealy's diary for November 10 adds weight to her statement: "We got the consent of the Casique [sic] to give up the images."[48]

Early on the morning of November 20, Tilly and Jim left Zuni for Santa Fe, stopping first at Fort Wingate to arrange transportation for their collection. En route to the territorial capital, they planned to secure additional artifacts at Laguna, Isleta, Santo Domingo, Sandia, and other Rio Grande pueblos. Hillers had started on his return trip to Washington a few days earlier, having exhausted his supply of negatives. Anxious to continue his ethnographic studies, Cushing persuaded James Stevenson to leave him behind while awaiting Powell and Baird's approval for his stay. Although he planned to remain in Zuni for no more than two months, Cushing would not return to Washington for nearly two and a half years.[49]

The 1879 expedition to Zuni was critical in establishing Tilly's credentials as an anthropologist. She had an excellent teacher in her husband, who got on well with people, despite Cushing's complaints against him. Her deep affection and respect for Jim seemingly grew during their shared experiences. She obviously relished her first prolonged fieldwork, possibly because it freed her from the constraints of polite Victorian society and appealed to her adventurous spirit. In the field she was free to explore an exotic world unlike her own. Unperturbed by the hardships and uncertainties of western travel, she showed an equal tolerance for the "strange" foods, habits, and living conditions of her Indian hosts. The challenge to document the lifestyles of Indian societies before they disappeared and to make her mark in the scientific community would keep her returning to the Southwest for the rest of her life.

Motherhood, however, would have limited Tilly's freedom to accompany Jim to New Mexico and to continue her career as an ethnologist. But the Stevensons never had children, a condition probably the result of medical complications and not a conscious decision on their part. Letters that Jim wrote while on a trip to New York City in 1880 strongly suggest that the couple had been looking forward to becoming parents. On July 10 he reported to bureau headquarters, "I arrived safely here yesterday with my invalid." About two and a half weeks later, he implied in a letter to Powell that Tilly, at age thirty-one, had suffered a miscarriage. "My wife's misfortune as well as mine," he lamented, would delay their return to Washington. Nowhere in extant letters did either Jim or Tilly mention anything specifically about having children.[50]

After leaving New Mexico late in 1879, the Stevensons stopped overnight in Chicago before continuing to New York and then to Washington. They now resided at 1303 P Street NW (only a few blocks from the Evanses' current residence on N Street) in a three-story house that Tilly would finally sell nearly two decades after Jim's death. The couple decorated their home with Indian pottery, baskets, blankets, and other craft work obtained during their western travels. Living on the premises in 1880 were two female servants (an Irish woman and possibly her daughter) and a male driver, presumably for the Stevensons' carriage.[51]

As the decade of the eighties got under way, Washington was poised on the brink of becoming one of the nation's most important intellectual centers. Many of its scientists and intellectuals were employed in government service, and came together in professional organizations to advance national culture and their own careers. By mid-decade, several such societies had growing memberships: the Philosophical Society of Washington, the Anthropological Society of Washington (founded in 1879 with John Wesley Powell its first president), the Biological Society, and the Chemical and Entomological societies. Many of Washington's intellectual elite also met at the prestigious Cosmos Club, a social club designed "to create the proper . . . atmosphere for intellectual activity." Following a national trend, almost all of these establishments were open to men only, leaving a growing number of professional women to work out their own support structures.[52]

A few years would elapse before Tilly took the lead in organizing the Women's Anthropological Society of America. In the meantime, she worked in other ways to enhance her professional status. The winter following her return from Zuni, she had helped Jim complete the catalogue of the artifacts they had collected, a manuscript that Powell published in the bureau's second annual report (1883).[53]

Tilly also devoted considerable time to writing "Zuni and the Zunians," her first attempt to describe an Indian society, which was privately printed in 1881. At the start of this thirty-page treatise, she identified herself as having accompanied the scientific expedition sent west by "Prof. J. W. Powell, U.S. Ethnologist," thus establishing her qualifications for writing about the Zunis. She also thanked the many officials who had aided in this enterprise— personnel of the railroad, General Sherman, Colonel Hatch, and especially Powell, who allowed her to illustrate her piece with Bureau of Ethnology drawings.[54]

Stevenson's essay was largely descriptive, based on her observations of the Zunis. She reported on their crops, animals, daily labors, agricultural practices, housing, layout of the town, and the general appearance of men and women. She recognized the difference that wealth made, even among the Zunis, who exhibited "little or no social distinction." She included a long section on pottery, probably (as Eliza McFeely contends) "[drawing] heavily on the notes she and her husband made for the catalogue." And although she spoke of Zuni dances and told something of their beliefs, she recognized her own limitations. "Little can be said respecting the myths and superstitions of this strangely interesting people," she wrote. "Without a knowledge of their language, only vague inferences can be drawn from witnessing the weird dances which form so prominent a part of their religious ceremonies."[55] Most importantly, this publication revealed two qualities that would characterize all of Tilly's work: careful descriptions of events and the environment she observed, and respectful treatment of Indian religious beliefs.

"Zuni and the Zunians" caught the attention of no less an eminence than Lewis Henry Morgan, a recognition that must have pleased Tilly. In his final work, *Houses and House-Life of the American Aborigines*, published in 1881 shortly before he died, Morgan devoted three pages to her description of Zuni Pueblo.[56]

The Stevensons had returned to Washington about the time its "fashionable season" got under way. From New Year's Day until the beginning of Lent, the capital was "extremely gay," the well-to-do and upper middle class flocking to dinners, balls, teas, and other forms of entertainment. Receptions arranged by the wives of leading statesmen and other notable figures were announced in the daily newspapers. Victorian etiquette, in fact, demanded that people of prominence not shirk their social obligations. In a political town like the capital, wives often were able to help advance their husbands' careers by adhering to protocol.[57]

Although preoccupied with her ethnographic work, Tilly undoubtedly attended her share of receptions during the first four months of 1880. A few years later, she and her mother would cohost regular Friday afternoon receptions, one of which the *Washington Post* described as among "the most delightful afternoon receptions on Friday last [1886]." On another occasion, she assisted Mary Logan, the wife of Senator John A. Logan, at one of her social gatherings, an event Mrs. Logan later described in her autobiography, *Reminiscences of a Soldier's Wife*.[58]

The Stevensons spent their second season of fieldwork collecting craftware from the Rio Grande pueblos. Before leaving the East Coast, Jim received written instructions from Powell. He was to proceed to the pueblos of New Mexico and Arizona with the following objectives in mind: "to make collections representing the arts and industries" of the Indians, "to make photographs and drawings" of their houses and scenes representing their daily lives, and to investigate their customs and lifestyles. Attached to the expedition were the photographer Hillers and two assistants, F. G. Galbraith and F. W. Morancy.[59] Among the credentials that Jim would carry with him was a letter written by his good friend and neighbor, Lieutenant Colonel Samuel B. Holabird, attached to the quartermaster general's office. In introducing the Stevensons to the commanding officer in Arizona, Holabird wrote, "We [the Holabirds] have come to esteem them most highly. You will find them most agreeable acquaintances as well as accomplished people."[60]

On September 9, the Stevensons traveled to New York, where Jim purchased a wide array of trade goods before starting by train via Chicago and Pueblo, Colorado, to Santa Fe. Earlier that year the AT&SF Railroad had extended its rails from Las Vegas down the Rio Grande Valley to Albuquerque, bypassing the territorial capital. An eighteen-mile branch, however, connected Santa Fe with the main line at Lamy. The Stevensons, Hillers, and the two assistants reached the capital on September 20, and took up residence at the Exchange Hotel, on the southeast corner of the plaza on San Francisco Street.[61]

Over the years, Tilly witnessed a remarkable transformation in Santa Fe's appearance, as city boosters worked to modernize the capital and regain its former economic prominence as the terminus of covered-wagon trade on the Santa Fe Trail. That enterprise ended with the arrival of railroads; thereafter the town's economic leadership was threatened by the upstart commercial centers of Las Vegas and Albuquerque, which were located directly on the railroad's main line and closer to regions that exported agricultural and other products.[62]

When the Stevensons arrived in 1880, Santa Fe's population stood at 6,635, many of whom were Spanish-surnamed farmers and farm laborers. A small community of Euro-Americans and Hispanic *ricos* (the wealthy class) dominated the town's commerce and elite society. The business district centered on the plaza, a park area in the middle of town that sported trees, benches, a bandstand, and a war memorial to Union veterans of the Civil War. The Palace of the Governors, a one-story adobe building containing government offices and the governor's residence, stretched along the plaza's north side; two-story frame business houses lined the other three sides. Although fairly wide dirt streets surrounded the plaza, elsewhere narrow ones predominated, often littered with garbage and wandering animals and flanked by flat-roofed adobe structures. An 1881 photograph of San Francisco Street west of the Exchange Hotel shows a number of burros sprawled in the dirt road.[63]

Reaching the Santa Fe train depot, Tilly and Jim would have taken a carriage for the one-mile trip to their hotel. A new gasworks to illuminate the town finally went into operation in December (after the Stevensons had left for home), and a system of regular garbage collection started some months later. The fashionable Palace Hotel (where Tilly often stayed in later years) was built in 1881 about a block northwest of the plaza to accommodate the influx of tourists and businessmen who arrived on the morning and evening trains. Not until March of the following year, however, did the town erect a modern water system with pipes laid through the principal streets.[64]

The day after reaching Santa Fe, the Stevensons made the acquaintance of forty-year-old Swiss-born Adolph F. Bandelier, sent west by the newly formed Archaeological Institute of America (AIA) to study Indian ruins. A former businessman and student of Latin American history, Bandelier had met Lewis Henry Morgan in 1873, and the two struck up a friendship. Morgan's influence helped Bandelier receive the AIA assignment and thus begin a career as scholar and anthropologist. Visitors to New Mexico recognize his name from Bandelier National Monument, created in 1916 to protect the fabulous Indian ruins located about twenty miles northwest of Santa Fe in Frijoles Canyon. During his researches in New Mexico, Bandelier, like Cushing, came to regard the Stevensons as competitors, although initially they seemed to be on friendly terms.[65]

While in Santa Fe, Jim again secured the assistance of Colonel Hatch, who furnished the expedition with two spring buggies, a six-mule team, tents, axes, and other camp equipage, as well as two men (presumably soldiers to serve as drivers and camp handymen). He also obtained bags of silver coins from the First National Bank to be used in purchasing Indian artifacts. More so than the Zunis, the Rio Grande villagers often wanted hard currency rather than trade goods for their craftware.[66]

James Stevenson's expedition visited the northern pueblos first, starting with Taos, some seventy miles north of Santa Fe. On October 2, the day after his arrival, Jim wrote in a letter to Powell, "Taos is a fine Pueblo, in structure, but comparatively nothing in the way of aboriginal productions is to be found among them." Still, the Stevensons managed to collect from Taos residents a substantial number of stone and clay objects. Hillers also took several excellent photographs of the village, which today are considered classics.[67]

Jim's crew stopped next at San Juan Pueblo, situated about fifty miles south of Taos on a major military wagon road. Because of its location, many of its "most valuable specimens" had already been bartered away to visitors. Even so, they left the village with between one hundred and two hundred objects.[68]

The Stevensons had better luck at Santa Clara Pueblo, a few miles south of San Juan, where they purchased a large amount of pottery, including jars, pitchers, cooking vessels, bowls, toy cups, and so on. Jim later described in great detail the process by which Santa Clara women produced their distinctive black polished earthenware. But he was most excited about the party's great archaeological "discovery" a few miles west of Santa Clara, the cave dwellings and ruins at Puyé, which the Santa Clara Indians had long considered the home of their ancestors. Guided by two Indians, each paid a dollar a day for his services, Jim explored the ruins, which he later described in a letter to Powell:

> In the faces of these cliffs [composed of a yellowish volcanic tufa], we found an immense number of cavate dwellings, cut out by the hand of man. We made no attempt to count the number of these curious dwellings, dug like hermit cells out of the rock, but they may be estimated with safety among the thousands. . . . They were excavated with rude stone implements resembling adzes, numbers of which were found here, and which were probably used by fastening one end to a handle. . . . Upon the top of the mesa of which these cliffs are the exposed sides we found the ruins of large circular buildings made of square stones 8 by 12 inches in size. . . . From four to five hundred people can find room within each inclosure.[69]

By October 15, Jim was back in Santa Fe to secure provisions and send an urgent plea by telegram to James Pilling, Powell's chief disbursing agent, to forward his salary to the Second National Bank. "Am seriously delayed for want of some money," he fretted. He also wired Tilly's father about his predicament, and received in short time additional funds.[70]

In the following days, the Stevensons and Hillers (sometimes accompanied by one or both assistants) visited the northern pueblos of San Ildefonso, Tesuque, and Nambé, and then returned to Santa Fe to pack the collection. It now amounted to fourteen hundred items, and would fill eleven large boxes. Toward the end of October, they started on a collecting trip to the southern pueblos, stopping first at Cochiti, about twenty-seven miles southwest of Santa Fe. Bandelier was there to witness their arrival and later recorded in his journal, "About 9 A.M. Stevenson, etc. arrived in two buggies. Went to the houses of the cacique and governor. Then called on me with his wife. Very pleasant visit."[71]

From Cochiti, the Stevensons traveled to Jemez, Zia, Santa Ana, Santo Domingo, and Sandia pueblos, amassing during the season a grand total of about twenty-eight hundred artifacts. At many of the pueblos, the expedition also purchased provisions, firewood, and the services of Indians as guides, hunters, and water carriers, thereby injecting additional money into the local economy.[72]

Bandelier, however, slowly came to look with jaundiced eye upon Jim's method of collecting. On November 1 (after his return to Santa Fe), he wrote, "Stevenson has bought nearly all the stone axes in town. Easy manner of collecting for the Smithsonian Institute!" Bandelier no doubt felt professional frustration after observing the Stevensons at work. He too had made important archaeological discoveries. On October 23, he became the first researcher to descend into Frijoles Canyon (with a Cochiti Indian guide) and explore its extensive ruins of a prehistoric civilization; a few days later he apparently became the first to view the mountain lions carved into rock near Cochiti, although James Stevenson also visited the site that fall. Writing to Professor Charles Eliot Norton of Harvard University, the first president of the AIA, Bandelier asked that a notice about his latest discovery be published before "the Government surveys" (presumably the Stevensons) took credit for it.[73]

Bandelier then allowed his resentment to overflow. "These Surveys of Major Powell are really ludicrous," he wrote. "I have but to be grateful, personally, to the gentlemen connected with them, but it is absolutely ridiculous.—Not one of Mr. Stevenson's party knows a word of Spanish,—they travel from Pueblo to Pueblo in carriages, with all the apparel of comfort, & spend (besides the salaries) $1500.—in 4. months. They have made a great bluster about discoveries in the Cañón of Santa-Clara; it is nothing but what I have seen at the Rito de los Frijoles." Vain about his own fieldwork at this early stage of his career, Bandelier (like his friend

Cushing) envisioned enemies where none existed.[74]

The Stevensons spent the following winter and spring in Washington. Tilly finished her article on the Zunis, helped Jim complete an illustrated catalogue of their recent collection, and prepared for a new season in the field. By now the couple had established a pattern of wintering in the capital and returning to the Southwest in late summer or fall. Jim's responsibilities increased, however, when in 1881 Powell was named to succeed Clarence King as director of the U.S. Geological Survey. Now heading two government agencies, Powell moved several bureau employees, including himself and Stevenson, to the payroll of the more liberally funded survey, thus releasing thousands of dollars from the bureau's budget for ethnological work. Jim apparently continued to receive his old salary of $3,000 a year, although he served as executive officer for both organizations.[75]

The Stevensons' third season of fieldwork, like their first, would later involve them in controversy. Before heading west, Jim purchased nearly $1,500 worth of trading goods in New York City—beads, necklaces, cloth, shirts, mirrors, needles, hammers, saws, and axes— items he believed the Zunis and Hopis coveted.[76] In late July 1881, they left Washington for New Mexico, accompanied by Victor Mindeleff, a young member of the bureau staff, whose assignment was to measure and map Zuni and then construct a scale model of the pueblo for the National Museum. Photographer Hillers and at least two volunteer assistants also joined the party.[77]

Once they reached New Mexico, their work was made more difficult by unusually heavy rains, which often caused train delays while crews rebuilt tracks and bridges washed away in prodigious runoffs. Their arrival at Fort Wingate was witnessed by Washington Matthews, the post surgeon. "Stephenson [*sic*] came down on us a week ago with half a dozen tenderfeet," he wrote to his friend Frank Cushing on August 8. Matthews had met Cushing earlier that year, and the two men quickly discovered a shared interest in ethnology. Cushing probably also shared with the army doctor his complaints against Tilly and Jim. "Stephenson staid with us [presumably Matthews and his wife], and we blew your trumpet all the time he was here," the letter continued, "& he kept rather 'mum.'"

Tilly, who apparently had stopped off at Crane's Ranch, also received Matthews's mocking attention. "We have not seen her fair face nor listened to her gentle voice. Perhaps she wanted an invitation to Wingate but she didn't get one."[78]

The Stevensons soon returned to Santa Fe to gather supplies that Jim was unable to obtain at Fort Wingate. They made the return trip to the post in the company of paleontologist Edward D. Cope, formerly of Hayden's survey and now looking for fossils in New Mexico. The ride from Albuquerque to Fort Wingate usually took a day, but on this occasion it took two. In a letter to his wife, Cope vividly described the difficulties they encountered.

> We rattled as far as Laguna and had to take a wagon and go around a broken bridge and damaged track [due to rains], meeting another train 4 1/2 miles beyond. The driver was very slow and when we reached the place, the train was gone! We sat down in the weeds and waited two hours and it came back, quite accidentally the conductor said, and we got aboard and rode some 25 miles. Then at 9 p.m. he put us out at a place called McCarty's and turned about and left us as soon as possible. We were not pleased and looked around for lodgings, but found none. There were two houses, station house with no waiting room, and a section house for work-men. I got out my blankets and laid down on the platform between some boxes and trunks, and got to sleep. A cold wind sprang up and gave me the creeps. . . . In the meanwhile we had telegraphed for relief, and learned that a train would come down from near this end, and take us off. It arrived at 3 A.M. and we got in and steamed away. By 8 A.M. we were at Wingate Station, where a box car serves as a station house. We sat on the mail bags and ate breakfast from our satchels.

A sergeant on the same train walked three miles to the post to secure a carriage, which finally carried the weary scientists to their destination.[79]

At Fort Wingate the Stevensons met up with two of Powell's geological survey parties, one headed by Powell's brother-in-law, Almon "Harry" Thompson, a man Tilly came to greatly admire. Within days, however, Jim, Tilly, Hillers, and two assistants set out for the Hopi villages, spending approximately one month in the area adding to the Smithsonian's collection.[80] Jim made Keams Canyon his headquarters, again enlisting Keam's aid in obtaining Indian artifacts. By the end of the season, the expedition had accumulated about twelve thousand pounds of material from the Hopis, mainly pottery and stone implements. Expedition members also explored the ruins of Awatovi, a once-thriving Hopi village located about ten miles southeast of First Mesa, and known to the Navajos as Tally-Hogan (Singing House).[81]

In an interview with a *New York Tribune* correspondent after his return from the field, James Stevenson touched upon highlights of the expedition's visit to the seven Hopi villages. He said that the residents of Oraibi, the westernmost village and the one most resistant to Euro-American influences, "became so much alarmed [by the approach of the ethnologists] that they abandoned their homes, leaving only the aged and the bed-ridden." The visitors investigated the nearly deserted village at their leisure, with Hillers taking a number of "fine" photographs. The party showed some restraint, however, for according to Jim, "it was thought best not to carry away any of the utensils or curious articles of furniture with which the village homes were filled."[82]

The Stevensons spent most of October and November in Zuni, collecting artifacts and continuing their observations of Zuni rituals and ceremonies. Tilly may have helped Jim prepare the catalogue of this year's collection, but in his reports he gave credit only to the men who assisted him. On November 10, he informed Powell that he, Cushing, and Mindeleff had been "at work night and day for a week numbering and labeling the specimens, the [manuscript] has reached 200 pages of foolscap, and will reach about 600 pages by the time we get them all catalogued." Cushing's help was indispensable. Having mastered the Zuni language, he recorded the Indian name of most items collected from the village. These materials, amounting to about twenty-one thousand pounds, with articles of clay predominating, were packed in large wooden boxes and hauled in army wagons to the railroad, then forwarded to Washington.[83]

Sometime during their stay at Zuni, the Stevensons went in search of Kolhu/wala:wa (Zuni Heaven), located near the confluence of the Zuni and the Little Colorado rivers in Arizona. According to Zuni religion, this is the place "where all Zunis go after death and where the supernatural Kokko [gods] reside under a sacred lake fed by the waters from a precious spring." Once every four years, a delegation of Zunis went on a religious pilgrimage to the lake to make offerings and say prayers on behalf of all tribal members. Cushing had secretly visited the site late in 1880 or early 1881, and took away prayersticks and other religious items from nearby shrines. When the Zunis discovered his theft, he was tried before a council of priests. Fortunately, he was released unharmed, though the penalty might very well have been severe.[84]

Most likely, the Stevensons first heard of Kolhu/wala:wa from their young colleague. Determined to see it for themselves, they set out with a Zuni guide, who had not been told of their intentions. After spending a night in St. Johns, Arizona, they "cautiously" broached the subject with the guide. Years later, Tilly remembered that "extreme persuasion was necessary to induce him to guide them to the sacred spot." As they neared their destination, the Zuni said to her, "If you insist on going, I will show you the way, but I shall offend the gods and I shall surely die." Disregarding the man's fears, the Stevensons pushed on and descended into the cave shrine adjacent to the lake. In writing about this excursion, Tilly unabashedly noted that the guide, lacking permission to visit the lake, faced "not only death within four days by the anger of the gods, but severe corporal punishment and perhaps death by order of the Ko'mosona."[85]

The Stevensons showed a similar disregard for Zuni customs when they acquired an Ahayu:da, a carved wooden image of a Zuni war god. Each year Zunis created new images of the Elder Brother Ahayu:da and the Younger Brother Ahayu:da, and took them to shrines outside the village. Their powers, it was believed, were capable of bringing rain and prosperity to the Zunis and of "promoting good in the world." Images carved in earlier years were allowed to disintegrate in their outdoor shrines, a process that dissipated their vast and potentially dangerous powers. Both Cushing and Jim threatened to upset this annual procedure when they obtained Ahayu:da for their personal collections and thereby unleashed these destructive powers on society at large.[86]

During his years at Zuni, Cushing acquired two Ahayu:da, selling one to the Berlin Museum. Jim obtained his Ahayu:da in 1881 from the Stevensons' friend Nai'uchi, the Zuni elder brother Bow priest, who took it from a shrine on nearby Corn Mountain. Several years after Jim's death, Tilly deposited this Ahayu:da in the National Museum; Cushing's widow sold the Ahayu:da her husband had collected to the Smithsonian. Despite these infractions of Zuni conventions, Nai'uchi and other Zuni elders continued to cooperate with the Stevensons and Cushing, probably for political reasons. With more and more outsiders encroaching on their territory, they hoped that these government scientists would champion their interests in the capital. And, in fact, over the years they did aid and support the Zunis, both locally and in Washington.[87]

Before the Stevensons left Zuni, they encountered John G. Bourke, an army officer and ethnologist who arrived to witness the annual Sha'lako festival. Earlier in the year, Bourke had met Cushing and Matthews at Fort Wingate, established a friendship with each, and learned of Cushing's resentment of the Stevensons. Bourke soon came to share his friend's biases, writing in his journal especially negative accounts of Tilly. On one occasion he recorded that Pedro Pino had told him that the new schoolmaster Samuel A. Bentley and Tilly Stevenson had said that Cushing "is not a chief at all . . . that he is only a muchacho (boy) and has not been sent here by order of the Great Father." Pino wanted to know if this were true. Bourke responded: "Cushing is one of the President's favorite sons and has come here by his, the Great Father's orders." He told Pino that Bentley had lied to him, and that Tilly did not know. "Among us," he continued, "women don't know much about what the [Great Father] is doing." Bourke's domineering male arrogance is clearly at work here.[88]

In early December, the Stevensons returned to the Hopi villages, presumably to arrange for the transportation of artifacts, before starting for home.[89] In Washington, they would write up their notes, attend social and professional events, and prepare for the next field season.[90] They may also have helped organize the reception that Senator and Mrs. Logan held at their home for a delegation of visiting Zunis. Cushing had arranged for five influential tribesmen, including Governor Patricio Pino, Pedro Pino, and Nai'uchi, in addition to one Hopi, to travel with him to the capital in March 1882. Here they met with President Chester A. Arthur and visited several Washington tourist sites. The Stevensons escorted them to Mount Vernon, where the ninety-plus-year-old Pedro Pino was overcome with emotion while standing before Washington's tomb. He regarded the nation's first president "as the Great Cacique of the American chiefs," and had longed to visit the site where Washington had lived. "Miss Grundy," a newspaper correspondent at the scene, later reported that for several minutes the "old man . . . stood clinging reverently to [the iron grating] until at last Mrs. Stevenson gently drew him away." The Indians also visited the Washington Monument; against Cushing's advice, the elderly Pino climbed to its top and "grew sick from all the exertion." While the rest of his party went on to Boston, Pino stayed with Tilly and Jim to recuperate.[91]

Pino quickly recovered after only a few days with the Stevensons and continued his sightseeing. He was "delighted" by a visit to the Government Printing Office, where he viewed women sewing pages together to make books. When it came time for him to return to Zuni, he again was overcome with emotion. He had grown fond of Tilly and Miss Grundy, and called them his daughters. "Both Mrs. Stevenson and I were much affected by Pedro Pino's unfeigned grief at saying goodbye to us," Miss Grundy later reported. "He so evidently realized his age and the unlikelihood of his ever coming here again."

The journalist writing under the pen name of Miss Grundy evidently was a good friend of Tilly's, for in this same article she expressed her admiration for the budding ethnologist. "She is a very gifted woman in respect to physical endurance as well as mental endowments. . . . She does not seem to mind hardships or fatigue, she is so interested in the Indians and collecting their antiquities."[92]

The Stevensons returned to the Southwest in late August 1882 to carry out Powell's instructions to Jim to explore and study the ancient ruins in Arizona and New Mexico, commonly known as "cave and cliff dwellings." Jim also was to provide logistical support for Senator and Mrs. Logan's visit to Zuni. Although the Logans had journeyed west primarily to see their daughter Dollie and her husband, Major William F. Tucker, recently attached to the paymaster's department in Santa Fe, the senator—as a member of the Senate Committee on Indian Affairs—also planned to visit Zuni, Hopi, and other Indian sites before returning to the capital.[93]

On September 10, the Logans, their son John, Jr., the Stevensons, and several other guests left Santa Fe for Albuquerque, where they boarded a special train that took most of the party to the end of the tracks, which now extended to Williams Station, nearly eighty miles west of Winslow, Arizona. The Stevensons most likely left the party at Wingate Station, so that Jim could obtain tents and other camping equipment from the military at Fort Wingate. A news dispatch dated September 13 indicated that Jim and his party would leave the post that day to set up camp at Zuni before the Logans arrived on the 14th. During the senator's six-day tour of Zuni territory, Tilly served as his interpreter. This seemingly innocent visit set the stage for a long drawn-out controversy, in which Logan was accused of conspiring with his son-in-law to secure Nutria Spring, a vital source of water for one of the outlying farming villages.[94]

Once the Logan party left Zuni, Jim set about preparing for the major expedition of the season, a reconnaissance of Canyon de Chelly, located in northeastern Arizona on the Navajo Reservation. Other government expeditions had traveled through the canyon, but none had as its specific mission the exploration of archaeological remains in its vast interior. As in past years, Stevenson received vital support from the military; Colonel Luther Bradley, commanding officer at Fort Wingate, supplied an ambulance, a freight wagon to carry supplies, and an escort of four soldiers. One of Jim's guests on the expedition, Henry C. Rizer of the *Eureka Herald* (Kansas), wrote in an early dispatch from the field, "For the ambulance we are probably more indebted to the fact that the Colonel [Jim] is accompanied by his courageous wife, who is familiar with frontier life, having been with him on various similar expeditions heretofore."[95]

In letters to his home newspaper, Rizer furnished the most detailed and colorful account of the entire expedition and mentioned Tilly more frequently than did her own husband in his report of the three-week journey. On October 3, the Stevensons, Rizer, and the army escort set out from Fort Wingate en route to Keam's ranch, where they would rendezvous with other expedition members. They traveled forty-eight miles to Fort Defiance on the first day, twenty-eight miles to Williams's ranch on the second, and forty-three miles to Keam's place on the third. On this final stretch, they found water only once, at a "muddy pool," where they stopped for an hour to let the animals rest. "For ourselves," Rizer explained, "we carried an abundance of water in canteens, and the mules were glad to take that afforded by the mud hole." He then provided another glimpse of the only woman on the expedition: "Mrs. Stevenson had been thoughtful enough to provide a lunch which was rapidly consumed by the Colonel and myself, of course out of compliment to her. Among other things she produced a quantity of tea which she consented to entrust to me for preparation."[96]

Other members of the exploring party were on hand to greet them when they reached Keam's ranch. When fully organized, the party included six government employees (in addition to Stevenson): ethnologist Victor Mindeleff, the photographers John K. Hillers and Benjamin Wittick, Joseph Stanley Brown (Powell's secretary and disbursing officer for the expedition), Major Alfred J. Gustin (artist), and Edward A. Oyster of the U.S. Geological Survey. Rounding out the roster were Tilly, Keam, Thomas A. McElmell (Keam's guest), Rizer, four soldiers, two teamsters, and two Navajo guides (George and Charlie).[97]

The trip proved arduous—the terrain often rough, the weather often nasty—but also breathtakingly beautiful once the travelers reached the majestic canyon lands. Tilly shared the rough conditions of camp life with her congenial traveling companions. On the second day out from Keam's ranch, October 8, they made camp near several ponds of murky water, of which Rizer claimed, "when boiled with a sufficient quantity of coffee in it the very marked yellow tinge with which it was decorated was entirely destroyed." That evening, after obtaining a sheep from a passing Navajo herder, they feasted on broiled mutton, "the best broil of mutton I have ever tasted," Rizer exclaimed. From then on, he said, "we scarcely ate a meal during our trip without mutton in some form." When the temperature dropped that night, ice formed in their canteens. But a hearty breakfast, featuring "an excellent mutton stew prepared under the directions" of Keam and McElmell, must have revived sagging spirits.[98]

Later that day, October 9, the party traveled through deep sand for several miles before reaching the mouth of Canyon de Chelly. According to Jim, "The wagon and other vehicles of our party sank deeply into the sand, rendering it extremely difficult for our animals to draw them." They moved three miles into the canyon before establishing camp for the evening. But a cold wind "swept in whirling eddies around us so fiercely and steadily," he noted, "as to render it extremely difficult to cook our supper." Tilly ate her food that night "highly seasoned with grit."[99]

The following morning, October 10, they proceeded up Canyon de Chelly while "squalls of rain and hail succeeded each other every few minutes." They soon entered a large side canyon, which Jim later designated as Canyon del Muerto ("of the dead"), a name suggested by Thomas McElmell because of the human burials the expedition discovered. Almost immediately they came upon some of the canyon's numerous ruins, most located on rocky shelves protected by overhanging cliffs from one hundred to three hundred feet above the canyon floor. For three and a half days they explored several of the cliff dwellings from their base camp at "Royal Arch," named for the huge "oven-like" cave directly across the way. Here they found the remains of a prehistoric village, as well as artifacts of its inhabitants—two sandals made of yucca fiber, and "several pieces of well-constructed cord."[100]

But, as Jim reported, "the most interesting discovery of all awaited our search, two miles further up the canon," where "we found an immense double cave containing the well-preserved remains of a village" at least the size of some of the Hopi towns. To reach the site, they had to climb "a steep bank of sand and broken stones," which had fallen from above. Once there, Joseph Stanley Brown discovered a burial crypt enclosing two skeletons, which appeared to have been buried "in a sitting or rather a squatting [posture]."[101]

Jim's party returned to Canyon de Chelly on October 13, lashed by fierce winds that carried "clouds" of sand. In Rizer's words, "There seemed to be no cut off, no shelter from the pitiless pelting of sand and pebbles and the suffocating dust." The explorers finally made camp under some cottonwood trees to wait out the storm—unable to light a fire to prepare their "long delayed dinner" until late at night. They spent the next four days probing the nooks and crannies of Canyon de Chelly. By the time Jim's crew started its return to Keam's place, on October 18, it had visited forty-six cliff villages, several of which they surveyed, photographed, and sketched.[102]

The Stevensons reached Fort Wingate in time to meet John Wesley Powell before he left the post in late October for the Grand Canyon. Early the following month the husband-wife duo headed for Acoma Pueblo, but a smallpox epidemic there prevented them from staying very long. Jim devoted the rest of November to studying the ruins in Frijoles Canyon. Tilly, however, may have stayed several days in Santa Fe to recuperate from the ordeal of Canyon de Chelly. Bandelier called on her there one afternoon in mid-November, and noted in his journal, "She has recovered and is pleasant." En route to Washington in early December, the Stevensons stopped for a few days in Denver, where Jim gave an interview to the local press about their recent exploits.[103]

The Stevensons spent most of the following field season (1883) exploring and excavating ruins in northeastern Arizona. Near the start of their investigations (in August), they encountered the

Dutch anthropologist Herman ten Kate at Fort Defiance, where Almon H. Thompson also had a camp for his geological survey crew. "The arrival of Mr. Stevenson and his wife, charged with a scientific mission from the Smithsonian Institution," Ten Kate recorded, "and of General [Samuel C.] Armstrong, superintendent of the Native school in Hampton, Virginia, injected considerable liveliness into the camp."[104]

For parts of August and September, the Stevensons were accompanied by Otto Gresham, a college student and son of Postmaster General Walter Q. Gresham. Because young Gresham's health had deteriorated during a strenuous academic year, Jim had agreed to take him along, at the request of President Arthur. Otto was with Tilly and Jim when they visited the seven Hopi villages, where they collected more items for the National Museum. Later, while digging at a group of ruins elsewhere, they were deserted by the hired help (most likely Indian laborers), who feared an outbreak of Navajo hostilities. Much later, a story was told about this incident; possibly the tale is apocryphal, and yet it is in keeping with Tilly's known fearlessness in the field. It also demonstrates her awareness that her gender could be useful in difficult situations. As the three continued their excavations (so the story goes), two Navajos passed nearby. Tilly offered them employment, but they declined, one saying that they were en route to a war dance and then planned to "kill all Americans." "Mrs. Stevenson—though knowing her action would have meant death to a man—laid her hand on the old man's arm and said smilingly, 'But you will come for me and help me.'" Eventually the two Navajos went to work for the ethnologists.[105]

The Stevensons also visited Zuni sometime that summer. Tilly would incorporate the information she acquired during this and previous stays in her essay "The Religious Life of the Zuni Child," published in the bureau's annual report for 1883. In Powell's introduction, he publicly recognized her contributions to ethnology for the first time, but he couched his praise in terms acceptable to male scientists. Mrs. Stevenson's research, he assured them, was "mainly among the women of the tribe and directed to the understanding of domestic life." Her work therefore was "complementary to that of Mr. Cushing." Tilly never limited her studies to family matters, but this essay does focus primarily on ceremonies relating to the initiation of children (mainly boys) into the order of the Kok-Ko. And in later publications, she included much information about women and their offspring, which caused anthropologists Margaret Mead and Ruth Bunzel to call her "the first American ethnologist to consider children worthy of notice."[106]

Many nineteenth-century scientists believed that women researchers, like Tilly Stevenson, were essential to the task of understanding nonwestern societies. They (more readily than men) could tap into Indian women's knowledge about childbirth, female rituals, and other topics pertaining to their sex. No anthropologist better expressed this sentiment than the distinguished Oxford University professor Edward B. Tylor, who praised the Stevensons' husband-wife approach to their studies. Tylor, Professor Henry N. Moseley of Oxford, Moseley's wife, and Grove Karl Gilbert of the U.S. Geological Survey had visited the couple at Zuni in September of 1884. They were enchanted by their visit, traipsing to Corn Mountain with Tilly to examine shrines and witnessing a dance held in their honor. Afterward, Tylor sent a scarlet blanket to the governor of the village to express his appreciation, and he also spoke "in unbounded terms of admiration and gratitude for the zeal and kindness" of the Stevensons on behalf of his party.[107] When Tylor addressed the Anthropological Society of Washington later that year, he singled out the couple for special recognition and emphasized the importance of welcoming women into the profession.

> It was interesting at Zuni to follow the way in which Col. and Mrs. Stevenson were working the pueblo, trading for specimens, and bringing together all that was most valuable and interesting in tracing the history of that remarkable people. Both managed to identify themselves with the Indian life. And one thing I particularly noticed was this, that to get at the confidence of a tribe, the man of the house, though he can do a great deal, cannot do all. If his wife sympathizes with

his work, and is able to do it, really half of the work of investigation seems to me to fall to her, so much is to be learned through the women of the tribe, which the men will not readily disclose. The experience seemed to me a lesson to anthropologists not to sound the "bull-roarer," and warn the ladies off from their proceedings, but rather to avail themselves thankfully of their help.[108]

It was during this field season that the Stevensons received permission from a priest to travel with a Zuni guide to the Zunis' sacred salt lake, located about forty miles south of the pueblo. This was a special privilege, since women never went on salt-gathering pilgrimages. When the men went forth, they deposited prayer plumes at the several shrines situated between Zuni and the lake. Tilly learned that other Indians, including the Hopis, Navajos, and Apaches, also gathered salt from this source, and that the area surrounding the lake was considered neutral ground. In olden days, in times of war, she later explained, "one was safe from the attacks of the enemy so long as one remained within the recognized limits of the lake."[109]

Tilly also wrote that she and Jim took from the site several religious articles, which later were deposited in the National Museum. Neither they nor Powell questioned the propriety of their actions, believing that material objects, especially sacred ones, helped scientists unravel the mysteries of exotic societies. In his summary of bureau activities for the season, Powell praised the Stevensons for the large collection they had made at Zuni (approximately thirty-five hundred objects), and forthrightly stated that some of them had been secured from "sacred springs, caves, and shrines."[110]

The Stevensons ended the season in Santa Fe, where Tilly's sister Georgie and her husband, William H. Patterson, now resided. Patterson had been hired as an assistant to New Mexico's surveyor general, but had come west mainly for his health. While the Stevensons were in the capital, the local press carried a long article on their work, and noted that Tilly evidently had "captured the admiration and esteem of the Zuni war-chiefs," for they had allowed her to place two Zuni children in the U.S. Indian Training School in Albuquerque. The four-year-old facility offered a curriculum that was meant to speed the integration of Indian youngsters into American society.[111]

Ironically, although Tilly dedicated her life to preserving Indian culture on paper, she and her husband, like so many other anthropologists of their era, became catalysts for change within the Indian communities they were studying. By encouraging Zuni children to attend government schools, the Stevensons hastened the speed with which Pueblo people learned English and adopted Euro-American customs and values. And by exchanging manufactured items, such as tools, cloth, windowpanes, doors, and candles, for Indian craftware, the Stevensons contributed to the vast changes taking place in Indian homes, architecture, and material culture.[112]

In the spring of 1885, Jim (and possibly Tilly) Stevenson attended two lectures that Washington Matthews presented to the Philosophical Society of Washington. Matthews summarized for his audience his investigations into the Navajos' Nightway ceremony and their use of drypaintings (or sand paintings). Prior to this time, ethnologists had thought that Navajos lacked any religious art, but Matthews proved otherwise.

Spurred on by Matthews's discovery, Jim delivered an illustrated talk on Zuni sand paintings later that year, at a meeting of the Anthropological Society.[113] In his presentation, he explained that sand paintings formed "only an incidental part" of Zuni religion, but they were much more important to the Navajos, "constituting the entire decorative plan of one of their most impressive ceremonies." The ceremony that he and Tilly observed at Zuni continued for four consecutive days and nights, the first three nights lasting until midnight, and the fourth until sunrise. The sand painting was made on the fourth day. On that evening, Jim recalled, the ceremonial room had become "stifling from the heat, smoke and additional [people]" who crowded in for the healing rituals. Jim readily acknowledged Tilly's help in gathering materials for this lecture. "Mrs. Stevenson who accompanied me to Zuni," he told his audience, "attended their daily and nightly exercises, and gave much time and care to the study of their religious life. I am indebted to her for many points of information regarding their Altar worship, and the sand painting connected therewith. The illustrations I have here tonight are from her field sketches." Nancy Parezo rightly notes that this acknowledgment is more than other scientists typically gave their spouses, "and demonstrates that James thought of his wife as a colleague."[114]

That summer, the Stevensons accompanied John Wesley Powell on a research tour of archaeological ruins near Flagstaff, Arizona, where a local news correspondent noted their presence on August 27. Later they visited the cavate dwellings near Santa Clara Pueblo in New Mexico, taking time to photograph, sketch, and take measurements so that models could be made.[115]

After leaving Powell, the Stevensons traveled to Keams Canyon, where they had the "good fortune to arrive . . . a few days before the commencement of a Navajo healing ceremony," the Nightway, which began on October 12. For nine days they observed and documented the entire performance, with the assistance of their Navajo interpreter, John, and Keam's protégé, Alexander M. Stephen. In his annual report for 1885–86, Powell singled out Tilly, rather than Jim, in summarizing this portion of their fieldwork: "Mrs. Stevenson was also enabled to obtain a minute description of the celebrated dance, or medicine ceremony, of the Navajos, called the Yéibit-cai [Nightway]. She made complete sketches of the sand altars, masks, and other objects employed in this ceremonial." Although James Stevenson often is touted as author of the first published account of the Nightway, "Ceremonial of Hasjelti Dailjis and Mythical Sand Painting of the Navajo Indians" [1891], anthropologist Louis A. Hieb is convinced (because of Powell's statement and other circumstantial evidence) that Tilly deserves credit as author of the essay. He also believes that Stephen (and to a lesser extent, Keam), being familiar with this and other Navajo rites, supplied texts of prayers and other details for Tilly's essay, which was still unfinished at the time of Jim's death in 1888. When Powell subsequently hired her to put it in final form, she chose (undoubtedly with Powell's blessing) to place only her husband's name on the report.[116]

Not surprisingly, given the competition that existed among the nation's natural scientists, Washington Matthews resented the Stevensons' encroachment upon an ethnological topic he claimed as his own. "I suppose that you have heard that the Stevensons poached on my preserve last fall," he groused to Cushing in August 1886. "They went there to duplicate my work, with a stenographer and far more means and materials than had ever been placed at my disposal." When "Ceremonial of Hasjelti Dailjis" finally appeared in print in 1891, Matthews never doubted that it came from Jim's pen. And by becoming the first to publish a description of the Nightway, and failing to acknowledge Matthews's prior research, Jim (rather than Tilly) earned the army doctor's undying enmity.[117]

Hieb's assessment that Tilly's account of the Nightway is "a remarkable field/research achievement at that time in the 19th century" finds support in the work of James C. Farris in his history of the Nightway. After examining all major published descriptions of this ceremony, Farris concluded that the Stevenson account, which he assumed had been written by Jim, is "the best description of a single specific Nightway" ever recorded. Conversely, although Alexander M. Stephen was not so complimentary, he rightly credited Tilly as the author, writing to anthropologist J. Walter Fewkes in 1893, "Tilly's contribution [to Powell's report featuring the Stevenson essay]—viewed as a votive offering to the manes of Colonel Jim—is highly laudable—otherwise I should call it a fragmentary tissue of absurd blunder."[118]

For the remainder of the field season (1885), the Stevensons concentrated their studies upon the Hopi villages, where during parts of October and November they secured more than seven hundred artifacts.[119] When they went to Oraibi, the largest of the villages, they became caught up in an episode that modern writers have used to highlight Tilly's alleged overbearing personality. But the story changed drastically in the telling, proof that anecdotal history is often unreliable. The Stevensons probably were aware that Cushing had experienced opposition at Oraibi in the winter of 1882–83 when he attempted to trade for goods in a kiva. In the heat of the confrontation, he drew a pistol, but then left the village when he realized that to continue collecting would lead to bloodshed.[120]

As Jim recounted the story, the Stevensons had camped one night at the base of the mesa on which Oraibi was situated. Having received an invitation from friendly Hopis to visit the village, they rode ponies to the top of the mesa the next morning, walked to the plaza, and then climbed a ladder to the top of the cacique's house. Almost instantly, a great clamor went up. Several Hopis opposed their presence and seemed to threaten violence. Jim later played down the danger, saying that the situation "was probably less alarming than it would have been to people unacquainted with the natural timidity of the Pueblos." Tilly apparently shook her fist in the face of one of the most vocal Hopis as she and Jim started to descend the ladder and make their way to their ponies. Later, Keam received word of the incident and traveled to Oraibi with a small party to investigate. He returned to his ranch with two of the most troublesome of the protesters, holding them prisoners until they promised "good behavior in the future."[121]

The Oraibi incident was described in full detail in articles appearing in mid-February 1886 in the *Washington Post* and the *New York Times*. About three weeks later, the *Illustrated Police News* ran the story with the sensational headline "Cowed by A Woman, A Craven Red Devil Weakens in the Face of a Resolute White Heroine." The article was accompanied by a caricature depicting Tilly grasping an umbrella in one hand and shaking the fist of the other in the face of a startled Indian, whom she has backed against a wall. Jim calmly stands behind her with the butt of his rifle resting on the ground. The sketch implies that Tilly defended her passive husband by aggressively confronting the Indian. When the story was retold by J. Walter Fewkes more than thirty years later, it had changed. In his version, Tilly (presumably with Jim) "was detained as prisoner in [an Oraibi] kiva from which she was rescued by Mr. Thomas Keam." It is this last account that seems to have stuck in the public mind.[122]

By the end of 1885, Tilly had completed seven field seasons among the Pueblo Indians; she had written two important essays on the Zunis, compiled a detailed account of the Navajo Nightway ceremony, helped collect the enormous treasure trove of Southwest artifacts now housed in the National Museum of Natural History/National Museum of Man, and assisted her husband in writing his reports. By anyone's standards, she had become a competent ethnologist, and had more field experience than most men who belonged to the Anthropological Society of Washington. Yet when she applied for membership that year, she was rejected, simply because of her gender. Tilly did not waste time bemoaning the injustice. With characteristic determination, she set about to organize the separate Women's Anthropological Society of America, its members dedicated to advancing the science of anthropology. For the rest of her life, Matilda Coxe Stevenson had to fight to achieve professional recognition within this male-dominated discipline.[123]

CHAPTER 4

"A Foundation upon Which Students May Build"

When Tilly returned to the capital in December of 1885, she was accompanied by her friend We'wha, the Zuni lhamana. For approximately six months, We'wha lived with the Stevensons at 1913 N Street, near Dupont Circle, a residence they shared with Tilly's parents. The Stevensons had not yet discovered that We'wha was anatomically a male, and introduced her to Washington society as a woman. During her stay in the capital, We'wha served as a "cultural ambassador" for her people; she met with national leaders, demonstrated Zuni weaving at the National Museum, attended social functions, and aided Tilly in her studies of Zuni culture and language.[1] Her presence in Washington also helped validate Tilly Stevenson's professional status as an anthropologist.

At the time of We'wha's visit, Tilly was in the midst of organizing the Women's Anthropological Society of America (WASA), one of the first professional associations for women scientists.[2] Because the all-male Anthropological Society of Washington barred women from their society, Tilly decided to establish a parallel organization for intellectual women who wished to help solve the "problems" of anthropology. Although not opposed to his wife's endeavor, Jim thought the project was "impracticable," for he believed that "not a half-dozen ladies could be found deeply enough interested in science to form the nucleus."[3]

Tilly proved him wrong. In June of 1885, she assembled at her home nine women who supported her plans. Several were well known in Washington society—Eliza Nelson Blair, wife of Senator Henry Blair; Jane Lawrence Childs, wife of the Reverend Thomas Spencer Childs (the first archdeacon in Washington); Emma Louise Hitchcock, wife of chemistry professor Romyn Hitchcock; and Mary Parke Foster, wife of the ex-minister to Mexico. Tilly was the only one who had done scientific work. At this preliminary meeting, the women elected Stevenson as the society's president (a position she held for three and a half years), Foster as treasurer, Hitchcock as recording secretary, and Sarah A. Scull, a teacher of ancient history, as corresponding secretary. They also adopted a constitution, and formulated two major objectives of the society: "first, to open to women new fields for systematic investigation; second, to invite their cooperation in the development of the science of anthropology." They then adjourned until November 28. Sometime late in the year, the society proposed bylaws, and elected as vice presidents Lida L. Nordhoff (wife of Charles Nordhoff, the Washington editor of the *New York Herald*) and Mary E. James (wife of Representative Darwin R. James).[4]

By January 31, 1886, the WASA was flourishing. Among its thirty-four active members were "some of the most cultured" women of the capital, including two additional senators' wives, Harriet Foote Hawley of Connecticut and Harriet M. Teller of Colorado. The society's first honorary member was Rose Cleveland, the president's sister and the official hostess of the White House until her brother's marriage in June. The *Washington Evening Star* credited her for suggesting the name of Stevenson's organization, and she often attended its meetings.[5]

A large number of Washington's medical women quickly joined the WASA, among them Clara Bliss Hinds, daughter of the prominent Washington physician Dr. D. Willard Bliss and the first woman to graduate from Columbian University Medical School, in 1887; Anita Newcomb McGee, daughter of astronomer Simon Newcomb and wife of William (W J) McGee of the U.S. Geological Survey, who also would graduate from Columbian University Medical School in 1892; and German-born Sofie Nordhoff-Jung, a specialist in gynecology, who became one of Tilly's closest friends. The society particularly valued its women physicians for their insight into "the workings of human nature in its normal and abnormal conditions."[6]

Several scientists who resided outside of Washington became corresponding or honorary members. Their numbers included such luminaries as Rachel Bodley, dean of the Women's Medical College of Pennsylvania; astronomer Maria Mitchell; chemist Ellen Richards; mathematician Christine Ladd Franklin; archaeologist Sophie Schliemann; and ethnologists Erminnie Smith, Zelia Nuttall, and Margaret Kalapothakes. Alice Fletcher, a resident of the capital and a scholar of the Omaha Indians, joined soon after the society was formed, and would serve as its third president. Other members who had ties to the scientific and scholarly world through their husbands were Ellen Powell Thompson (wife of Almon H. Thompson of the U.S. Geological Survey and sister of John Wesley Powell) and Matilda Bancroft (wife of historian Hubert H. Bancroft). Also on the roster was the inimitable Kate Field, actress, author, world traveler, popular lecturer, advocate for women's rights, and (later) publisher of a weekly newspaper, *Kate Field's Washington*. She became "one of the nation's best-known women in America," according to the *New York Tribune*, and counted Tilly among her friends.[7] Like Field and Stevenson, many of these remarkable women achieved great success in their chosen professions.

The society held regular meetings on alternate Saturday afternoons from November through May, usually at Tilly's home. By 1887, however, the women met in reception rooms at Columbian University. The more scholarly of the group gave thirty-minute papers, which were followed by discussion. The seriousness of their enterprise was evident in their decision not to serve refreshments except at once-yearly receptions, when invited guests were present and the outgoing president gave an address. Among the earliest papers presented were Clara Bliss Hinds's "Child Growth," Sarah A. Scull's "Topics for Anthropologic Study," Alice Fletcher's "Omaha

Child Life," and Erminnie Smith's "Reminiscences of Life among the Iroquois Indians in the Province of Quebec."[8]

Tilly Stevenson read her presidential address, "The Religious Life of the Zuni Child," at the society's first annual reception, held on the evening of March 30 at the Stevensons' residence. Decidedly a social and political coup for the ambitious president, the event received coverage in both the *Washington Post* and the *Washington Evening Star.* Despite pouring rain, a large number of guests were present: Senator and Mrs. Henry Dawes (Henry Dawes, the sponsor of the General Allotment Act of 1887); Senator and Mrs. Henry Teller; Representative and Mrs. Darwin James; anthropologists Albert Gatschet, Garrick Mallery, Otis T. Mason (curator at the National Museum), and John Wesley Powell; and many other members of the society. Following Tilly's paper, which the *Evening Star* reported as being well received by the distinguished scientists, refreshments were served, "and it was not until a late hour that the entertainment finally terminated, with everybody pleased."[9]

Like Fletcher's and Stevenson's presentations, many papers that followed focused on domestic issues. Anthropologist Nancy Lurie points out that WASA members "emphasized the special work they could do as women. . . . Seeing themselves as capable of making special contributions to anthropology because they were women, and subscribing to views of their day that the infancy of the individual reflects the infancy of mankind, they engaged in further rhetorical questioning. In the 'earliest unfoldings of thought, language and belief, who can collect so valuable materials as mothers?'" Yet, the subjects of their papers were diverse, ranging from Indian music, Basque marriage customs, house-building in Alaska, ceramic art of Pacific Coast Indians, and ancient ruins of Mexico to asylums in Brooklyn, comparative human growth, and "the motor element in memory." Tilly presented six papers, the most delivered by a single member, during the first four years of the society. Her presidential address in 1886 was followed by "The Moki Indian Snake Dance," "Mission Indians," "The Thirteen Medicine Orders of the Zuni," "The Sand-Paintings of the Navajos," and "Zuni and the Zunians." That more than twenty-five women contributed a total of forty-seven papers during this time demonstrates the society's vitality, which Anita McGee, the group's historian, attributed to Tilly's "energy, ability, and fostering care."[10]

For Erminnie Smith, Alice Fletcher, and Matilda Coxe Stevenson, the nation's pioneer women anthropologists, membership in an organization of like-minded women reinforced their identity as professionals and serious scholars. Fired by ambition and scholarly zeal, each made significant contributions to the discipline. Smith, the oldest of the trio, was born in 1836 in Marcellus, New York. Like Tilly, she developed an interest in geology as a child. She graduated from the renowned Troy Female Seminary in 1853, and within the following year married the wealthy Chicago lumber dealer Simeon H. Smith. In the 1870s, she and her family of four sons moved to Germany, where she took a degree at the School of Mines in Freiburg. Upon their return to the United States, the Smiths settled in New Jersey, where Erminnie developed an interest in the Iroquois tribes of her native state. Lurie believes that she initiated fieldwork among the Tuscarora in Canada either in 1878 or 1879 (the same year Tilly visited the Zunis). Thereafter John Wesley Powell funded at least part of her work, stating in his first annual report that she had "undertaken to prepare a series of chrestomathies [learning aides] of the Iroquois language, and has already made much progress. . . . She has also collected interesting material relating to the mythology, habits, customs, etc., of these Indians, and her contributions will be interesting and important." Her "Myths of the Iroquois" appeared in Powell's second annual report, the first paper by a woman to be published by the Bureau of Ethnology. Powell continued to comment on her work each year until, in his seventh report, he noted her untimely death at her home on June 9, 1886.[11]

Two years Smith's junior, Alice Fletcher had also conducted fieldwork by the time she joined the WASA. Born in 1838 during her parents' temporary residence in Cuba, she later attended a female academy in New York City, and as a young woman traveled in Europe. In the 1870s, she made the acquaintance of Frederick W. Putnam, director of the Peabody Museum at Harvard, who fostered her interest in archaeology. Perhaps even more important to Fletcher's decision to become a scientist was her encounter, in 1879, with Susette and Francis La Flesche, a sister and brother from the Omaha tribe, and Thomas Henry Tibbles, a Nebraska journalist, during their speaking tour in the East. The La Flesches and Tibbles were protesting the removal of the Ponca Indians from Dakota Territory to Indian Territory (present-day Oklahoma). Inspired by their message, Fletcher determined to go live among Indians and study their lives. In 1881, at the age of forty-three, she did just that, aided by the newly married Susette La Flesche Tibbles and Thomas Tibbles, who, in the fall, took her on a camping trip of several weeks among the Sioux Indians. She then went to live with the Omahas through the winter. Like Tilly, she would spend the rest of her life studying the lifeways of American Indians, becoming in the process an expert on Omaha culture and Indian music.[12]

Smith, Fletcher, and other members of the WASA must have met We'wha during her lengthy stay with the Stevensons. Tilly, in fact, introduced her friend to the elite of Washington's intellectual and cultural community. Dressed in Zuni clothes, We'wha greeted Tilly's Friday-afternoon guests, and together they called upon other society women. She met scientists and political dignitaries, including Speaker of the House John G. Carlisle. Years later Tilly recalled that "the Speaker and Mrs. Carlisle were very kind to We'wha, and upon her return to Zuni she found a great sack of seed which had been sent by the Speaker." We'wha retained fond memories of the Carlisles for the rest of her life.[13]

By the 1880s, Washingtonians had grown accustomed to the arrival of Indian delegations, but Indian women rarely came with them. We'wha's presence was a novelty, and the local press seemingly followed her every move. Both Tilly and We'wha received a great deal of publicity during these months, which bolstered Tilly's reputation as an anthropologist. One newspaper wrote about We'wha's entrance into Washington's privileged circles, "Society has had recently a notable addition in the shape of an Indian princess of the Zuni tribe. This is the princess Wawa. She is the guest of the wife of

Col. Stevenson of the geological survey. Princess Wawa goes about everywhere at all of the receptions and teas of Washington wearing her native dress."[14] Another news article described the ethnological connection between the two women: "[We'wha] was brought to this city by Mrs. Stevenson last fall, when that lady returned to Washington from Zuniland. Wa-wah is well versed in all the mysteries of the Zuni religion and the customs of her people, and Mrs. Stevenson has obtained from her much valuable information."[15]

They spent long hours together documenting various aspects of Zuni culture in the quiet of the Stevenson household. In midsummer, Otis T. Mason told readers of *Science* that for six months We'wha "has taught her patroness the language, myths, and arts of the Zunis,—now explaining some intricate ceremony, at another time weaving belt or blanket under the eye of the camera." In June, Tilly took We'wha to the National Museum, where she helped to arrange and interpret various Indian objects in the museum's collection. She also demonstrated Zuni weaving, using a loom and instruments crafted by Zuni artisans. "She worked on silently, patiently in the stolid Indian way," wrote a reporter who witnessed the scene, "apparently not noticing the spectators that gathered about her or the photographer's camera which was leveled at her."[16]

In Stevenson's ethnography of Zuni, published eight years after We'wha's death, she acknowledged her friend's assistance, naming her among the tribal members "who faithfully served the writer." She paid further tribute by describing We'wha as "the strongest character and the most intelligent of the Zuni tribe." Her friend, Tilly recalled, "had a good memory, not only for the lore of her people, but for all that she heard of the outside world. She spoke only a few words of English before coming to Washington, but acquired the language with remarkable rapidity, and was soon able to join in conversation." A newsman also noted that "Wewha, who knew no English when she first came here, and who had never before traveled beyond the immediate neighborhood of Zuni, has rapidly learned to understand our language and to speak a little in it very distinctly."[17]

We'wha continued to observe Zuni religious practices while staying with the Stevensons. Probably with Tilly's aid, she received sacred cornmeal "by express from Zuni regularly." Each morning and evening, whatever the weather, she went into the street in front of the Stevensons' residence "to pray to the sun and offer cornmeal to the six directions." She also followed the Zuni ritual of offering prayer plumes to the gods on the summer solstice. With the Stevensons' help, she obtained the supplies she needed from the National Museum—shells, turquoise, and feathers from the golden eagle, wild turkey, mallard, and bluebird. Letters were sent to New Mexico to find out the date the ceremony would take place at Zuni. According to Mason, on Saturday, June 19, at 2:00 P.M., in a "retired garden in Washington" [presumably the Stevensons'], We'wha "performed the ceremony of planting the plumes. Her time was arranged so as to act simultaneously with her people at Zuni." At the end of the ritual, she poured a small amount of sacred meal into her own hand and "into that of each of her two friends [Tilly and Jim], who were watching with the deepest interest. Each, in turn, sprinkled the meal over the shrine, blowing gently with the breath."[18]

But We'wha probably did not share with her friends all she knew about Zuni religious practices. This is hinted at in a news article that described her adverse reaction when she saw photographs of Zuni sacred objects that Tilly intended to publish in her book. In this instance, however, she came to accept the ethnologist's explanation. According to the *Washington National Tribune*, "At first [We'wha] was much shocked, for the Zunis, like most other Indians, do not think it right to make pictures of such things. . . . But when she was kindly told what use Mrs. Stevenson would make of the pictures, and that they would be in a book in which her people would be most kindly mentioned, Wewha became reconciled, and said: 'It is all right if it rains. If it rains I will know you have told the truth about us.' So, when shortly after the rain began, Wewha was very happy."[19]

In the parched lands of the Zunis, rain had religious significance. While in Washington, We'wha apparently viewed rain storms as good omens, which allowed her to behave in ways that might otherwise have been considered inappropriate. Thus she became a main attraction in the Kirmes, a major social event organized by society women to benefit Washington's National Homeopathic Hospital. Tilly had volunteered to help organize the Indian dance, one of several dances—or tableaus—in which dancers moved about the stage in choreographic arrangements and then froze to depict a theme. We'wha accompanied her to several rehearsals, but when asked to participate, she at first declined. "It required much coaxing before she gave her consent," a reporter noted, "for as a priestess in Zuni dancing is to her a religious rite, and she had conscientious scruples about being in a dance given for the amusement of spectators. So she spent three hours praying aloud to seek guidance of her gods on the day before the Kirmes, and finally consented to take part in the Indian dance. . . . When it rained next day she felt sure she had decided aright in agreeing to be in the dance."[20]

On the evening of May 13, the first night of the Kirmes, a brilliant crowd filled the National Theater. "The galleries overflowed with Congressmen from every State in the Union," the *Washington Post* reported the next morning. "Judges abounded, Senators did much more abound, and the old families of Washington were largely represented." President Grover Cleveland sat near the stage in a box that had been sold for two hundred dollars, the guest of Representative W. L. Scott. Also in the audience were the Stevensons, the Evanses, and Georgie Patterson, in town visiting her parents.[21]

When the curtain rose, the 280 young men and women performers were seated on the stage in colorful costumes. Then came the dances. The *Evening Star* called the Indian dance "the novel event of the evening." Attempting to look the part, the dancers (twenty-five unmarried couples) had "bronzed and blackened their faces and wore the most barbarous of costumes. There were buckskin breeches, painted blankets, muskrat skins, feather head-gear, tomahawks, hatchets, and bushels of beads and chains." The dance itself had been created by the director of the Kirmes, Professor Marwig of New York. The presence of We'wha, "a [real] Zuni priestess," one newsman reported, "added to the realistic effect of the warlike spectacle. She was the central figure in several of the tableaux, being dressed in the complete costume of her tribe." What We'wha made of all this is uncertain. The strange movements in the dance seemed to surprise her, and she later told a reporter that "she had not seen anything just like it among her people, but it was very nice notwithstanding." Even though she represented a peace-loving pueblo, the audience expected the dancers to depict warlike Indians, a stereotypical image that Marwig delivered. Whether Tilly influenced his staging of the spectacle is to be doubted. But the publicity she received because of We'wha's participation helped to generate public interest in anthropology and fortify her status as a scientist.[22]

In the months that We'wha spent in Washington, the bond between her and Tilly deepened. This was "a genuine friendship," a relationship that went beyond the typical rapport established by ethnologists and informants. Nancy Lurie believes that Stevenson's "deep affection and admiration for this remarkable person [We'wha] were entirely those of a close and unquestioning friendship between any two women." They shared certain personality traits; both were enterprising, self-confident, eager to understand the other's culture, and willing to take risks. And each wanted to preserve the traditional lifeways of the Zunis, which may have been a major reason why We'wha cooperated with Tilly, at Zuni and in Washington. For We'wha, however, the trip to the capital also was a great adventure, reminiscent of the grand tour that Pedro Pino and his fellow tribesmen had made with Cushing. Her curiosity probably had been aroused by the stories they told upon their return, and as a prominent Zuni she determined to go see for herself when the opportunity arose.[23]

For most, if not all, of their friendship, Tilly was unaware of We'wha's birth as a male. Early on, she may have suspected that her friend was a hermaphrodite, although she denied this in her Zuni ethnography: "Some declared [We'wha] to be an hermaphrodite, but the writer gave no credence to the story." Cushing identified her as such in his 1881 census, yet two years earlier he had spoken of her as a woman. The missionaries Taylor and Mary Ealy also believed her to be a woman.[24] Still, the question often is asked—how could Tilly continue to ignore We'wha's masculine features, so evident in extant photographs? A reporter for the *Evening Star* acknowledged that "folks who have formed poetic ideals of Indian maidens, after the pattern of Pocahontas or Minnehaha, might be disappointed in Wa-wah on first sight. Her features, and especially her mouth, are rather large; her figure and carriage rather masculine." And yet, he continued, her "manner is very gentle." Like Tilly, this reporter, as well as members of Washington's elite, set doubts aside and accepted "the Zuni princess" as a woman.[25]

In mid-June, sometime prior to We'wha's departure for home, Tilly sought an audience with President Cleveland and his new wife. In a note to the president's private secretary, she explained that We'wha, "a Zuni Indian priestess who has been spending the winter with me for the purpose of Ethnological study," wished "to extend to [the Clevelands] a greeting from her people," and to present to Mrs. Cleveland a wedding gift she had made herself. "May I ask your kindness to arrange for a time," Tilly concluded, "when it will suit the convenience of the President and Mrs. Cleveland for me to present Wéwhá to them."[26] The meeting took place on June 23, an event described the next day in the *Washington Post.* "We-Wah, the Zuni princess, walked up the broad entrance to the White House yesterday, and, in company with Mrs. Col. Stevenson, was shown into the Green Room. She was dressed in her aboriginal costume, and wore a head-dress of feathers. Her conversation with the President was mainly in monosyllables, but Mrs. Stevenson and the President had quite an interesting talk"—a talk, it might be added, that kept Tilly and ethnology in the public eye.[27]

As Will Roscoe has so eloquently described, We'wha made an excellent ambassador for her people. She met national leaders and socialites with aplomb, and helped to strengthen the reputation of the Zunis as an industrious, peaceable ally of the United States. By the end of the 1880s, partly because of We'wha's visibility in Washington, the Zunis had become one of the best-known tribes in the country.[28]

For Tilly and We'wha, the first six months of 1886 had been filled with novel events, interspersed with the mundane activities of the household. Other notable occasions included the celebration of the Evanses' forty-second wedding anniversary and a reunion with

Tilly's sisters, Georgie and Betty; Betty's husband, Commander Kellogg, recently had been assigned to the navy yard in Washington. The Kelloggs took up residence at 1919 N Street, only a few doors down from the Evanses and Stevensons, continuing a family pattern of dwelling near one another.[29]

During this time, the Stevensons also helped their friend Thomas V. Keam lease his facilities in Keams Canyon to the government for use as an Indian industrial school. Jim spoke to the Indian commissioner on several occasions on Keam's behalf, and Tilly penned an editorial entitled "An Arizona School Site," which was published in a reform journal in February. To buttress his case, Keam sent to the commissioner a petition signed by twenty Hopi elders requesting a school so their children would "learn the Americans' tongue and their ways of work." This same petition, with slight changes, was sent to Tilly in hopes of enlisting her aid. Keam's friend Alexander M. Stephen, a man who devoted the last fourteen years of his life to studying Navajo and Hopi culture, served as the elders' amanuensis. Calling Tilly "our good friend," they declared, "We remember your kind talks with us, and your promise to help us. We therefore send our petition to the Great Father to you, asking you to take it to him. You have dwelt among us and know our hearts, and our needs, and can speak for us." Education was to become a divisive issue among the Hopis, but their apparent unanimity on this occasion gave weight to Keam's proposal. On October 3, 1887, the Keams Canyon school opened with fifty children in attendance.[30]

In the fall of 1886, the Stevensons returned to the Southwest to carry out Powell's orders to Jim to investigate Indian ruins in Arizona. En route to Flagstaff, they may have stopped off at Zuni to see We'wha before they went on to examine archaeological sites north of the San Francisco Mountains. From there, they traveled to San Diego, where, again following Powell's instructions, Jim inquired into the possibilities for conducting a geological survey of southern California. While in the region, they visited several tribes of the Mission Indians, from whom they obtained "much valuable ethnologic data . . . including portions of the dialects of two of the Mission tribes."[31] In an address that Tilly later delivered before the Women's Anthropological Society, she described how she overcame the reticence of some elderly Diegueño Indians (who had claimed they knew nothing of the old ways) by demonstrating her knowledge of other tribes. When she began to dance, she reported, "it worked like magic, for in a few minutes the oldest man of the tribe . . . becoming excited, rose to his feet and began vigorously to dance and sing."[32]

The Stevensons' final work together as a research team took place a year later when, at the start of their field season, they spent the months of August and September (1887) with John Wesley Powell exploring the numerous ruins in the Jemez Mountains and adjacent plateau northwest of Santa Fe. They were joined by Samuel P. Langley, who had assumed the secretaryship of the Smithsonian after Spencer F. Baird resigned in May on his doctor's orders. During their investigations, the party collected numerous pottery fragments and stone implements, including arrow points and awls.[33]

Late in September, about the time the Stevensons left to visit the pueblo of Jemez, William H. Holmes, curator at the National Museum, joined Powell and Langley in the mountains for what was to be for him a memorable and painful excursion. As he later recalled, "in descending on horseback from a high peak, I had the misfortune to suffer a serious [back] injury," which left him incapacitated. The Stevensons came up from the valley to help out. Jim constructed a travois, upon which Holmes would be transported by mule power over the rough mountain trails to Jemez, while Tilly cared for him during the two days it took to reach a physician. Years later, in a memoriam to Tilly at the time of her death, Holmes gratefully paid tribute to both Stevensons for their "heroic service" in his behalf.[34]

The Stevensons spent ten days among the Jemez Indians, studying their customs and religion. Although they found these Indians "much less tractable" than the Zunis, still, Jim reported, they won the confidence of the priests and obtained "quite a little store of valuable knowledge." From Jemez, the Stevensons went on to Zia Pueblo, eight miles to the south, where they remained for six weeks, engaged in what proved to be their most profitable ethnological work of the season. They gained "the complete confidence" not only of village officials, but also of the "entire population," which at the time may have numbered about one hundred people. They were invited into ceremonial chambers, where they witnessed sacred rituals and observed the highly decorated altars and walls that were "hung with various mythologic emblems of great beauty and delicate texture." They inspected shrines that were scattered about the pueblo, some guarded by "large crudely carved stone animals."[35]

The highlight of their visit came after Jim persuaded a priest of the Snake Society to show them the location where the Zias held ceremonies involving live rattlesnakes. Early one morning, the Stevensons and the priest set out on a six-mile ride that brought them to a small log structure (known as the snake house) hidden among some hills. After further persuasion, the priest then guided them to a cave where two vases used in the ceremony were concealed. Jim offered to buy one, only to be rebuffed. According to Tilly, the priest explained, "These can not be parted with, they are so old that no one can tell when the Sia first had them; they were made by our people of long ago; and the snakes would be very angry if the Sia parted with these vases." On several occasions thereafter Jim made known his desire to acquire one of the vases, each decorated with snake, cougar, and bear images. His persistence paid off, perhaps because he offered a hefty sum of money to the reluctant Zia. Late on the night before the Stevensons left the pueblo, the priest appeared at their camp with one of the vases in a sack. He was "much excited and also distressed," Tilly reported. "He would not allow a close examination to be made of the vase, but urged the packing of it at once; he deposited a plume offering in the vase, and sprinkled meal upon it and prayed while tears moistened his cheeks." Despite the man's obvious distress, the Stevensons went away with the vase, which they ranked as one of the finest specimens they had collected for the Smithsonian that summer.[36]

Before starting for home, the Stevensons returned to Zuni, where they spent two weeks securing more detailed information about its secret medicine orders. But Jim may already have fallen victim to a second attack of "mountain fever," presumably Rocky Mountain spotted fever, which he first contracted two years earlier. When he reached Washington in December, he "was literally prostrated," although he seemed to rally in following weeks. The Stevensons again took up residence at their old address, 1303 P Street, while Tilly's parents shared a home on G Street with their daughter Georgie and her husband, William, who had entered into law practice with his father-in-law.[37]

Tilly soon resumed guiding the affairs of the Women's Anthropological Society. On March 8, 1888, she delivered her presidential address "Zuni Religion" before an audience that included, according to one observer, "the most accomplished anthropologists in Washington," all of whom "pronounced it to be the best presentation of a savage religion yet written." She told of Zuni origin stories and of the Zunis' migration to their present home, and she enumerated the medicine orders and gave descriptions of their ceremonials. She treated Zuni beliefs with respect, as attested by her closing remarks:

> The medicine practices of the Zuni are therefore religious observances and rites; and the daily life of the Zuni, under the guidance of their priests through the agency of the medicine order, is so controlled that every act of life assumes something of a religious character. To them their religion is fraught with much fear; to them it brings many trials, many privations, and much suffering. Notwithstanding this, they derive from it much amusement and great joy, and in it all their hopes and aspirations are centered.[38]

Sometime that spring, Tilly must have conferred with Alice Fletcher about their joint project to obtain federal legislation that would protect and preserve the Indian ruins west of Santa Fe. During the previous year, the American Association for the Advancement of Science (AAAS) (apparently at Fletcher's request) had appointed the two women as a committee to draft such a proposal. Early in July

1888, they submitted a report to the AAAS, and included a copy of their proposed bill, which already had been introduced into Congress. But Jim's declining health prevented Tilly from actively lobbying among the legislators, and the bill failed to gain their approval. Still, as Joan Mark points out, their bill "was a prototype for the Lacey Act of 1906," the first major federal legislation for the preservation of American antiquities. Tilly never lost her commitment to the preservation of ancient Indians ruins. A year before she died, she supported efforts to establish a federally funded National Park of the Cliff Cities, which would have protected many of the archaeological sites that she and her husband had explored in New Mexico.[39]

For several weeks prior to his death, Jim traveled the countryside hoping to regain his health. He first went to Fortress Monroe, and then Waterford, Virginia, followed by a visit to Boston and finally a stay in a seaside cottage, probably in Gloucester, Massachusetts. Tired and sick when he reached the latter spot on June 21, he wrote a brief note to his wife, telling of his arrival. Bidding her "good night with a kiss," he said he would write more the next day, and signed off, "your loving husband." Tilly and her father accompanied Jim during some of his travels, and were with him when he became dangerously ill while on the way back from Massachusetts. They were forced to stop at the Gilsey House in New York City, where he died on July 25 from heart failure brought about by Rocky Mountain fever. Alexander Evans and John D. McChesney of the Geological Survey accompanied his body to Washington, where it was taken to the Stevensons' residence. Funeral services were conducted there on the 27th, after which the remains were placed in a vault at Rock Creek Cemetery. Several of Jim's closest friends served as pallbearers, including Senator Henry Teller, Otis T. Mason, General Samuel Holabird, John D. McChesney, and Henry W. Elliot.[40]

   An outpouring of sympathy helped Tilly through this awful ordeal, made especially difficult because Jim's condition had seemed to improve after each of his trips. Her grief and sense of loss must have been immense. She had telegraphed news of his death to their old friend, Robert Adams, Jr., who was absent from Philadelphia at the time, but soon wrote to express his shock upon receiving her telegram. Otto Gresham, the former college student who had accompanied them to Arizona, now an attorney in Indianapolis, also sent condolences, adding, "I often think of the kindness of both you and [Col. Stevenson] to me during the trip to Arizona and shall always remember him as one of the few real kind hearted and agreeable gentlemen I have ever met."[41]

In extending their sympathy to Tilly, Charles Walcott and Otis T. Mason both remarked on the strong bond that had united the couple. Mason closed his letter with these consoling words: "I trust your own life will be long spared to complete the work which you both so dearly loved." None shared Tilly's grief more intensely, however, than the Stevensons' longtime friends Dr. and Mrs. Louis Sayre of New York City. Dr. Sayre, a professor of orthopedic surgery at Bellevue Hospital Medical College, attended Jim during the final days of his life. In a letter to Tilly dated August 6, Sayre wrote that "next to yourself I think [Jim] was loved best by all my family. Poor Mrs. Sayre has felt his death quite seriously, and grieves over your loss every day." He too referred to the Stevensons' special bond: "My dear friend you have now only to remember the happy hours you had together, the immense advantage you always were to him—and how he appreciated it—and the faithful manner in which you nursed him—and these memories must make you happy."[42]

Tilly's parents undoubtedly provided strong and loving support at this time. Within a year of Jim's death, they moved into the Stevenson residence on P Street, and later would share a home with Tilly on Connecticut Avenue.[43]

Grief stricken, the thirty-nine-year-old widow set about to forge a new identity as a woman without a husband, without the devoted partner who had fostered her ethnographic studies and satisfied so many of her emotional needs. What surely saved her from despondency in the months ahead was her professional work—for the National Museum, the Bureau of Ethnology, and other scientific organizations. In November she entered into negotiations to sell her collection of Indian artifacts to the National Museum for $500.

In recommending the purchase, Otis T. Mason wrote to Samuel P. Langley, "I am extremely anxious to retain her attachment to the [National Museum], for she knows more about the collections from the Southwest than any one else. She will give us a minute account of each piece to enable us to label her collection and also others of the same character not well identified." It was a large collection indeed, consisting of 152 pieces of Pueblo pottery, 42 pieces of Hopi basketry, 35 pieces of Navajo silver jewelry, 12 Zuni idols and rattles, 2 Navajo blankets, 1 Hopi sacred blanket, and miscellaneous other items. Mason judged that some of the pottery and basketry were rare, and all would form valuable additions to the museum's collection. By the end of the month, Langley had approved the purchase, and Tilly set to work writing detailed instructions for labeling and mounting the articles.[44]

Within a few years of Jim's death, Stevenson became active in two scientific organizations (in addition to the Women's Anthropological Society)—the Anthropological Society of Washington (ASW) and the American Association for the Advancement of Science. The all-male ASW voted to admit her as its first female member on November 17, 1891, which caused Anita McGee to announce jubilantly in a congratulatory note written to Tilly the next day, "Hurrah! You are a member of the Anthropological Society." McGee passed along information gleaned from her husband, who had attended the meeting. Eight of twelve members present had supported Tilly's membership, including William McGee, Otis T. Mason, Lester Frank Ward, William H. Holmes, and Garrick Mallery, all employed either by the Smithsonian or the Geological Survey.[45] The ASW and the WASA would finally merge in 1899, probably, as Gloria Moldow contends, less "an acknowledgment [on the part of the men] of women's abilities than an admission of their own group's decline." By the mid-1890s, ASW meetings were poorly attended, and Washington's influence as a center of anthropological studies was being eroded by university-driven programs.[46] The American Association for the Advancement of Science also elected Stevenson a member in 1892. It was one of the first scientific organizations to admit women to membership, Maria Mitchell having joined in 1850.[47]

And most likely by the end of the decade, Tilly had joined the exclusive Washington Club, founded in 1890 by prominent Washington women to generate the kind of atmosphere that men found in the Cosmos Club. It welcomed women of "well-regarded families who boasted scientific, scholarly, or civic distinction." Among its members were Anita McGee, Sofie Nordhoff-Jung, Alice Fletcher, and statistician Clare de Graffenreid, all active in the Women's Anthropological Society. Tilly must have enjoyed the ambience of the club's elegant headquarters, a block from the Cosmos Club, for she remained a member long after she had resigned from other organizations.[48]

But what mattered most to Tilly was to continue the work she had shared with Jim. "My whole heart is in the work my husband left me to do," she once remarked. Fortunately, Powell also believed their studies were important to science, and consequently hired her in 1889 to complete the unfinished manuscript on the Nightway ceremony, and to organize Jim's notes on the Zia. This temporary position became permanent on March 15, 1890, when he placed her on the payroll as an assistant ethnologist (the first and only professional woman permanently employed as a staff ethnologist by the Bureau of Ethnology). Her salary of $1,500 seems to have been the same amount paid to male assistant ethnologists. Yet for several years thereafter, almost all of Stevenson's male colleagues received higher salaries than she did, a discrepancy she would finally protest after working at the bureau for fourteen years.[49]

Tilly's first assignment was to complete the study of Zia Pueblo that she and Jim had begun the year before he died. Powell issued specific instructions on the day he hired her: "You will . . . proceed at once to Silla, Jemez, and Zuni, New Mexico, for the purpose of investigating the customs of the Indians of these pueblos, especially their history, mythology, medicine practices, usages with regard to the training of children, the rites and privileges pertaining to their secret societies, etc." She was allotted $1,400 for travel and other expenses for herself and one assistant, Miss May Clark, one of Powell's secretaries. She was also instructed to send in monthly reports.[50]

Tilly's first letter from the field was dated Zia, New Mexico, April 29, 1890. She had arrived there on the 16th, and already had attended all-night rain ceremonies of two of the medicine orders. "The altars were most elaborate and I succeeded in having Miss Clark photograph one of them by flash light," she informed Powell. Years later, Clark's remembrance of this event was not as sanguine as Tilly's. She recalled that Stevenson had informed her on the day she arrived at Zia—sometime after Stevenson's arrival—that an important kiva ceremony was being held and that they would attend. Thrusting a camera into her assistant's hands, she assigned Clark the task of taking pictures. May protested—she knew nothing about using a camera, she said. "Never mind that, I'll show you!" Tilly replied. When they reached the kiva, Stevenson ignored the remonstrances of the Zia guard at the entrance, and urged Clark forward. "Frightened half to death, May, clutching her camera in one hand and her skirts in the other, entered the dark and smoky chamber; Tilly right behind her. They sat in a vacant spot against the wall until their eyes adjusted to the darkness." But they would have to return another day to get Tilly's photographs, for the Zias stopped what they were doing upon this intrusion, and sat silently until finally, after a half hour, "Tilly gave up and left."[51]

Stevenson presently made amends for her brash behavior, and won the cooperation of several priests and villagers. Her chief advisors were six aged "theurgists," or priests, one of whom was acknowledged as the pueblo's "oracle," the keeper of its ancient traditions. When he passed away during the summer, Tilly relied on the other five— the only men, in her opinion, "from whom any connected account of their cosmogony and mythology may be gleaned." In a poetic passage, she later wrote, "Each shadow on the dial brings nearer to a close the lives of those upon whose minds are graven the traditions, mythology, and folklore as indelibly as are the pictographs and monochromes upon the rocky wall."[52]

One of Tilly's staunchest friends at Zia was a vice-theurgist of the Snake Society, who on one occasion "rode many miles to solicit her prayers for his ill infant." The distraught father, she recalled, placed in her hand "a tiny package of shell mixture done up in a bit of corn husk, and, clasping the hand with both of his, he said: 'Your heart, being good, your prayers travel fast to the sun and Ko'pishtaia.'" He then recited a long prayer, in which he addressed Tilly, "You will be to the child as a mother, and the child will be as your own for all time to come; your thoughts will always be for one another."[53]

From women informants, Tilly obtained information about marriage and childbirth. One woman allowed her to be present during the birth of her child, and to participate in the rituals surrounding this event. Upon the baby's arrival, Tilly was asked to "rub the father's moccasin down the woman's back." "The toe of the moccasin must be downward," she was told, "to hasten the passage of the placenta." After the "doctress" in attendance had bathed the boy infant and wrapped him in a sheet, he was placed in Tilly's arms, after which the grandfather offered a prayer, sprinkled meal upon Stevenson, and gave her "a pinch of it." Referring to herself in the third person, as she usually did in her professional writing, Tilly noted, "[The writer] could not dream what was expected of her, but she ventured to make four lines on the child's breast, and sprinkled the remainder of the meal to the east." This proved the right thing to do, for the grandfather responded, "The child is yours; I make it a gift to you," in effect making Tilly the boy's godmother.[54]

Tilly went to great lengths to accurately record Zia's elaborate ceremonies. During the four-night ceremonial of the Giant Society for healing a sick boy, she placed a lamp on the wall to illuminate every detail. "The child was afflicted with a severe sore throat," Tilly later reported, "caused by ants having entered his body when he was in the act of micturition upon their house." During the ceremony, members of the society dipped eagle plumes into medicine water, and then passed them down the boy's body from head to foot to brush away the ants. In reality, Stevenson noted, tiny pebbles were dropped to the blanket on which the boy stood. But even though she positioned herself close to the group and a lamp lit up the chamber, "the conjuration was so perfect the writer could not tell how or whence [the pebbles] were dropped."[55]

While engaged in these studies, Stevenson and Clark lived in government tents on the edge of the pueblo. May apparently took most of the photographs that appear in Tilly's ethnography, several of which show women and girls at work renovating the earthen floors of the tents, the women by tradition performing much of the labor in house building. Many of the drawings in the monograph are also based on Clark's pictures.[56]

A break in the Zia round of ceremonials came in mid-June, at which time Tilly temporarily moved her camp to the small village of Archuleta, located in the mountains about twenty-six miles above the pueblo. Here she could "quietly" pursue her studies by having Indians come to her, away from the watchful eyes of other Zias who might oppose her gathering of data.[57] She later employed this same technique, interviewing Indians in secret away from their village, when she sought information from the Taos Indians, many of whom strenuously resisted her efforts.[58]

Tilly returned to Washington in late September. She had found so much of interest at Zia that she never did extend her studies that summer to the Jemez and Zuni pueblos. Once back home, she immediately set to work writing up her notes, and by the end of June 1891 she had completed a 148-page manuscript. Powell congratulated her "on collecting so much good material and putting it in such good shape." He called her monograph "a valuable contribution to anthropology." But he also asked for revisions, suggesting that she provide more background information to some sections to aid general readers. And in an ironic twist, in view of his later tiff with Tilly over delays in finishing her Zuni ethnography, he advised, "It is a good paper. Do not be in a hurry, but put it in just the shape you want it. It will be very widely read and give you reputation and you can afford to treat your subject with great care."[59]

Stevenson's "The Sia" was published in the *Eleventh Annual Report of the Bureau of Ethnology* (1894). In his introduction, Powell complimented her work, stating that it had been carried on "with indefatigable energy and zeal." He then described how she had achieved her success by using a method that would later be known as "participant observation." "The fact that she shared the daily life and habits of the Sia people for long periods gave her indeed the inestimable advantage of fully comprehending their idiosyncracies [*sic*] and esoteric concepts." He called her report "unique," "an excellent paper." It was, as Nancy Parezo has stated, the first major ethnography of a Rio Grande pueblo.[60]

On the very first page, Tilly acknowledged her indebtedness to her late husband, whose field notes she freely had incorporated and "whose life interest in the North American Indians [had] been her inspiration." With much sympathy, she depicted the Zias as living in dire poverty, the pueblo's one hundred or so residents only a small remnant of a former thriving community. Although she devoted more than half of the monograph to their myths, tales, and rain ceremonies, she also offered accounts of childbirth, weddings, healing ceremonies, their form of government, clothing, house building, and the pueblo's difficult relations with neighboring Santa Ana and Jemez Indians. She wrote positive vignettes of Zia family life, describing the children as "industrious and patient little creatures, the boys assisting their elders in farming and pastoral pursuits, and the girls performing their share of domestic duties. A marked trait is their loving-kindness and care for younger brothers and sisters." And she allowed Indian voices to be heard in the text (a goal espoused by modern-day anthropologists), recording verbatim, for example, a woman's story of her sexual relations with men.[61]

Still, Stevenson's attitude toward the Zias was ambivalent. She described some individuals as intelligent, hospitable, and loving, yet depicted Indians in general as childlike. And in one sentence, she wrote that their philosophy "scintillates with poetic conceptions," yet was "fraught with absurdities and contradictions."[62] Nonetheless, her publications show that she possessed more compassion for American Indians than did the majority of her fellow citizens.

Upon publication of "The Sia," Daniel G. Brinton, an eminent anthropologist at the University of Pennsylvania, wrote to congratulate Tilly for having written such a "fascinating monograph." He singled out the main factor that distinguished it from all others: "the genuine sympathy revealed throughout its pages" for the people of Zia. "You have brought forward the *human* elements of their lives," he asserted, "a feature so often overlooked in the descriptions of scientists."[63]

Tilly must have been pleased with Brinton's remarks. She was less happy, however, with those of J. Walter Fewkes, a renowned marine zoologist who recently had embarked upon a second career as ethnologist and archaeologist. Starting in 1891, he began fieldwork among the Hopis, and subsequently, with Alexander M. Stephen's assistance, wrote an important description of their snake ceremonies. With publication of Tilly's report, he undertook to compare the snake ceremonies of the two pueblos. At the start of his article, published in the *American Anthropologist* (1895), Fewkes frankly stated that Stevenson's study was "not all that I had wished." He found several passages in her description of the snake ceremony difficult to comprehend, and suggested that in one instance she was in error. Although he admitted that Stevenson had performed valuable pioneer work, he called for a reinvestigation of the Zia snake ceremony before "it passes away forever."[64]

Throughout her career, Stevenson demanded to be treated fairly, and refused to accept criticism meekly that she believed was unwarranted. In this instance, she wrote a politely worded but resolute rejoinder to Fewkes, expressing "regret that you question the care taken in my observations and the accuracy of my statements." She believed that after he had undertaken further studies among the Hopis, "you will be more inclined to agree with me on points where we now differ." Whether he ever came to fully agree with Tilly is doubtful, but in an essay that he wrote following additional fieldwork, he showed more respect, referring twice to Stevenson's "valuable account of the Snake dance of Sia."[65]

Tilly resumed her studies at Zuni Pueblo in August 1891. From the time of her arrival until she departed in March, she observed Zuni ceremonials "almost continuously." Through the intercession of her friend Nai'uchi, the elder brother Bow priest, she witnessed one of the pueblo's most sacred festivals—Hla'hewe—a ceremony for rain and growth of corn, enacted quadrennially in August "when the corn is a foot high." Because the drama had been performed the previous year, the rain priest of the north strongly opposed staging it again simply for Tilly's benefit, but after consultation with Nai'uchi, he acquiesced (so Tilly reported), deciding that the ceremony could be performed to counteract a threat made by Hopi sorcerers to cause a drought throughout Pueblo country.[66]

If there was one field experience that encapsulated Tilly's personality—her ingenuity, arrogance, boldness, ability to persuade Indians to assist her—it came at the close of the Hla'hewe ceremony, when Zuni elders delegated members of the Flute order to accompany her to a shrine located in a cave several miles east of the pueblo. To reach this sacred place, seldom visited and "barely accessible," it was necessary "to scale an almost vertical rock for 12 or more feet," Tilly reported, an act easily accomplished by Zuni men, who used crevices for finger holds and toeholds. Determined to reach the spot, she persuaded two Indians to form a ladder, one standing on the shoulders of the other, and then scrambled to the cave's entrance. Once there, she discovered that the interior was too shaded to allow its contents to be photographed, so she proceeded to place the sacred objects in the sunlight. One of her guides begged that they "not be taken from the place where they had rested undisturbed" for years. "But it had to be done," Tilly recorded without apology. After the items had been photographed, she and the Indian "tenderly returned" them to the cave.[67]

Stevenson was hardly alone in her use of aggressive field techniques. Frank Hamilton Cushing, J. Walter Fewkes, Adolph F. Bandelier, Washington Matthews, John G. Bourke, and Franz Boas (all contemporaries) were equally assertive in the field and, like Stevenson, disregarded Indian resistance to their intrusive behavior. For example, Bandelier's photography, his constant stream of questions, and his rude behavior to officials in Santo Domingo Pueblo generated such hostility that he was forced to leave the village. Washington Matthews noted, as he prepared to view a Navajo Night Chant, "Now we go out to see sweating. Jack says I can't go, but I do all the same." Franz Boas disregarded Indian protests when he photographed totem poles and painted houses in the Pacific Northwest; he also stole Indian bones from burial sites. "It is unpleasant work to steal bones from a grave," he declared. Using words similar to Stevenson's, he continued, "[But] someone has to do it." Moreover, as Nancy Lurie points out, by the turn of the twentieth century, when university-trained ethnologists appeared on the scene, "they still obtained their data by whatever rough and ready methods would accomplish the task."[68]

In October (1891), following her trek to the Zuni shrine, Tilly witnessed the initiation ceremony of the Bow priest society, an event that lasted for several days. In earlier times, a warrior had to secure an enemy's scalp to become a member of the priesthood; now, since scalping had ceased with the end of intertribal wars, the ceremony was carried on using scalps "taken from the scalp vase, in which such trophies have rested since the establishment of the present Zuni." During the ceremony, Zunis boisterously fired rifles and pistols, shouted war whoops, and danced nightly around a scalp pole, behavior that Tilly found to be excessive. "The worst element in their barbaric nature seems to be aroused," she wrote. "If the mere dramatization produces such frenzy, what must have been the scenes when the victor in reality returned from battle with scalps of the hated Navaho!"[69]

In November she was present for the great Sha'lako festival. Even more so than in previous years, Sha'lako attracted droves of visitors, which Stevenson captured both on film and paper. "Every house of any pretensions has guests, welcome or otherwise," she noted; "nearly every pueblo is represented, and large numbers of Navahos are here to enjoy the lavish hospitality of the Zunis. The house tops on the south side of the village are crowded with men, women, and children, while the streets are filled with pedestrians and equestrians." But a disturbing new element had been introduced since her first visit in 1879, and that was whiskey. Although federal law prohibited selling alcohol to Indians, it was not enforced. Gallons of whiskey were now brought in kegs by the Rio Grande Indians and sold to Zuni men, who then resold it in bottles to the Navajos. The scenes brought about by this potent intoxicant disgusted Tilly—drunken men staggering through the streets both morning and evening, some of them not older than fourteen or fifteen. "Numbers of Navahos are fighting with one another or with the Pueblos," she reported, "drawing knives and pistols. The wonder is that some of the disturbers of the peace are not trampled to death, for many fall from their saddles during their quarrels; others lie motionless in the streets, too drunk to move away from approaching hoofs. Native police are kept busy in their efforts to quell disturbances and to clear the streets for the processions."[70]

During Sha'lako, Stevenson spent many days and nights observing its multiple events, which she later described in exacting detail, demonstrating once again her skill in collecting ethnographic data. She documented the movements of participants, their colorful attire, the trappings of indoor chambers, and the kaleidoscope of outdoor scenes. Her growing familiarity with the daily life of the Zunis allowed her to delineate differences in social status. "Zuni, like more civilized places," she wrote, "has its exclusive set, and at no time is this more in evidence than at festivals, some women especially holding themselves aloof from others, whom they esteem less fortunate." On the night the Sha'lako gods appeared, she noted, the elite gathered in the inner rooms of the largest house in Zuni, where one god was to be housed and ceremonies performed. Through large openings in the walls, the elect—from their box seats, so to speak—could observe events unfolding in the large ceremonial chamber.[71]

We'wha was of immense help to Stevenson during her visit to the pueblo, taking great risks to assist her in one instance, for example, when she attempted to photograph ceremonies of the Hle'wekwe fraternity. At the time, Stevenson occupied "the upper story of the ceremonial house and her door opened upon the roof to which the members resort." But residents of the house so feared the "powerful medicine of the fraternity" that they opposed her efforts to capture on film the events that transpired outside her door. In Tilly's words, We'wha "was untiring in her efforts to detain an old father below while the writer secured photographs on the roof, and several times released her when the father had barred the door of her room with heavy stones."[72] Tilly's flurry of activity did not go unnoticed by Washington Matthews, who referred to

her in a letter to Frank Cushing as that "learned authoress and sci-
entistess," and told his friend in another that she was still "working
her sponge for all it was worth."[73]

After Stevenson's return to Washington in the spring of 1892, she
concentrated on organizing her notes for publication.[74] More than a
decade would elapse, however, before her long-awaited Zuni ethnography appeared in print. Still, her focus remained on her Zuni
friends. In December of 1892, after she read disturbing accounts
in eastern newspapers of Zunis being arrested for the murder of
two alleged witches, she met with Washington officials and wrote to
Governor L. Bradford Prince of New Mexico, seeking further information as well as leniency for her friends. Tilly had long been aware
that Zunis and other Indians believed that witches and sorcerers
caused most of their misfortunes—drought, sickness, death, the
failure of crops—and that the cause of the evil had to be destroyed,
death being the usual punishment. Although she could understand
their reasoning, she also believed that such beliefs "had to be rooted
out" before Zunis could advance to civilization.[75]

During episodes of witch hunting, Stevenson, Cushing, and
Taylor Ealy, as well as other Euro-Americans, attempted to prevent
the execution of alleged witches, with varying degrees of success.
Ealy had alerted the Pueblo Indian agent in Santa Fe, in 1880, that
an innocent victim had been sentenced to death, but after the agent
met with Zuni officials and then left, the sentence was carried out
in secrecy. Cushing, too, intervened, pleading successfully with
Zuni priests on one occasion for a more lenient sentence, but failing
on another to prevent the execution—even after warning that U.S.
officials surely would retaliate.[76]

Stevenson described two incidents in which she successfully
subverted Zuni "justice." As she later recalled,

> Near midnight the writer was notified that this man [accused
> of being a witch] was to be put to death. It seemed too ter-
> rible to believe, and hastening from her camp to the village
> she met Nai'uchi as he was returning from the deathbed

of his patient. The great theurgist and elder brother Bow priest was urged to withdraw his verdict on the ground that he might be mistaken. Since he was obdurate, he was told that the United States Government would certainly punish him. He retorted: "I am your friend. Friends do not betray one another. Would you betray me to the soldiers?" . . . The position of the writer was a delicate one. The man must be saved, but she must not make an enemy of a tried friend and one of the men most important to her in her studies. . . . [The following day] she held a court of her own, Nai'uchi, the younger brother Bow priest, and the accused being present, and the result was the unfortunate was released. This was brought about by a declaration on the part of the writer that she had deprived the man of his power of sorcery; and he was soon at work upon his house, fitting it for the reception of a Sha'lako god.

She saved another condemned Zuni using a similar ploy when, after exhaustive questioning by Nai'uchi, the accused was brought to Tilly's camp, where she talked to him "and doctored him a little." She then assured Nai'uchi that the young boy "would never again be able to practice his diabolical art," and after the boy admitted that he had lost his powers after visiting "my mother's camp," he was released. Grateful for Stevenson's intervention, Nai'uchi expressed regret that she could not stay forever among them to "rob all witches of their power to destroy."[77]

Tilly had returned to Washington before a deputy marshal and troops from Fort Wingate arrived in late December 1892 to investigate new allegations that Zunis had killed or were about to kill alleged witches. Although far from the scene and lacking knowledge of details, she sought to engage the help of Governor Prince for the accused. She pictured the Zunis as having fallen on hard times. Once prosperous, they were being robbed of their cattle and horses "on all sides with no human soul to do one thing for them." Her sympathy was with the Zunis: "It is the same old story. The Indians are in the way of the white settlers." When disaster struck, she explained, "they believe they must destroy the curse of the evil and so poor wretches must be accused of witchcraft . . . and are punished with death." She recalled the early history of the United States, telling Prince, "Believing as implicitly in witches as did our Puritan forefathers, they hang them as destroyers of life just as we condemn the criminal to capital punishment." She pleaded with the governor to intervene and secure leniency for the accused Zunis (one of whom she suspected was her friend Nai'uchi). If they "could be made to clearly understand that the thing must not be repeated," she believed they would abide by the decision. She described Nai'uchi as "one of the few Zunis loyal to our Government, ready to serve an American, as they call us, in every possible way. The Bureau of Ethnology owes more to him than any other man in Zuni."[78]

As it turned out, not only Nai'uchi but We'wha and the Zuni governor had been arrested. One alleged witch had been severely beaten, not killed, but when the deputy marshal and a captain commanding a troop of twenty-five soldiers from Fort Wingate arrived to investigate, matters turned ugly. We'wha physically prevented soldiers from entering a house to arrest her older brother. The confrontation escalated as the captain deployed his troops, an action that angered the Zunis, who then quickly armed themselves. Shaken by this show of force by a people thought to be peaceful, the soldiers withdrew to await reinforcements. When they arrived, a total of 193 armed men, along with artillery, surrounded the village. Appalled by this show of military power, and believing they might die, the Zunis allowed the soldiers to take away Nai'uchi, We'wha, and the governor. It is unclear what happened next; the arrested Zunis may have spent a month or more in jail, either at Fort Wingate or Gallup, before making their way back to the pueblo.[79]

Tilly must have learned of these events while in Washington, but nowhere is her reaction recorded. Instead, the records show that she spent much time after returning from Zuni preparing exhibits for two expositions commemorating Columbus's "discovery of the New World," the first held in Madrid, Spain, and the second in Chicago. The Madrid Columbian historical exposition, which opened on October 30, 1892, was "relatively small, dignified, and scholarly." The exposition was meant to illustrate "the arts and cultures of the Old and New worlds at or about 1492." Several employees of the Smithsonian and the Bureau of Ethnology, including Tilly, contributed to the exhibits that were sent from the United States and that eventually filled six rooms in the newly built Museum of Madrid. Among the displays were pottery, craftware, and ceremonial objects from Southwestern pueblos, models of the pueblos, sand paintings, colored engravings of prominent Indians leaders, and some thirteen hundred photographs and transparencies of Indians, many by John K. Hillers and William Henry Jackson. Several exhibitors from the United States were awarded medals and diplomas by exposition officials. Among the gold medal recipients were G. Brown Goode, director of the National Museum, and J. Walter Fewkes, who had mounted an impressive Hopi exhibit. Stevenson received a silver medal for her efforts, along with Otis T. Mason, William H. Holmes, and Zelia Nuttall (who presented a paper at the exposition and exhibited some of her "remarkable studies" in Mexican archaeology).[80]

In contrast to the small and poorly attended Madrid celebration, the Chicago World's Columbian Exposition (which opened on May 1, 1893, and was commonly referred to as the World's Fair) sprawled over 686 acres of land bordering on Lake Michigan. It featured a mile-long "honky-tonk" sector of popular amusements and sideshows, called the Midway Plaisance, and attracted hordes of ordinary citizens to its lecture and exhibition halls. Its central theme was America's progress since 1492, as depicted in huge exhibits touting the industrial, agricultural, and cultural accomplishments of the United States. The fair featured numerous anthropological and archaeological displays. The largest, located in the Anthropology Building, was assembled by Frederick Ward Putnam of Harvard and his assistants, who aimed to illustrate the life of the Indians of North and South America at the time of Columbus's arrival. Near the Anthropology Building was an Indian village, where several Indian groups—Cree, Kwakiutl, Iroquois, Sioux, Apaches, Navajos, and others—lived in traditional houses.[81]

The Smithsonian's anthropological exhibits, prepared by the staffs of the National Museum and the Bureau of Ethnology, were housed in the Government Building. Earlier in the year, twenty-five carloads of materials had been shipped to Chicago, and although museum personnel had begun installing the exhibits in March, the work remained unfinished on opening day. Tilly Stevenson, Frank Cushing, and William H. Holmes all helped with the displays once they reached Chicago. Tilly also would serve as one of the judges of awards for the exposition's Department of American Ethnology.[82]

While in Chicago, Stevenson took part in the fair's Auxiliary Congresses, a series of meetings devoted to literature, the arts, and the sciences. During the six-month-long celebration, nearly six thousand speeches or papers were given by 3,817 individuals at the various congresses—"a veritable glut of verbiage," in the words of Don Fowler. The World's Congress of Representative Women, which convened on May 15, drew one of the largest crowds, with more than 150,000 people jostling for seats or space to stand in meeting rooms and halls in Chicago's Memorial Art Palace. As a member of the congress's science and philosophy committee, Tilly surely attended some of the sessions. A series of smaller congresses were held in the Woman's Building, where Stevenson delivered an address on "The Zuni Scalp Ceremonial," probably in late May.[83]

Midway through the World's Fair, on July 29, Tilly's father died (at age seventy-five), an event that may have affected her emotionally more than she would ever admit. Probably she and her four siblings gathered at the family home in Washington to console their grieving mother (and one another) and to attend the funeral. Sometime after her return to Chicago, she became ill and was forced to spend several days in bed. Although she was scheduled to deliver a paper at the International Congress of Anthropology, which opened on August 28, her illness kept her away, and her paper, "A Chapter in Zuni Mythology," was read for her. True to form, Cushing called it "a poor effort, rambling, superficial, and in its differences from my own well-known statements, really silly and somewhat venomous."[84]

Tilly's health remained precarious for the following six months; Powell's annual report for 1893–94 made note that "unfortunately [her work had] suffered interference through serious illness." By the end of that fiscal year, however, she had completed "preparation of most of the illustrative material of the [Zuni] monograph and made progress in the final revision of the text."[85]

John Wesley Powell's own health was in serious decline, a factor that entered into Tilly's later troubles with the bureau. He had arrived at the World's Fair with his wife and daughter in July, where for four days William H. Holmes had escorted him around the grounds. On the 27th, Holmes reported in a letter to his wife, Kate Holmes, "[Powell] is quite weak and I had to take great care not to let him get tired out." Earlier in April, a colleague of Powell's in the U.S. Geological Survey had reported that he was "by no means well" and "seems to shirk his duties as much as possible." Powell resigned from the Geological Survey in 1894, about the time he had surgery performed on the stump of his right arm, which had been amputated during the Civil War. After that, he delegated much of the administrative chores of the Bureau of Ethnology (soon renamed the Bureau of American Ethnology) to W J McGee, formerly of the Geological Survey and now Powell's surrogate and presumptive heir to the bureau's directorship. From then until Powell's death in 1902, McGee was the de facto head of the bureau. He later confided in a letter to Mrs. Powell that following the surgery, her husband remained "ever afterward an invalid. . . . [He] never wrote a report or any other important official paper; for while sometimes he was undoubtedly able to do so, he was oftener unable. . . . During later years in this Bureau he seldom saw the reports until they were shown him in printer's proofs."[86]

Under both Powell and McGee, Stevenson and other bureau staff members enjoyed considerable independence in their intellectual pursuits. Tilly later testified that before going into the field, her instructions from Powell were usually these: "Go and do the best you can, you know best how to pursue your work and I know that you will accomplish all that is possible." She never had her own office at bureau headquarters until after the turn of the century, but this may have suited her just fine, as she enjoyed working independently in the quiet and comforts of her own lodgings. For the remainder of 1894 and all of 1895, she worked at revising her manuscript on the Zunis. The bureau's reports for this period (probably written by McGee) acknowledged that her ethnography had "been in preparation several months." This delay seemed justified, however. "In view of the great number and interest of the ceremonials and the significant nature of the beliefs of the Zuni Indians, it is thought desirable to spare no pains in making it as nearly exhaustive as possible, and thus all details of ceremonial and belief are receiving special attention, necessarily at considerable expense in time."[87]

Tilly's work was further interrupted by the illness of her mother. In June of 1894, Maria Evans's sister Theodosia had written to encourage both mother and daughter to join her in the resort town of Atlantic City, New Jersey, believing "it would do you both so much good." Maria in fact went to the seashore in September, but the ocean's invigorating breeze failed to restore her health. Tilly's mother died in Washington on November 20 at the age of seventy-three.[88]

Over the years, Tilly was to seek relief from her own stress and ailments at various health resorts on or near the seashore. About thirteen months after her mother died, on January 1, 1896, she wrote to Powell from Carrabelle, Florida, located on the Gulf Coast southwest of Tallahassee: "This place is an ideal spot for one suffering from nervous exhaustion. I am really a new person since coming here, and I expect to return home in a short time with all my old steam power returned. . . . I spend much of my time, by day and moonlight, on the gulf, I think the water so restful."[89]

Powell also had experienced the restorative powers of the ocean. In the mid-1890s, he began spending summers away from Washington to escape the heat, a time-honored tradition among the capital's more affluent residents. In August 1895, he had written to McGee from Gloucester, Massachusetts (expressing sentiments similar to Stevenson's): "Here I find I can work; the temperature, especially the sea breeze, is delightful and I spend much time on the water." Starting in 1896, he would summer in the village of

Brooklin, Maine, but by 1900 (according to his biographer), he "was sinking fast into incapacity."[90]

Tilly left Washington to return to Zuni on July 8, 1896. She was "in good health and spirits and full of enthusiasms," McGee reported to Powell. Her goal was to collect additional material that she thought she needed to complete her manuscript. She took with her ninety-six skins of hummingbirds (provided by the National Museum), the feathers to be used in bartering with Indians. Once she reached the pueblo, she rented two rooms from her friend the trader Douglas D. Graham, to provide greater privacy during interviews. Over the years, Graham, who spoke Zuni fluently, often assisted her in her research, and she acknowledged his "generous aid" in her Zuni ethnography.[91]

Tilly spent about seven months at Zuni, returning to the East Coast in February 1897. During this time, she observed and photographed several ceremonies, one of which—the winter retreat of Nai'uchi, the Shi'wanni (rain priest) of the Nadir—she thought was among the Zunis' "most pleasing ceremonies." The retreat lasted one day and night, with the day spent in silent prayers for rain, and the night in sacred ritual. With Nai'uchi's approval, she photographed by flashlight the elaborate pollen and meal painting he created during the evening hours. Nai'uchi also allowed her to photograph and make sketches of the Ahayu:da altar as it appeared in his home during winter solstice ceremonies. She convinced him and other religious elders to make replicas of objects associated with the Ahayu:da (war god), all of which she used—in conjunction with the Ahayu:da her husband had acquired in 1881—to create an impressive display in the National Museum upon her return home.[92]

During this field season, Tilly added to her knowledge about childbirth and medical practices among the Zunis. In two labor cases she offered crucial assistance. One involved "a child wife, not more than 15 years old," who went into labor at midnight on October 20, and did not give birth until six o'clock the following evening. For four days the mother failed to produce milk that the baby would accept. "The infant was so weak from lack of nourishment," Tilly later reported, "that the writer prepared condensed milk, upon which it was fed for some days." On a second occasion, the wife of Nai'uchi's son, who lived at an outlying farming village, delivered a baby who died at birth. Because she suffered a severely lacerated perineum, she was rushed to Zuni, where Nai'uchi examined her in Stevenson's presence. After he removed some of the woman's diseased flesh, Tilly instructed an attendant to bathe the affected area in a solution of carbolic acid diluted in water. Nai'uchi also sprinkled a powder upon the same area. Although at first not expected to live, the patient resumed her normal activities after more than a week of Nai'uchi's and Tilly's treatment.[93]

Stevenson also was on hand to aid and comfort her dear friend We'wha during her final illness, brought on in part by the long hours she worked to prepare her home to receive a Sha'lako god. Too sick to witness the ceremony, she fell listless and kept to herself as much as possible. A week or so after the close of Sha'lako, Tilly dropped in to see her friend, and found her much changed. She later wrote a moving account of We'wha's death, which appears in her Zuni ethnography. Now fully aware that We'wha was a lhamana, she explained to readers, "As the writer could never think of her faithful and devoted friend in any other light [than as a woman], she will continue to use the feminine gender when referring to We'wha."[94]

When Tilly entered the room that day at sunset in 1896, she found We'wha "crouching on the ledge by the fireplace," unable to breathe when she tried to lie down. Tilly sent to her camp for a comfortable chair for the sufferer, but there was little else she could do. "Death evidently was rapidly approaching," Stevenson reported. "Only a few days before this strong-minded, generous-hearted creature had labored to make ready for the reception of her gods; now she was preparing to go to her beloved [Kolhu/wala:wa]."

Three times Nai'uchi came to minister to We'wha, declaring that a witch had caused her illness, although Stevenson avowed that she suffered from heart disease. Realizing that the end was near, We'wha's foster brother, "with streaming eyes," prepared prayer plumes for his dying sister. We'wha called Tilly to her side, and in a feeble voice said in English, "Mother, I am going to the other world. I will tell the gods of you and Captain Stevenson. I will tell them of Captain Carlisle, the great seed priest [John G. Carlisle, former Speaker of the House of Representatives], and his wife, whom I love. . . . Tell all my friends in Washington good-by. Tell President Cleveland, my friend, good-by. Mother, love all my people; protect them; they are your children; you are their mother." We'wha died with her family and Tilly at her side. It was, as Will Roscoe has stated, "a personal loss for Matilda Stevenson."

We'wha's female relatives prepared the body for burial, and her two brothers carried it to the grave. Later, one brother gave Tilly and each member of the family prayer plumes, which they planted on the bank of the Zuni River, a small stream that flows by the village. After that, the grieving mother gathered We'wha's possessions so they could be destroyed in accordance with Zuni tradition. But she could not force herself to sacrifice certain of We'wha's cherished gifts from her Washington friends—pictures of the Carlisles and James and Tilly Stevenson. "These were left in their frames on the wall," Tilly recorded. "With another outburst of grief the old woman declared they must remain, saying: 'We'wha will have so much with her. I can not part with these. I must keep the faces of those who loved We'wha and whom she loved best. I must keep them to look upon.'"

Undoubtedly with a heavy heart, Tilly continued her studies; she had few precious days left before her allotment ran out. And she was determined to secure duplicates of sacred masks used in Zuni ceremonials. By mid-January 1897, she had convinced two priests to duplicate nine masks, even though they risked severe punishment if discovered. To provide them a safe place to work, she rented a house far from Zuni, apparently in Gallup. The masks would cost more than she had originally estimated: about fifteen dollars a piece, including incidental expenses, such as rental of the house and the cost of material that went into the masks. To make certain they were identical to the originals, for example, she bought two embroidered kilts to obtain the native cotton fabric that was used in two of the masks. On the 25th she shipped these treasures in four boxes to the National Museum, writing to Otis T. Mason to request that the boxes not be opened until she returned home, "as no one can receive the masks as I can." She had taken great care in their packing so they would arrive undamaged. With a spark of humor, she told McGee at the bureau, "[I] think any museum would be glad to have me as chief mask packer—but I want five years rest on mask collecting." As it turned out, before she returned home, she obtained additional masks at Zia pueblo.[95]

Shortly after Tilly departed from Zuni, members of the Bow priest society held a witchcraft trial for the old woman suspected of having caused We'wha's death. News of her severe beating soon reached government officials; troops were dispatched, and for the second time in the decade, soldiers occupied the homeland of the Zunis. Four Bow priests were arrested, including Nai'uchi, and sent to jail. For six months, soldiers remained camped near the village. The imprisoned Zunis were finally released eighteen months after their arrest (without ever having come to trial), but this entire unfortunate affair helped to undermine the power of the Bow priesthood. Tilly probably received news of these events and of Nai'uchi's incarceration; whether she attempted to intervene as she had done before is not known. In her Zuni ethnography, she made only passing reference to Nai'uchi's imprisonment and subsequent loss of status.[96]

Before returning to Washington, Stevenson spent a few days in Philadelphia, and then took refuge on the seashore at Atlantic City. She had been working twenty hours a day at Zuni and was exhausted. In a letter to McGee seeking approval of her travel plans, she said that she wanted "to go somewhere and sleep for a week, a whole week, then I will go to Washington in good shape for work." She was anxious to get home, she wrote in another letter, to "unpack my precious parcels" and see how the masks had weathered the trip. She had fallen victim to "the grippe" in Philadelphia, however, but went to the seashore anyway on the advice of her physician. She would spend the rest of the year revising her Zuni manuscript.[97]

Tilly took a break from fieldwork from 1897 to 1902, during which time she sought relief at various resorts from intermittent illnesses. In July 1898, she wrote to McGee from West Chop, Massachusetts, "Dr. Sayre [Reginald Sayre, the son of Dr. Louis Sayre] writes me I must work with great care for some weeks yet in order to thus more surely return to perfect health. This is a very lovely spot and the climate is charming." That same year she published an article on "Zuni Ancestral Gods and Masks" in the *American Anthropologist*, and became a charter member of the Washington Academy of Sciences. Although she immersed herself in these and presumably other professional activities, the bureau's annual reports for this period contain virtually the same perfunctory notice: "Although retarded by ill health, Mrs. M. C. Stevenson made substantial progress in her analysis and discussion of Zuni mythology during the year."[98]

Stevenson rarely described the exact nature of her illnesses. She simply informed McGee or Powell that she had been "ill during the night" or was "confined to her bed," unable to work or to sit up. Powell later said that she was suffering from neurasthenia, a sickness of near epidemic proportions among educated, urban, middle-class women at the turn of the century. Symptoms included (among others) headaches, neuralgia, depression, insomnia, and exhaustion. George Beard, the neurologist who introduced the term "neurasthenia" in 1869, described it as a state of nervous exhaustion, the natural result of overwork and overtaxing the nervous system. According to late-nineteenth-century medical wisdom, women who competed with men outside the home were prime candidates for neurasthenia. Dr. Margaret Cleaves, herself a sufferer, may have been describing Tilly's position when she attributed this ailment "not simply to overwork but to women's ambitions for intellectual, social, and financial success, ambitions that could not be accommodated within the structures of late-nineteenth-century society." The standard treatment was rest, usually under a physician's care.[99]

Although Tilly would deny that she was neurasthenic, she seems to have suffered from numerous ailments. Even during bouts of illness, however, she continued to work on her ethnography. In a letter to Powell dated August 15, 1900, she stated that in former days, she had worked ten or twelve hours a day at her desk, but now was unable to put in such long hours. Still, since returning from Zuni she had taken "*all told* including the times I have been confined to my bed, not four months from my work." At all other times, "whether in Washington or at the sea-shore, or mountains I have worked from four to seven hours a day. I have never ceased working on account of ill health unless I have been in my bed."[100]

It is not clear whether it was Powell or McGee who placed the most pressure on Tilly to finish her manuscript. In her August 15th letter to Powell, she sought to justify the delay, but she would not be rushed, for she wanted her work to be "thorough and classic." Respectful of his vast experience, she wrote, "I think you who have a far deeper knowledge of American Aboriginal life than most men, must agree with me that preparing a number of separate or isolated papers is one thing and writing a comparatively complete and connected history of an aboriginal people whose thoughts are not our thoughts, weaving all the threads into an intelligent and satisfactory whole for the civilized student is quite another." Then in a brilliant passage, she revealed the vision she held of her own work:

> It is my wish to erect a foundation upon which students may build. I feel that I can do the most for science in this way. I make no claim that my paper on Zuni will exhaust the subject, on the contrary it but opens the subject but I think and hope it may open wide the gates for other students to pass the more rapidly over the many, many paths which I have left unexplored.[101]

Within twelve months of writing this letter, Stevenson faced dismissal from the bureau; or, as Powell put it, she was placed on furlough due to "ill health and severe depression."[102] But he had not reckoned on Tilly's steadfast resolve to continue her life's work. She fought back, with all the resources at her command, including her friendships with influential national figures. And in the end, she won this battle that had pitted one strong-willed woman against the combined wills of McGee and Powell, although Powell was to suffer a severe stroke before it was over.

CHAPTER 5

The Zuni Ethnography

On June 3, 1901, Matilda Coxe Stevenson penned a letter to Major Powell, expressing regret that on the previous day when he visited her lodgings she had failed to inquire about her next assignment. She wrote enthusiastically about her desire to work among the Santa Clara and San Juan Indians, and reported that Dr. Sayre said that "the one thing which would restore me to my old condition of health would be a return to the dry clear climate of the Rocky Mountain region." Moreover, she continued, "I could not endure weeks and weeks of idleness [and] much of my work in the West would keep me out doors which is what I most require."[1]

At this point, Tilly had no idea that Powell intended to place her on furlough. She had considered Powell's recent visit "of purely social character," as he made little reference to her work. The first intimation she had of Powell's plan was in a note W J McGee sent her on June 5. He realized that she and Powell had not fully understood each other as to her "future connection with the Bureau," he explained, and since Powell had left town, he felt duty bound to set the record straight. "Over a year ago," he wrote, "the Major had it in his mind to change your status so that you would be paid on the basis of purchase of manuscript rather than on the monthly basis, and would accordingly be free to work or not as your state of health might permit from time to time." But Powell had delayed making the change after discussions with McGee (or so McGee reported). Then in mid-May of the current year, Powell had sent his plan of operations to Secretary of the Smithsonian Samuel P. Langley, with the recommendation that Stevenson be paid by purchase of manuscript, since her "state of health does not permit regular duty."[2]

Other scientists not on the bureau payroll, such as Franz Boas and Alice Fletcher, similarly had been paid for ethnographic manuscripts. In Tilly's case, however, Powell's move—as it would become clear—was an effort to rid the bureau of a staff member slow to publish (although no slower than other members of the bureau) and to fill the opening with a younger, university-trained anthropologist. After Tilly received this bombshell from McGee (who seems to have backed Powell all the way and to have initiated the hiring of her replacement), she was dumbfounded. And in her bewilderment, she made an all-too-hasty reply to McGee, in which she expressed regret that she had not "given satisfaction to the Bureau," and volunteered to resign. "As soon as I shall have completed the present work," she wrote, "I shall be ready to sever my connection with the Bureau of Ethnology," a statement she would later retract.[3]

Powell only muddied the waters when he wrote to Stevenson on June 20th from his summer cottage at Haven, Maine. He had delayed answering her June 3 letter, he explained, to allow time "to fully and carefully consider the matter." He expressed sympathy for her loss of health: "I can appreciate it the more because my daughter is troubled in the same manner with neurasthenia." He never mentioned the word "furlough," but stated his belief that her health could not be restored without "complete rest." He thought it unwise for her to resume work among the Indians. And her manuscript was "in such shape that it can be published" with only some additional editorial work, which McGee could do. "By all means I should advise you to seek that rest and retirement from active life which will conduce to your restoration to health. This seems to me to be your duty to yourself," he concluded. Tilly later was to state that Powell's letter was "the first knowledge" she had that she suffered from neurasthenia.[4]

Tilly quickly responded to Powell's communication. She still had several weeks' work to do on the manuscript, she reported, but would take the rest he suggested after she had gone over the proofs. She nonetheless strongly defended her record. "I am now doing as good work as I have ever done in my life. . . . Please permit me to say you are mistaken in thinking my work has been intermittent and that any ordinary amount of work ever effected [sic] my health. On the contrary, although I have suffered from ill health since my last visit to Zuni, I have worked steadily with but few interruptions, with the one desire—to have such a publication as would live, and be of permanent good to ethnology."[5]

Thereafter Tilly continued to work on her manuscript, on the assumption that she remained employed by the bureau. The first "definite word" of her furlough came from Tolly Spriggs, a "colored" messenger, when he "expressed regret [to Tilly] that such action had been taken." Shortly after this, she sent for her mid-July salary statement, only to be informed that no salary was due her. What followed was a tangle of communications between Tilly and her supporters and bureau and Smithsonian officials. Tilly best described the situation a couple of years later in testifying before a committee investigating administrative affairs at the bureau: "This is such a mixed up affair the only way it could be understood would be to see the correspondence."[6]

The ensuing fight to keep her job at the Bureau of American Ethnology was one of the most difficult periods in Stevenson's life. A woman of lesser determination and strength of character might very well have folded her tent and quietly departed the scene. At her insistence, she finally received official notice of being placed on furlough, which now was to start the end of July, rather than the end of June as Powell had intended. McGee was the one, not Powell, who had written to Langley on July 22 suggesting that Tilly be formally informed that she was to be furloughed, without pay, due to her failure of health. McGee's communication, however, only raised more doubts about the bureau's wisdom in pursuing this course. He told Langley that he made this recommendation with great regret, and he went on to praise Stevenson's performance. "Her work in the field was always excellent, and was pursued with such zeal and enthusiasm that her health suffered seriously even under conditions otherwise most favorable[;] her office work has been carried forward with great energy, intelligence, and persistence, even when her physical suffering was very great." Senator Henry Teller, one of Tilly's staunchest supporters, later remarked, "If your work has been faithful in the field and it has been pursued with such intelligence and persistence in the office, why then do they put you on furlough?"[7]

Tilly now began to object in earnest to efforts designed to remove her from her job. In a July 31 letter cosigned by Gasch Brothers (her legal advisers) and sent to the director of the bureau, she protested being placed on furlough while in the midst of completing important work, and objected to any portions of her manuscript being published "in any other than complete form." She then agreed to complete the manuscript, but "only on condition that my status is continued as before." If these terms were not granted, she vowed to "lay the matter before Congress."[8]

When responses to this and further correspondence proved unsatisfactory, Tilly carried copies of letters bearing on her case to the White House for President Theodore Roosevelt to peruse, and sought the advice and support of two congressional friends, Senator Teller and Representative Robert Adams (also a regent of the Smithsonian). Then in December she informed Secretary Langley, "While I was ready at one time during the discussion of this matter with the Director, to resign, I now beg to state that I do not intend to resign from the Bureau of American Ethnology." Moreover, she found Powell's statements to others regarding her performance highly insulting.

The Director expresses himself as dissatisfied with my work and he under-values my years of service in the Bureau and grossly offends me by pretending that I have not rendered value received for the small salary which has been paid me, and proposes to defend the unjust treatment accorded me, by claiming that my retention in the Bureau of Ethnology had been based upon his generosity, and consideration for the memory of my late husband, eliminating altogether the contributions which I have made to the National Museum and my scientific work.[9]

By mid-January 1902, a compromise of sorts was reached, whereby Tilly agreed to produce the finished Zuni monograph within four months, after which she would receive $525, a sum equivalent to her monthly salary.[10] Sometime later, Stevenson's superiors reinstated her as a bureau ethnologist, although it remains unclear how or when they reached a decision to do so.

There still remained, however, the issue of payment for the work she did on the ethnography during the period of her furlough, August 1 to January 9. At first, Langley and Powell resisted payment, saying she had not been employed by the bureau at this time and presented no evidence of having performed bureau work.[11]

Before the matter of this back pay was resolved, Powell attempted to justify his actions in regard to Tilly's furlough in lengthy letters to both Teller and Adams. Powell's health was precarious, however. In his message to Teller dated January 21, 1902, he said that when Teller and Stevenson had called at his office several days before, "I was exceedingly ill, and really not able to be on my feet and scarcely able to speak." Within ten days of writing this letter, Powell suffered a stroke, which left him incapacitated. Late in May, he was well enough to travel with his wife and daughter to their cottage in Maine, but he had only a few more months to live.[12]

Langley's sympathies were clearly with Powell, one of the few friends he had made since coming to Washington. Now, in addition to handling the Stevenson situation, he had to plan for the contingency of Powell's death. Harboring an intense dislike of McGee, in February he asked William H. Holmes, curator for anthropology at the National Museum, to take over the bureau upon the director's death. During these difficult days, Langley—an astronomer—

continued with his research in aerodynamics. The previous year he had built the nation's first gasoline-driven airplane, and now he intended to construct one capable of carrying a man. Whether he succeeded would be decided only after Tilly's troubles at the bureau had ended.[13]

With these matters weighing heavily on his mind, especially Powell's deteriorating condition, Langley sent a private communication to Congressman Adams in which he denigrated Stevenson's work. He claimed that during most of her employment at the bureau, she "might be called an invalid. . . . During the later years Mrs. Stevenson has rendered little or no service except in the preparation of a manuscript," which remained unfinished. "We all here were friends of Colonel Stevenson," he wrote. Then he made the outrageous claim that "his widow on her husband's account has been living on the Government in a condition as near that of a pensioner as any one could be allowed to do without direct violation of official duty." With more than a touch of bitterness, he described Tilly's efforts to keep her job. "During the last year she has kept up in every way, not excepting the public press, by threatened legal process, and in other ways, a warfare on her generously indulgent friends. . . . Mrs. Stevenson has kept up this incessant attack on an invalid, and as he grew worse and worse she has had no pity." He stopped just short of blaming Tilly for Powell's stroke. "My friend, Major Powell, is dying; his end has not been brought about by this affair, but it has been hastened by it." Knowing that Adams championed Tilly's position, Langley admonished him to "receive my word that the facts are as stated here and not as you have received them from Mrs. Stevenson." Given Langley's vitriolic remarks, the wonder is that he sanctioned Stevenson's return to the bureau.[14]

While Tilly spent the first four months of 1902 completing her manuscript, her chosen replacement, Frank Russell, a recent Ph.D. graduate of Harvard University, was in Arizona at the behest of McGee, working among the Pimas. Knowing of Powell's plans to furlough Tilly, McGee had contacted Russell as early as January 3, 1901, about possible employment in the bureau. "A contingency is arising which makes it desirable to contemplate an addition to the corps," McGee explained. Russell's salary was to be approximately the same as Tilly had received. Upon being hired in April, the young scientist immediately headed to the Southwest, but his employment with the bureau ended once Stevenson was reinstated.[15]

Tilly finished her monograph in timely fashion, but not without frustrations caused by McGee's bungling at headquarters. Sometime in January 1902, the bulk of her manuscript, which she had previously sent to the main office, was returned to her missing four chapters. Although she had retained duplicate copies, she was exasperated by McGee's conduct. First he told her that all chapters had been given to her, then he sent Tolly Spriggs to her rooms at the Lenox with the missing material and with a note from McGee saying that the chapters had been found in the vault, and that Spriggs would explain. Spriggs took the blame; he said he had placed the chapters in the safe and forgotten to tell anyone. Under Tilly's intense questioning, however, he admitted, "I never knew anything about the manuscript until Mr. McGee gave it to me this morning, and that is the way they always make me do, they always make me do all the lying for them." That McGee had involved the messenger in his "trickery" offended Tilly's sense of decency.[16]

On May 13, Stevenson notified the director of the bureau that her Zuni monograph was completed and could be picked up the next day by "some responsible person." A few days later, her furlough was terminated.[17] She continued to press the issue of her back pay, however. With the help of Senator Teller, who wrote letters to Langley on her behalf, and after submitting proof that she had worked on the manuscript during the furlough, she received a sum equal to her regular salary for the period August 1 to January 9. Stevenson's victory was complete. With "everything she had worked so hard to achieve" at stake, including her professional standing in the scientific community, she had fought and won a fierce battle against formidable adversaries.[18]

Yet Tilly's fight to obtain fair treatment within a male-dominated bureaucracy is but one example of the struggles facing professional women in late-nineteenth and early-twentieth-century America. Historian Margaret Rossiter posits that "ejecting women [from scientific organizations] in the name of 'higher standards' was one way to reassert strongly the male dominance" in these associations. Women scientists who successfully maneuvered around roadblocks erected by males often adopted, like Tilly did, a "confrontational strategy": they demanded full equality with their male counterparts. "This involved writing angry letters and otherwise documenting the 'unfairness' of the unequal opportunities open to men and women." And these successful, talented, stubborn, ambitious women never gave up. In Rossiter's words, "one can only marvel at what these earlier women . . . were able to accomplish" before the era of "federal legislation and executive orders."[19]

Stevenson never ceased working on her scientific projects during the furlough imbroglio. As it was winding down, she sent to Washington Matthews, now retired as an army surgeon and living in Washington, a copy of a paper she had written on Zuni medical practices. Apparently the two ethnologists had put aside their past differences, for Matthews now sent a warm note in return, thanking her for the chance to read her work before it was published. He called it "one of the best articles" he had read on the "rational medical practice among Indians." Many of her observations were "valuable," he said, including her discovery of the use of corn smut among the Indians. "This is probably the *Ustilago maidis* [*sic*] of our practice, which we employ for the same purpose as the Zuni doctors employ it." The irony is, of course, that Stevenson had written this valuable article at a time when Langley and others had consigned her to a sickbed.[20]

Tilly would later defend Matthews's scholarly reputation, shortly after his death in 1905. Although he had left behind a legacy of many first-rate ethnographic studies of the Navajos, some critics questioned the accuracy of his observations because of his deafness. In a short piece published in the *American Anthropologist*, Stevenson stated that most of his work among the Navajos had been done before his hearing became impaired. "His careful, painstaking, honest work," she concluded, "must ever stand as a beacon to students of ethnology to lead them on over the path followed by this noble, high-minded, modest scholar," a remarkable statement, considering that it came from a woman once mocked by this noble scholar.[21]

Once Tilly submitted her Zuni monograph, Langley approved her request to return to the field. She had two goals in mind: to collect "the ethnic flora" of Zuni Pueblo, and to begin a comparative study of the Pueblo Indians. She claimed that on previous field trips, she had discovered that each of Zuni's thirteen esoteric fraternities used an Indian language other than its own in its ceremonies. She now intended to investigate this phenomenon in greater detail.[22]

Stevenson set out from Washington on July 1, 1902, and subsequently spent three days in Albuquerque and two at Fort Wingate gathering supplies. She was further delayed in Gallup, awaiting the arrival of a camera, but finally left without it, reaching Zuni on the 13th. Somewhere along the route, probably in Albuquerque, she hired an assistant, Dora Pracher, who, for health reasons, remained but a short time in Tilly's employ.[23]

In her first message from the field, Stevenson reported with delight, "The Zuni gave me a warm welcome [after an absence of six years]. Many of the older men have passed away but Naiuchi [sic] with a number of others are eager to aid me in every possible way." During the month of August, she observed a series of dances associated with the retreat of the rain priests, which gave her the opportunity to substantiate the descriptions in her monograph. She also visited the Zunis' sacred salt lake in company with the younger brother Bow priest, and discovered that "quite a Mexican settlement" had sprung up since her last visit, "the people earning a living by selling salt." Two dressing rooms had been constructed of stone beside the lake, leading her to speculate that only the scarcity of drinkable water prevented this sacred spot from becoming a "white man's" resort. "It is a great cause of distress to the Zuni," she reported, "that the sacred lake in which the 'Salt Mother' resides is being desecrated by Mexicans."[24]

She noticed other disturbing changes at Zuni as well, among them a decline in the quality of ceramics. In her eyes, women potters no longer produced the exquisite pieces that she and Jim had collected on their first trip to the Southwest, but instead manufactured "large quantities of exceedingly poor pottery" to exchange with traders for china and tinware, items that now were being used even in religious ceremonies. More than before, she passionately believed it a moral duty to preserve Indian traditions. The sense of urgency that propelled her is eloquently expressed in an August letter to the bureau: "I realize more fully each day, that every moment is golden for the ethnologist, for changes in the life of the Indian are becoming more rapid each year."[25]

Tilly soon set forth with three Zuni guides on a venture that again showed her willingness to take risks and endure the hardships associated with her profession. She had persuaded the guides (one of whom was the younger brother Bow priest) to take her to Hanlipinkia, a sacred site far to the west of Zuni, which they said had never been visited by an "American." They set out from the pueblo twice. On their first attempt to reach the site, they followed "the old California wagon road" through a desolate countryside devoid of water. After making two dry camps and sharing water from their keg with their thirsty animals, they turned back. The guides had been "so anxious that I should not be disappointed," Tilly later reported, that they separated, each going miles on foot in a different direction to find water, but without success. On the next attempt, they took a longer and more southern route. On the second morning out, they faced a difficult climb to the top of a mesa, which required the Indians to unpack the wagons and carry supplies to the top. An excellent horsewoman, Tilly had let the Zunis know that she objected to them driving her team. When it came time to make the treacherous descent, however, one guide ignored her admonition. Fearing she might be killed if she tried it herself, he jumped into her wagon without warning and drove it rapidly down the makeshift road.[26]

After several more difficult miles of travel, they made camp, one guide going ahead to find water for the animals. The next morning they arrived near the site of Hanlipinkia. Here they made a second camp and proceeded by foot, descending into a canyon whose walls were covered with pictographs. At one point, the party squeezed through an opening in a chamber wall only by "lying flat on the ground." They spent a day or two at the site, discovering nearby a sun shrine, which Tilly photographed and sketched and then removed "to be deposited in the National Museum." Once again, Stevenson displayed no moral qualms about raiding a religious shrine in the interest of scientific inquiry.[27]

The saddest event for Tilly during this field season was the death of a young Zuni girl. Stevenson often wrote with affection in her ethnography about her Indian friends, and these passages, including the ones devoted to this fifteen-year-old child, allow us to glimpse the anthropologist's own humanity. The girl had first caught her attention in 1896, when, at the age of nine, she suffered with curvature of the spine. "She had a beautiful face and was so patient and gentle," Tilly recorded, "that she won the heart of the writer, and the two became fast friends." When she returned in 1902, Stevenson discovered that "her little friend" suffered "from a large lumbar abscess with probable caries of the vertebrae. . . . Her sad face and ever gentle bearing were profoundly touching." Wishing to be of help, she sent for Dr. Wood, a Bureau of Indian Affairs physician, who had been dispatched to the village to stem a diphtheria outbreak. With Tilly's assistance, Wood won the cooperation of the Zuni doctor who had been treating the sufferer. But there was little he could do beyond sprinkling the wound with boracic acid, wrapping it with gauze, and making the patient comfortable. A short time later, the girl whispered to Tilly that the pain had lessened considerably. "And so this little soldier," Tilly wrote, "who had endured so much, lay in comparative comfort and peace for two days, when she fell into her everlasting sleep, leaving her 'Washington mother' to tell of her beauty of person and soul."[28]

Before Tilly returned to Washington, she obtained several ceremonial masks for the National Museum, and collected a herbarium of two hundred edible and medicinal plants, which she planned to describe in a later publication. Among the most important specimens in the collection, she believed, was *Datura stramonium*, or jimsonweed, which the Zunis used as a narcotic during surgery and to treat wounds and bruises.[29]

Clearly pleased with the results of this year's fieldwork, as well as the accuracy of her earlier studies, Stevenson described in one of her final reports from Zuni how the priests had her read to them what she had written in her monograph, "and they are deeply gratified that I have so clear an understanding of their philosophy, religion and sociology." Still, she acknowledged her own limitations: "My present season's work convinces me all the more . . . that I have but opened the doors for the study of these most curious and interesting people. The field ethnologist must realize that a life time is not sufficient to fully understand a people as profuse in legend and ritual as the Zuni."[30]

When Tilly returned to the capital in December, she found the bureau in a state of disarray. Powell had died in Maine on September 23, and William H. Holmes had taken over his job as chief in mid-October. The scientific community had expected McGee to succeed Powell, as did McGee himself. But he had mismanaged bureau affairs during Powell's declining years, a factor that must have entered into Langley's decision to appoint Holmes. Embittered by the secretary's action, McGee mounted a campaign to undermine Holmes's authority.[31]

By the turn of the century, the bureau's importance as a scientific agency was already in decline, although its ethnologists—Matilda Coxe Stevenson, James Mooney, J. Walter Fewkes, and John N. B. Hewitt among them—continued to do good anthropology and publish important ethnological work. Under Powell's direction in the early years, the bureau had become, in the words of Bruce G. Trigger, "the leading centre of anthropological research in North America." After Powell's death, no leader emerged who matched his vigor and purpose. Holmes avoided controversy, and was more willing than Powell to accept Langley's supervision; nor did Holmes implement any new research programs himself. More importantly, professional training in anthropology had become available at universities, at Harvard under Frederick Ward Putnam, at Columbia under Franz Boas, and (shortly) at the University of

California under Alfred L. Kroeber. These and other institutions, rather than the bureau, would become the central agencies that directed the discipline's future.[32]

Tilly must have been aware of these developments when she gave testimony before a committee that Langley appointed in June 1903 to investigate the bureau's internal operations. In fact, she had played a key role in the creation of this committee. Sometime in April, after her return from the field, Tolly Spriggs had intimated to her that a clerk, Frank M. Barnett, had fraudulently cashed government checks. After Tilly alerted higher authorities, Barnett was arrested for forgery and embezzlement. Langley immediately instigated a preliminary inquiry, followed by a full-scale investigation, into this and other irregularities that may have occurred during the tenures of Powell and McGee. Ultimately, Langley hoped that evidence the committee uncovered of sloppy administrative procedures or downright mismanagement, particularly under McGee, would justify his exerting greater control over the bureau (which had operated as a semiautonomous agency under Powell).[33]

The committee consisted of Cyrus Adler, librarian of the Smithsonian (chair); William de C. Ravenel, administrative assistant of the National Museum; and Frank Baker, superintendent of the National Zoological Park. For nineteen days, they heard testimony from bureau employees, including clerks and stenographers, amassing more than one thousand pages of testimony and four boxes of correspondence and other related material.[34]

Tilly's testimony on July 14 ran to thirty-nine typed legal-size pages. She told in some detail what transpired after Spriggs came to her with his suspicions about Barnett, but the core of her testimony concerned McGee's failures as an administrator, especially his treatment of her during the furlough episode. She gladly turned over to the committee a letter she had solicited the previous year from Caroline Brooke Dinwiddie, McGee's former stenographer. This vengeful letter seemed to support the committee's growing conviction that McGee had conducted private business on company time, and had been an inept administrator at the very least.

Dinwiddie, who had worked at the bureau for five years, claimed that "Professor McGee devoted the major portion of his time, and mine[,] . . . to the work made necessary by his connection with innumerable scientific organizations." At other times, she helped prepare articles that he published in popular journals, "for which he was paid magazine rates." He had called upon her to work on Sundays and holidays to finish other reports. The last straw was the year he required her assistance on Christmas day and the day following, a Sunday. "From that time I left no stone unturned until I was transferred to the Library of Congress. . . . In my judgment, such a man is absolutely unfit for an administrative officer. His whole policy is autocratic in the extreme," she concluded.[35]

Stevenson also recounted to the committee her most recent difficulties in getting her Zuni ethnography published. Last spring before she went into the field, McGee had assured her that it would be published without delay, and later implied that the proofs would be ready to read upon her return. On the contrary, during her absence the manuscript apparently remained in the safe, and the accompanying illustrations on a shelf, where she found them "looking like they had been in the furnace room, they were so black." She blamed McGee. "It is my opinion," she stated, "that my book would not have been published if it could have been prevented, unless there had been a change in the directorship."[36]

In a parting shot, Tilly referred to one of McGee's most serious blunders, publishing inaccurate statements in the annual report about Fewkes's work among the Hopis. She held a lofty view of the bureau and of the labor performed by ethnologists. Shoddy work by McGee reflected badly on the institution to which she had pledged her loyalty. "[The bureau] should be a Mecca for scientific men to come to and to believe in," she told the committee, "and not a place at which scientific men all over the country shrug their shoulders." Unfortunately, she continued, "so long as they make publications of this nature, that is all that you can expect."[37]

During the long, hot summer of 1903, Stevenson added to her manuscript the new material she had obtained on her recent visit to Zuni.

She apparently spent most weekdays at bureau headquarters, where she now had an office. Langley, in fact, may have imposed as a condition of her reinstatement that she work at the bureau, rather than at home, where her labors would be under greater scrutiny by the new chief. This arrangement probably was not burdensome, however, for starting in 1904 she was more often in the field than in Washington.[38]

In the fall of 1903, Stevenson's article entitled "Zuni Games" appeared in the *American Anthropologist.* The essay was based on her own observations as well as on information gleaned from Zuni rain priests, the elder and younger brother Bow priests, and other important personages. In the opening paragraph, she explained that "the ceremonial games of the Zuni are for rain, and they constitute an important element in their religion and sociology." She then described in detail seventeen games, some involving races and gambling, and many providing much merriment. These descriptions were later incorporated into Stewart Culin's massive eight-hundred-page annotated catalog, "Games of North American Indians." She must have found this professional recognition especially satisfying, coming as it did on the heels of her recent troubles.[39]

Stevenson left Washington on January 27, 1904, to return to Zuni to resume her comparative study of the pueblos and to collect material illustrating Zuni symbolism for the bureau's forthcoming exhibit at the Louisiana Purchase Exposition, which was to open in St. Louis on April 30. Long before this, she had sought to play an even larger role in assembling the fair's ethnological exhibits. As early as August 1901, while fighting to retain her job, she had submitted plans to assemble a living exhibit of Pueblo Indians in St. Louis. Holmes, Frederick W. Putnam, and F. W. Clarke (a top government official for the 1901 Buffalo, New York, exposition) wrote letters supporting her scheme and testifying to her qualifications. Clarke described her as "the foremost scientific authority" on the Pueblos.[40]

The Louisiana Purchase Exposition Corporation, the company that organized the entire fair, only finalized its plans for anthropology exhibits in mid-1903. The corporation hired W J McGee to head the Anthropology Department on July 31, the same day he resigned from the bureau under suspicion of fiscal mismanagement. McGee and the corporation planned for a much larger display of living American Indians than Tilly had proposed. Nonetheless, she still harbored hopes that McGee would accept her proposal to bring a contingent of Zunis to the fair (despite her previous testimony against him).[41]

The Bureau of American Ethnology would sponsor its own, much smaller, exhibit in St. Louis. With limited funds at his disposal, Holmes decided to focus on the field research of the bureau's ethnologists. The overarching theme was "the mythic symbolism of various tribes as embodied in their decorative arts." Housed in the Government Building, this display would feature the work of Fewkes at Hopi, Stevenson at Zuni, James Mooney among the Plains Indians, and John R. Swanton among the Northwest Coast tribes.[42]

Because of severe storms in the East, Tilly missed her train connection in St. Louis on the way to Zuni, a delay that allowed her to visit the fairgrounds for several hours. She was not impressed. "They looked forlorn," she wrote to Holmes, and advised him to "keep away until the weather changes." She also made inquiries about the cost of lodging during the exposition, and was astonished at the high prices. Apparently she already had given McGee an estimate for her proposed living Zuni exhibit, and now submitted new sums for her per diem and incidental expenses. She told Holmes that she had "made the figures as low as possible. . . . I know that no other person could make the exhibit for the amount I can simply because I can get more out of the Indians than a stranger could."[43]

Tilly understood that her stay in the field would end on March 31, when she expected "to go to work for the Indian exhibit." She hired her sister Nina Zevely, who joined her at Lamy, New Mexico, to serve as her paid assistant during February and March. Once they reached Zuni, the two sisters took up residence in an Indian house, outfitted with some furnishings—one table, heavy cooking utensils—that Tilly had stored with the missionary at the close of her previous field season. She had to borrow bedding, however, when she discovered that several boxes sent from Washington (including the one holding her bedding) were being held in Gallup until the bureau paid for expressage.[44]

There were other frustrations. Illustrations she needed for her study of Zuni symbolism failed to arrive from Washington when expected, causing her to lament to Holmes, "The time is so short I fear I cannot do the work as I had hoped to do unless the illustrations are sent to me without delay." Her typewriter broke down, forcing her to send it to Gallup for repairs, but the machine came back in such poor condition she still was unable to use it. Fieldwork was made especially difficult by New Mexico's notorious sandstorms. In March, she reported to Holmes, "There has seldom been a day that we have not had several hours, generally two thirds of the day, of sandstorms when I have found it necessary to dust off my papers every few minutes. And while observing the ceremonies my eyes fill with sand. I fear the photos will not be so good owing to the dust." After another month of such vile weather, she wrote, "Only those who have experienced these storms can imagine how horrible they are."[45]

For two months, Tilly diligently pursued her study of symbolism "on fabrics, ceramics, altars and other carved objects." While officers of the secret fraternities had knowledge of the symbolism on their altars, she found "but four persons who can read the beautiful sentiments expressed on their pottery." In a letter to Langley, she described her technique for obtaining accurate information: "This work has been verified by at least three Indians neither one knowing that another had explained the symbols to me." She was extremely thorough, and reported the significance of nearly every symbol used in Zuni art.[46]

In early April, she sent Holmes handwritten labels to accompany her St. Louis exhibit, but then encountered difficulties in locating packing boxes for shipping Zuni pottery. She finally purchased two dilapidated barrels in the pueblo, packed the specimens in wool (which she secured from Mr. Bennett, a local trader, with the understanding that she would sell the wool for him in Washington), and then with two Zuni assistants, drove the artifacts to Gallup in a wagon borrowed from the longtime trader at Zuni, Douglas D. Graham. Once there, she hunted "over all the alley-ways, barns, and back yards of all the shops" to find boxes, paying sixty cents for each one, which she then had to make over. "I never in my life worked harder," she told Holmes. By April 22, she had shipped eleven boxes of Zuni artifacts to the Government Building at the exposition. The shipment was missing one sacred image that she had promised to send, however, for she had given it up "to prevent the woman who sold it to me receiving a severe whipping." Her "mental suffering was so great," Tilly reported, "I had not the heart to drive her away without the image."[47]

In the midst of these activities, Stevenson arranged for Zunis to accompany her to St. Louis, although she still awaited McGee's final approval. She would take to the fair the finest potters and weavers, who would use native wool and dyes to demonstrate their craft, as well as some priests who agreed to go along with "their masks and all their religious paraphernalia." In April, however, McGee belatedly turned down her proposal, most likely because her cost estimates seemed excessive, possibly also because of a lingering bitterness occasioned by her testimony during the Smithsonian investigation. At any rate, she believed that she should have been notified much earlier. Now she was placed in "an awkward position" with the Indians who "had set their hearts on going with me to St. Louis," she informed Holmes. But she hastened to assure him, "all my communications to Mr. McGee have been of a strictly business character and right to the point."[48]

Since she would not be going to St. Louis, Tilly asked Holmes's permission to remain in Zuni until after the summer solstice ceremonies. "I should regret to leave Zuni just now as I am gathering some interesting material," she explained, and she vowed to stay longer at her own expense if necessary. She thought the cost would be minimal. About the time her sister left for home, she gave up the Indian house, and secured room and board at the residence of Andrew Vanderwagen (also spelled VanderWagen), a missionary turned trader, for $25 a month. Here she would find privacy when interviewing Indians, "and I can make golden use of every minute."

She estimated that her total monthly expense would amount to about $50.[49]

With Holmes's approval, Stevenson continued working at Zuni through July. As in past years, she spent many hours observing religious dances, including the quadrennial sun dance of the Cimex fraternity, a ceremony based on the Zuni belief that "the original fire was the gift of the Sun Father." During this four-night ceremonial, men and women members of the fraternity danced in a bed of coals. "There is no special time for remaining in the burning bed," she later explained. "Some are able to endure it much longer than others. The women do not remain in the fire so long as the men." But she discerned "a waning of enthusiasm" since she first had observed the ceremony; "the fire is not so great," and the men no longer "[run] their arms into the glowing coals in addition to dancing in them."[50]

In mid-May she again borrowed Graham's wagon to visit several shrines she had not previously known about, reaching one only after making "one of the hardest climbs of my life" and being drenched in the rain. Still, she told Holmes with some pride, "I was fully repaid for the effort." There seemed to be "no end" to Zuni shrines, however, which led Tilly to repeat that "no one life" is long enough "to complete the study of these people."[51]

During the summer solstice ceremonies, which began on June 23, Tilly chose to stay with the Galaxy fraternity, never before having observed its rituals. On two separate occasions, she spent an entire night recording the proceedings. "The prayers and songs at this time," she explained to Holmes, "are exclusively for rain." For the remainder of her stay, she spent a good deal of time verifying her previous observations of Zuni religion, and was gratified to find that she had no corrections to make.[52]

Aside from her systematic research into symbolism and ceremonies, Stevenson continued to collect artifacts for the National Museum, but on a much smaller scale than in the early days with her husband. Her aim now was to secure rare items that the museum did not have. The Indians asked higher prices than in the past, however, causing Tilly to grouse, "[They] have had their heads turned by those who have more money than we have." Her problems had been compounded by Stewart Culin's visit to Zuni the previous year on a collecting trip for the Brooklyn Institute of Arts and Sciences. "Mr. Culin has made the Zuni half crazy over money," she reported in March. When he returned to the pueblo during Tilly's stay in 1904, the two collectors alternately competed and cooperated with each other as they sought artifacts. Tilly told him about an old stone doorway that she dearly wanted, for example, but had not received permission to buy. "I am sorry the museum will not have it," she lamented to Holmes, "but glad some other is to preserve it."[53]

During this field season, Stevenson collected more than five hundred objects, ranging from pottery, raw materials, cooking utensils, and weaving tools to games, dolls, jewelry, clothing, and musical instruments. She paid $15 for an old drum of the Galaxy fraternity, $30 for an old shell set with turquoise, and $35 for a beautiful fetish, which she acquired only with great difficulty. The fetish had been handed down from father to son, and it took all of her persuasive powers (as well as money) to induce the son to part with it, "as he said he knew he would die if he let it go out of his possession."[54]

In accord with instructions, Tilly had sought Holmes's approval for the most expensive purchases. One such item that caught her fancy was a rare old necklace of shell beads and turquoise with an accompanying pair of turquoise earrings, which she persuaded "a warm friend" to leave with her until she heard from Holmes. The price of $250 seemed excessive, but she explained, "Collectors are buying these necklaces when they are so fortunate as to induce an Indian to part with them, at enormous prices." Occasionally she made purchases without prior approval, to make certain she secured the objects, knowing she could easily sell the items to other collectors should Holmes refuse payment.[55]

In late May, Tilly was forced to move out of Vanderwagen's complex when the trader needed the space to house visiting missionary inspectors. For the rest of her stay, she rented a house outside the village for $10 a month, but now had to cook for herself and employ an Indian "to look after various things that would consume too much of my time."[56]

She soon brought to this house several Zuni spinners and dyers to demonstrate the process of preparing and dyeing wool using native dyes—nearly a lost art, she believed, among the Pueblo and Navajo Indians, who now almost universally used commercial dyes. Although the Zunis willingly volunteered to do this work, they balked when she insisted they do it at her place, reasoning that "they could do much better work and would be less interrupted in their own homes." With considerable cajolery, Tilly had her way, or, as she later described the episode, "A little patience and perseverance on the part of the writer brought the men and women to her camp, the clouds of discontent disappeared, and they had a merrymaking time for some days. Not only the workers were present but numbers of their relatives and intimates, and the midday meal was much enjoyed amid jokes and laughter."[57]

Over the course of several days, the Zunis manufactured yellow, blue, dark blue, green, white, black, and red dyes, the red being the most difficult to produce. After six attempts by elderly women, the seventh was successful. Reconstructing the formula that her grandmother had used, an aged Zuni succeeded in producing the dye, which brought forth praise from the other workers, who were delighted that this knowledge of ancient ways had been recovered. Among the many artifacts that Tilly shipped to Washington were specimens of the native materials and tools used in creating the dyed woolen yarn.[58]

While these events unfolded, Stevenson's friend Nai'uchi—elder brother Bow priest and rain priest of the Nadir—died, on June 26. Two days prior to this, he had called Tilly to his bedside, taken her hand, and begged her to remain with him. Before drifting into unconsciousness, he uttered these last words: "I have waited and waited for you; you will not leave me; you will remain by me."[59]

Tilly had long held her old friend in high regard, believing that his bright mind "would have marked him as a superior man in any community." Earlier that year, Stevenson had served as his emissary when he reached out across the continent to another exceptional man, President Theodore Roosevelt. To show the "high esteem" he felt for the president "as a great hunter of the cougar and bear," he sent as gifts prayer plumes and a necklace composed of claws from a bear that he had killed more than fifty years ago. Since the killing of the bear, Tilly explained, Nai'uchi had worn the necklace in ceremonials of the Little Fire fraternity "when invoking power from the bear to discover disease and to heal the sick."[60]

But neither "American" nor Zuni medical practitioners were able to restore Nai'uchi to health. A government doctor had diagnosed his trouble as Bright's disease, and left medication and instructions for administering it with the sufferer's favorite grandchild, Nina, a bright young girl who had spent years in the local school and spoke English. After his death, the medicine bottles were found untouched, Nina offering as an excuse for not giving the medicine, "I am young and I could not do that to which my elders objected."[61]

Tilly took part in the rituals surrounding her friend's death. Her gift of a blanket was the one on which the body was directly placed, "as an expression of Nai'uchi's close ties with her." Before Nai'uchi's interment, she joined the immediate family in praying over the remains and sprinkling sacred meal on the blanket that covered them. The deceased's son and nephew carried the body to the grave. The next morning, Tilly, Nai'uchi's relatives, and an associate rain priest buried prayer plumes and his belongings, including his war pouch, near the Zuni River. Later that night, in a move that appears callous, yet epitomizes her single-minded devotion to her work, the ethnologist persuaded Ha'lian, the son, to remove Nai'uchi's war pouch from its burial place so that it might be sent to the National Museum. The purchase price was $25.[62]

Tilly incorporated a lengthy account of the events surrounding Nai'uchi's death into her as-yet-unpublished manuscript. Impatient to see her book in print, she had vented her frustrations in a letter to Holmes written on June 22: "I will be much indebted if you will inform me why there is still further delay. Nearly five months have passed since I left Washington[;] still my book seems no nearer being published than when I worried over it last summer and winter."[63]

Despite her disquiet, the delays allowed time for her to include the new information she obtained during this field season.

Finding time to work quietly on reports and the manuscript proved difficult, however, for visitors often dropped by. Although these distractions sometimes were annoying, she never turned Zunis away, for fear they might be bringing choice artifacts. She frequently offered food to her guests, a practice that led the bureau to inquire into her high commissary bills. Tilly took pride in having never overspent her allotment, and went to great lengths to show how frugal she was in the field. In explaining the commissary bill, she pointed out that prices changed from time to time, and that when she learned "of a cheaper grade I have secured it." Most of the items, she noted, "are for the Indians who have become very fond of our food."[64]

Tilly's other visitors that spring and summer included a student from Norway, who spent most of his time at the Hopi villages, and a group of fifteen Harvard students led by Professor William C. Farabee, on a tour of the American Southwest. She later sent copies of her Zuni ethnography to at least two of the expedition members, both of whom sent thank-you letters in return. One, James Switzer, expressed astonishment that she remembered him. "That I should remember you well is but natural," he avowed, "for you were so courteous and kind to all of the fellows who made up the Harvard crowd at Zuni." The other recipient, James N. Baldwin, went on to have a distinguished career as founder and director of the American Civil Liberties Union.[65]

During her six-month stay at Zuni, Stevenson had labored tirelessly in adding to her knowledge of ceremonials, symbolism, and the daily life of the pueblo's residents. She took photographs, added to the museum's collection of Indian artifacts, and explored numerous shrines. She believed her diligence merited an increase in pay. Before leaving the pueblo in early August, she sent Holmes a politely worded request to that effect, playing on his sense of fairness. She asked him to consider the character of the work she had done and was doing. "And if you regard it as valuable to science as that done by others in the field in which I work, you will do me the kindness to recommend that my salary be increased at the beginning of the fiscal year, to a sum approximating at least, that of other students who have been engaged in the same character of work, and for as many years as myself." Belatedly, Tilly's salary was increased—from $1,500 to $1,800 per year—in 1907.[66]

After leaving Zuni, Stevenson spent six weeks pursuing her comparative studies among the Rio Grande pueblos, stopping first at Santo Domingo in early August to observe and photograph the village's annual festival. She devoted most of the month, however, to expanding her study of Zia Pueblo, where she stayed only two days before a water shortage forced her away. Nevertheless, she worked with one Zia Indian for nine days at Jemez Springs, and with other villagers for several days at a nearby ranch. She spent two days among the Jemez Indians, and then returned to Santa Fe for a few days' interlude, during which time she likely visited her old friend former governor L. Bradford Prince, for she had requested that her mail be forwarded to his address. From Santa Fe she went to Cochiti Pueblo, whence she visited the stone lions some twelve miles distant on the 28th. Interestingly from Tilly's viewpoint, only the Zunis among all the pueblos considered this a sacred site.[67]

During the first half of September, she toured the cavate ruins twelve miles from Santa Clara, and then carried on her studies among the Tewa peoples of San Ildefonso, Santa Clara, and San Juan. What she learned among these Indians only reinforced her determination to continue her comparative investigations. "I found the cosmogony, rituals and old customs of these peoples to be so closely allied with the Zuni," she reported to Holmes, "as inevitably to lead to the conclusion that they are of the same origin were it not that the languages as spoken in every day life are distinctly different." Only detailed fieldwork in each pueblo would allow her to make meaningful statements "regarding the relations of the Pueblo tribes."[68] From then until the day she died, she dedicated her life to unraveling the connections among the various pueblos.

Stevenson left New Mexico on September 17, and spent about two weeks thereafter in St. Louis touring the Louisiana Purchase Exposition, held to commemorate the one-hundredth anniversary of the country's acquisition of the Louisiana Territory. Larger than any other world's fair ever attempted, the exposition covered 1,240 acres (nearly double the size of the Chicago fair), housed thousands of exhibits, and attracted 19 million visitors before closing its doors the first of December. The ubiquitous and popular anthropological exhibits were meant to educate the general public about the diverse peoples of the world, and "to trace the paths of human progress," which often meant reinforcing the fairgoers' feelings of racial superiority.[69]

Tilly must have been looking forward to seeing the elaborate exhibit she had designed and that others had assembled. Among the motifs she selected to illustrate Zuni symbolic decoration were the bird, butterfly, dragonfly, cornflower insect, serpent, frog, tadpole, mountain lion, the human figure, and "sundry cosmic phenomena, such as clouds, lightning, rain, sun, moon, stars, and the planets." These symbols, used to induce rain, were emblazoned on the many Zuni artifacts she had sent to St. Louis, and were featured in the illustrations prepared by artist Mary Wright Gill. In accompanying labels, Stevenson emphasized how important religion was in the Zunis' daily life, and how religious beliefs permeated their art. In recognition of her work, the Louisiana Purchase Exposition Corporation awarded her a commemorative diploma and medal at the close of the fair.[70]

Stevenson returned to Washington, D.C., in October, and soon began reading the final proofs of her ethnography of the Zuni people. Not until December of the following year, however, did it appear in the *Twenty-third Annual Report of the Bureau of American Ethnology*, which carries a 1904 publication date. She had taken great care in preparing this monumental work, and made sure that introductory remarks did not detract from its merit. Having read a draft of the report, she asked Secretary Langley to remove a portion written before Holmes became chief, statements to the effect that her work had been retarded by ill health and by having been placed on furlough. "The statements themselves are not only unjust to me," she argued, "but are absolutely without foundation. The delay in the publication of my work on Zuni has been beyond my control and in no sense dependent upon my health." The records tell a slightly different story. Certainly bureau officials bear responsibility for failing to publish the manuscript in a timely fashion after she had placed it in their hands. But health problems had contributed to Stevenson's slowness in completing it. Nonetheless, the offending statements were omitted.[71]

At the time it appeared, Stevenson's ethnography "The Zuni Indians, Their Mythology, Esoteric Fraternities, and Ceremonies" was, in the words of Will Roscoe, "one of the most comprehensive cultural descriptions of a single American Indian society ever written," and it remains the most complete account of the Zuni people.[72] Lavishly illustrated with 173 photographs and drawings, many in full color, it encompasses nearly six hundred pages of text. In the opening paragraphs, Tilly exhibited a deep sympathy for the Zunis and admiration for certain of their religious principles:

> The quest for happiness is universal, and in their endeavor to attain this the Zunis have developed a philosophy that has been profoundly influenced by their environment. Upon this philosophy is built a system of religion which, among its many interesting features, inculcates truthfulness. A Zuni must speak with one tongue in order to have his prayers received by the gods, and unless the prayers are accepted no rains will come, which means starvation. His voice must be gentle and he must speak and act with kindness to all, for the gods care not for those whose lips speak with harshness.[73]

She then briefly reviewed her early research among the Zunis with her husband, to whom she again paid tribute: "Whatever has been accomplished by the writer at Zuni and elsewhere is largely due to the training and instruction received from her lamented husband and companion, James Stevenson." She acknowledged many others who had helped with her studies, including W. H. Holmes,

Washington Matthews, Henry M. Teller, Robert Adams, Jr., Reginald H. Sayre, Douglas D. Graham, and several military officers. Among her Zuni friends, she singled out We'wha; Pedro Pino; Nai'uchi, his wife, his son Ha'lian, and his granddaughter Nina; Mesha (also spelled Me'she), the younger brother Bow priest; other priests and theurgists; as well as "the women and children, who ever manifested a pleasing readiness to serve her."[74]

Four-fifths of this massive work is devoted to Zuni religion, philosophy, and esoteric societies, in line with Tilly's belief that religion was the cornerstone of all Indian cultures. She gave minute descriptions of sacred rituals and ceremonies, incorporating Zuni words throughout, and presenting facts within the context of the Zunis' world as she understood it. She made no attempt to draw "final conclusions" about the origins of their religious beliefs and organizations, stating this would be possible only after she made a comparative study of the Pueblos.[75]

Tilly set forth her data in a straightforward manner—there are few frills in her writing—but frequent attention to the personalities involved enlivens the volume. Occasionally her prose is lyrical, as in this paragraph concerning the winter solstice ceremonies:

> The sun rose in splendor on the morning of the fifth day, making brilliant the mantle of snow that covered the earth. The valley was sparkling white, and the mesa walls were white, with here and there a patch of dark blue, the pines veiled by the atmosphere. The snowy plain was a vast kaleidoscope from morning until evening, the devotees in the bright clothing going to and returning from their sacred mission.

She often documented her interaction with the Zuni people and allowed multiple voices to be heard in the text. She told her readers, for example, that during the course of the winter solstice ceremonies, she joined a Zuni family in planting prayer plumes in a nearby melon patch. The male head of the household apparently had observed her activities as closely as the ethnologist observed the affairs of the pueblo. In handing her the plumes he had made for her, he said, "Though you are a woman you have a head and a heart like a man, and you work like a man, and you must therefore make offerings such as men make." This statement probably pleased Tilly, for she prided herself on her stamina in the field and on working as hard as her male colleagues. So, like the Zuni men, she planted one prayer plume "with its stick colored blue to the Sun Father, and four with sticks colored black" to ancestors. The women planted one prayer plume "with the stick colored yellow to the Moon Mother, and three with the sticks colored black" to their ancestors. When all the prayer plumes were planted, each person took a pinch of meal and, "holding the meal near the lips, repeats a prayer for health, long life, many clouds, much rain, food, and raiment, and the meal is sprinkled thickly over the plumes."[76]

Tilly devoted nearly one hundred pages to the history, arts, and customs of the Zuni people. She clearly admired many aspects of their society, including their family life, which she believed "might well serve as an example for the civilized world." "Members are deeply attached to one another," she wrote. "The writer found great enjoyment in her visits to the general living room in the early evening, after the day's labors were over. . . . The young mothers would be seen caring for their infants, or perhaps the fathers would be fondling them, for the Zuni men are very devoted to their children, especially the babies." Children were obedient, never quarreled with one another, and never touched other people's belongings. Nor did parents use harsh words with them or resort to physical punishment.[77]

She also respected many Zuni medical practices, including the use of antiseptics (which antedated the modern practice of surgery in Western medicine) and other useful drugs, although they were often employed "in conjunction with theurgism." The medicines of the Shu'maakwe fraternity, she reported, comprised "a variety of plants, several of which, after being ground, are compounded into small cakes and sun dried, and then used as medicine internally and externally." She could testify to one medicine's efficacy, for when applied externally, it relieved her rheumatism after other medications had failed. And in an aside, which might go unnoticed in the maze of her detailed report, she obliquely referred to the greater equality women doctors found in Zuni society compared to their counterparts in her own: "It can not be said whether the Zuni women ever had a struggle to enter the field of medicine, but to-day some of the most successful practitioners, both in legitimate medicine and in theurgy, are women."[78]

Tilly wrote about birth, puberty, marriage, and mortuary customs, often describing incidents in which she participated or intervened to relieve the suffering of a villager. In one case, she used "simple remedies" to end the cough and pain in the abdomen of a pregnant woman. In another, she offered helpful reassurance to a pregnant woman whom Nai'uchi had declared was carrying a serpent rather than a child. The distressed husband approached Tilly "and begged her to go to his wife, who was in such a wretched mental state that he feared she would die." After examining the woman, she pronounced that Nai'uchi was mistaken. Although it took several days for the young woman to accept the ethnologist's assessment, she eventually recovered her good spirits and gave birth to a healthy boy. In gratitude, the mother asked Tilly to name the child, and the husband, certain that she had saved his wife's life, delivered to her every week thereafter "the best products of his fields and garden" from several miles away.[79]

In sections on house building, agriculture, food and drink, and pottery, Stevenson described many of the women's contributions to the daily well-being of the pueblo, a boon to modern-day scholars of women's history. "The women delight in house building," she told her readers, "especially in plastering the houses," which they considered "their special prerogative." Even little girls helped by bringing water from the river, carried in small vases balanced on their heads, that would be used to mix the mortar. Women also raised onions, chiles, and a variety of herbs in small gardens, watering them daily with water carried from the river. And Stevenson described how women prepared and cooked several varieties of bread and mush, as well as other foods.[80]

She also gave a detailed account of the manufacture of pottery, an industry entirely dominated by women, most of whom learned the art at an early age. The black clay used in making the vessels came from Corn Mountain, where Tilly and her husband had once gone with We'wha on a collecting mission. "When she drew near to the clay bed she indicated to Mr. Stevenson that he must remain behind, as men never approached the spot," Tilly wrote. A short distance beyond, We'wha cautioned Tilly to remain quiet, saying, "Should we talk, my pottery would crack in the baking, and unless I pray constantly the clay will not appear to me." Stevenson described in detail the implements used in pottery making and the process of forming, decorating, and firing the vessels.[81]

Despite her high regard for the Zuni people, Tilly found some of their customs disturbing, especially their treatment of suspected witches. Nor did she approve of the antics of the Ne'wekwe fraternity, whose use of excrement and urine in their ceremonies shocked her Victorian sensibilities. But even after describing the "revolting sights" she had witnessed, she reported with some detachment, "This dose [composed of the aforementioned elements] is given and received with the same seriousness that Christian churches observe with their most sacred sacraments."[82]

In several sections, particularly in the one entitled "Recent Changes in Arts and Industries," Stevenson pictured Zuni society as being in a state of flux rather than static or frozen in some "ethnological present." She felt that some changes that had taken place since her visit in 1879 were for the better, others decidedly for the worse. Finer homes were now built entirely of stone, ceilings were higher, rooms were larger. Windowpanes, candles, and lamps were widely used, and some homes sported cooking stoves, curtains on windows, doors with locks, china closets, iron bedsteads, chairs and tables, and sewing machines. Men wore store-bought clothes; Zunis now laundered their garments; families purchased flour, lard, yeast, coffee, and sugar from local sources; and wheat fields were protected by barbed-wire fences. Increasing numbers of Zunis also spoke English.[83]

To Tilly's dismay, however, contact with "civilized man" had also adversely affected the pueblo people. "In 1879 no amount of money could have purchased a genuine Zuni mask," she avowed, "and not for the world would they have manufactured a bogus specimen, so great was their dread of offending their gods." That had changed; now "the less orthodox men will manufacture almost anything a collector may desire." And they made "spurious ancient fetishes" as well, passing them off as genuine. She also decried the increased consumption of alcohol, and the "trickery in dealing with the white man, whom they delight to lie to and cheat, though among themselves the Zunis are still honest."[84]

On the book's final page, Stevenson repeated her call for comparative studies before the Pueblo Indians lost their native culture. Still strongly committed to salvage ethnology, she professed, "For this work the passing hours are golden, for not only are the villages losing their old-time landmarks, but the people themselves are changing, are adapting themselves to [a] suddenly and profoundly altered environment."[85]

Stevenson's Zuni ethnography was well received within the scientific community. Walter Hough, curator at the National Museum, wrote in a congratulatory note, "The monograph takes a high place at once in the literature of anthropology and I am sure will be of permanent value on account of the accuracy, patience and skill with [which] you have made your observations." George H. Pepper, an anthropologist at New York's American Museum of Natural History, called it "a work of inestimable value." P. C. Warman, of the U.S. Geological Survey, recognized the passion Tilly put into her work: "I congratulate you on the appearance of what is probably your *magnum opus* thus far, and hope that you may be fortunate enough to continue your beloved work many years." Arnold Hague, also of the Geological Survey, conveyed to Tilly the prophetic remarks that her erstwhile defender Robert Adams had made concerning the Zuni book, just prior to his death: "It is really quite a remarkable publication. She will not receive much credit or applause while she lives, but it is a great monument to her industry and long after her death will be regarded as a most valuable publication and referred to by scholars."[86]

Friends also wrote notes of congratulations, among them Sofie Nordhoff-Jung, who had requested that copies of Tilly's ethnography

Matilda Coxe Stevenson as a young woman. Courtesy National Anthropological
Archives, Smithsonian Institution, Neg. No. 92-15408.

WASHINGTON, D. C.

Matilda Coxe Stevenson, 1879, the year she first went to Zuni Pueblo. Courtesy
National Anthropological Archives, Smithsonian Institution, SPC 01145300.

James Stevenson. Courtesy National Anthropological Archives, Smithsonian Institution, Neg. No. 76-13442.

Interior view of James and Matilda Coxe Stevensons' home, 1303 P Street, Washington, D.C. Shows Indian craftwork; also portraits of M. C. Stevenson's mother and father on wall of dining room. Courtesy National Anthropological Archives, Smithsonian Institution, GN 04910a.

Interior view of James and Matilda Coxe Stevensons' home, 1303 P Street, Washington, D.C. Shows Indian pottery, baskets, and other craftwork. Courtesy National Anthropological Archives, Smithsonian Institution, GN 04910g.

Exterior view of the Stevensons' home, 1303 P Street, Washington, D.C. Courtesy National Anthropological Archives, Smithsonian Institution, GN 04909.

Zuni Pueblo, Logan–Stevenson Party, September 1882. Photo by Ben Wittick. Courtesy Palace of the Governors (MNM/DCA), Neg. No. 16054.

Zuni Pueblo, gardens in foreground. Courtesy National Anthropological Archives, Smithsonian Institution, Neg. No. 47776-a.

Camp in Canyon de Chelly, October 1882. James and Matilda Coxe Stevenson to the far right. Photo by Ben Wittick. Courtesy Palace of the Governors (MNM/DCA), Neg. No. 15475.

Stevenson party at White House Ruin in Canyon de Chelly, October 1882. Matilda Coxe Stevenson in hat and long dress, standing in lower ruin. Photo by John K. Hillers. Courtesy National Anthropological Archives, Smithsonian Institution, Neg. No. 2005-31480.

We'wha and Zuni child. Probably Matilda Coxe Stevenson's shadow in foreground. Courtesy National Anthropological Archives, Smithsonian Institution, SPC 0241 2200.

Zia women and girls preparing clay floor for Matilda Coxe Stevenson's camp. Courtesy National Anthropological Archives, Smithsonian Institution, SPC 02407100.

Zia women and girls outside Matilda Coxe Stevenson's tents, pounding clay for new floor. Courtesy National Anthropological Archives, Smithsonian Institution, Neg. No. 02199 (gn).

Matilda Coxe Stevenson in her later years. Courtesy American Anthropological
Association, *American Anthropologist* 18 (1916).

be sent to several gynecology professors with whom she had studied in Germany. Professor Winckel, the father of modern midwifery, "is delighted with the book," she reported, and planned to introduce it "this winter in Munich before a selected company." "I do not see that there is anything left to know about the Zuni after your exhaustive work has appeared," she declared. "You see we Germans know how to appreciate such thorough investigation and what I am particularly proud to show them is that such work was done by a woman."[87]

A congratulatory letter from Victoria Siddons, who helped type the manuscript, turns upside down the stereotypical images that have long depicted the ethnologist as humorless, insensitive, and overbearing, and it deserves to be printed in full.

> The book came yesterday and I appreciate it very much indeed. It is something to feel that one has been permitted the privilege of having ever so humble a part in the production of a valuable work, but what stupendous pride you must experience at the result of your labor. I know that it was a labor of love with you and yet I dont [*sic*] believe there is another woman who could, under the same trying conditions which seemed to encompass you at the time—point to such successful culmination of their efforts. *Triumph!* Thats [*sic*] the word.
>
> Looking over the book recalled with much pleasure to me the hours spent in your society, hours during which you made me forget that I was *working* for my living and to which you lent a womanly sympathy and charm to the uncongenial office of "typewriter." The familiar, but unpronounceable words and quaint ceremonies stare at me from the pages of the monologue like old friends conjuring pleasant memories of you. With affectionate regard always and many thanks.[88]

Tilly was not at all certain how the Zunis would receive her book, however. At first she tried to keep copies from reaching the pueblo. She specifically requested that the bureau not send complementary copies to Indian traders Bennett and Vanderwagen, or to Dr. Edward J. Davis, a Bureau of Indian Affairs physician, fearing that the book, in their hands, "would cause me and any future workers in Zuni trouble." In a letter to Holmes written only a few months after the book's publication, she explained, "The Zuni know that I studied them for the purpose of making records for the high authorities in Washington but they would be crazy to find my book in the hands of people in the west and it would be disastrous to my work there." Of course they would see the book one day, she continued, but she would prepare them for this when she returned to Zuni for further study.[89]

Stevenson was not alone in her efforts to keep native peoples from seeing what an anthropologist had written about them. Washington Matthews had warned Thomas V. Keam not to let Navajos see his *Navajo Legends* (1897), and Elsie Clews Parsons admonished a young researcher in the 1920s that "for the sake of fellow workers one must never show Pueblo Indians any publications." Parsons went so far as to include in her agreement with Yale University Press the stipulation that her *Taos Pueblo* (1936) would "not be made available to people in New Mexico."[90]

Despite Tilly's efforts, a copy of her ethnography reached Zuni Pueblo before she returned, and she was delighted by its reception. From Douglas D. Graham, she learned that the Indians frequently had him read to them from the book. "They prize the work greatly, calling it their book[, saying] that their mother wrote it to preserve their history," she reported to Holmes. "Each fraternity thinks the part about them is the best in the book. I am surely pleased at their favorable criticism. It is above all others to me."[91]

As Robert Adams had predicted, Stevenson's ethnography became a standard reference for students of the Southwest. For the next generation of ethnologists, including Alfred L. Kroeber and Elsie Clews Parsons, it served as a starting point for their own studies, even though Parsons criticized Stevenson's technique and some of her findings. Kroeber, who trusted Stevenson's material over Cushing's, incorporated her data into his definitive "Zuni Kin and Clan" (1917).[92]

In later years, Stevenson's ethnography has been praised by some scholars and ignored by others. For example, Fred Eggan, in his 1968 overview of the past one hundred years of ethnology, and Keith Basso, in a 1979 essay on the history of ethnological research in the Southwest, fail to mention Tilly's work among the Zunis. Yet Eggan made amends in the prestigious *Handbook of North American Indians* (1979). In an essay on Zuni history, he and coauthor T. N. Pandey assert that Tilly's book, in conjunction with Cushing's work, provides "an important baseline for understanding Zuni society and culture in the 1880s and 1890s that is unrivalled [*sic*] for the Pueblo region." David M. Brugge, E. Richard Hart, and Nancy J. Parezo have expressed similar sentiments.[93]

Indeed, historians and anthropologists alike have mined Stevenson's book for its descriptions of Zuni society at a time when it was undergoing vast changes, and to document the lives of Indian women. More importantly, however, Stevenson preserved for modern Zunis a picture of their ancestors as they lived in the last quarter of the nineteenth century, and many since then have consulted her book to confirm the accuracy of certain rituals, a fact that surely would have pleased Stevenson. Anthropologist Barbara Tedlock succinctly pays tribute to her prodigious accomplishment in these words: "Oh, how that woman struggled to get it all down for science, before the Zunis either died off or forgot their old ways."[94]

CHAPTER 6

"I Will Make Any Sacrifice in Order to Go On with My Field Work"[1]

Tilly returned to fieldwork in late January 1906, filled with energy and enthusiasm for advancing her comparative studies among the Pueblo Indians. She planned to start the season at Taos Pueblo, where she and her husband had received a cordial welcome in 1880. On this occasion, however, she ran into a stone wall. A council of elders prohibited her from staying in the pueblo for more than a few weeks, and the Taos governor forbade his people to have anything to do with her. This resistance was unlike anything she had encountered before, and she vented her frustration in letters to William H. Holmes. Still, with a doggedness that characterized her entire career, Tilly persevered, and eventually obtained from key Taos villagers information about their language, philosophy, and customs, as well as "the only detailed and reliable account of the annual August pilgrimage of the Taos people to Blue Lake."[1]

Tilly left Washington on January 30 with an allotment of $1,000 to cover travel and subsistence expenses, as well as the services of interpreters, laborers, and a clerical assistant. En route to New Mexico, she stopped over in Denver to view an archaeological exhibit at the state capitol. By February 7, she and her assistant Jessica Hockenberry had reached Santa Fe, where she visited several old friends, including former governor L. Bradford Prince. She also gave an interview to the *Santa Fe Daily New Mexican*, a deed she soon had reason to regret.[2]

In due time, Stevenson and her assistant traveled north to Española, a small Hispanic settlement near the Indian pueblos of Santa Clara, San Ildefonso, San Juan, and Nambé, where Tilly outfitted for her anticipated six-month field season in Taos Pueblo. She hired a wagon to transport an ample stock of commissary goods and other supplies to the Indian village. She also became "better acquainted with the Santa Clara Indians," telling Holmes in one of her first letters from the field, "My Mexican [Spanish] is coming back to me rapidly so that I have no trouble in communicating with the Indians." She had spent two or three hours while in the area "winning over the old cacique of Santa Clara," she continued. "My description of the Zuni rain ceremonials was too much for him so he smiled and begged me not to stay too long at Taos as he and his people wished me with them."[3]

Tilly may have been introduced to the cacique by Clara D. True, the government teacher at the Santa Clara day school, whom Stevenson probably met toward the close of her 1904 field season. Whatever the case, Clara True was to cause Tilly a great deal of misery later on, but, of course, the ethnologist had no way of knowing this when she reentered True's world in 1906.[4]

On February 14, Stevenson and Hockenberry reached the remote settlement of Taos, New Mexico, tucked away in a beautiful alpine valley at the base of the towering Sangre de Cristo Mountains. The population of Taos (predominately Hispanic) stood at 1,309 in 1910; that of nearby Taos Pueblo at 521. Likely the two women checked into the local hotel, one of several adobe business buildings and dwellings located on the central plaza. Tilly spent the next few days becoming "acquainted with some of the Taos Indians," for as she explained to Holmes, with the pueblo less than three miles away, "large numbers of Indians come daily to Taos."[5]

Very likely Stevenson also met, or heard of, a trio of Euro-Americans living in Taos who were to affect the ethnologist's life and work in quite different ways. The one who impressed her the most was Arthur R. Manby, "a cultured Englishman," whose large adobe hacienda was near the plaza. Graced with fine English furniture and paintings, with an English-style park located on one side, Manby's residence must have appeared to Tilly as an oasis in this distant outpost. She looked less kindly upon the artist Bert Phillips, whose studio-home was directly across the street from Manby's residence, and the physician Thomas Paul Martin, Phillips's brother-in-law, who lived next door to Manby.[6] Tilly came to believe that both Phillips and Martin opposed her ethnographic work, especially the artist, who seemed to hold a proprietary interest in the Taos Indians, many of whom served as models for his paintings. "I presume [Phillips] feels determined that I shall not get what he has been striving for for years, a knowledge of the secret beliefs and ceremonies of the Taos Indians," she confided to Holmes.[7]

Tilly's problems started even before she reached Taos, for someone—she suspected Dr. Martin—had told the Indians about her Santa Fe interview. Although most of the article was innocuous, some passages might easily have upset the Indians. They heard of her plans to secure a house in the pueblo, for example, and to remain there for six months in order "to learn all about the practice of the priests, the religious ceremonials, the secret societies of which there are many and the general lives of men, women and children." Although Stevenson claimed that a reporter had fabricated much of the interview, it reflects accurately her research goals for the season.[8]

Tilly and her assistant rode out to Taos Pueblo on February 19, stopping first at the house of Lorenzo Martínez, the official interpreter for the pueblo. A former student at the Indian Industrial School in Carlisle, Pennsylvania, Martínez had once been to Tilly's home in Washington while visiting the capital as a member of a Pueblo delegation. She had hoped to rent two rooms from Martínez, the only available rooms in the pueblo, but refused to pay the exorbitant sum he demanded—$4 per day. As a consequence, Tilly reported to Holmes, he decided "to act against me when I met the Council [the next day] composed of fourteen men, the Governor presiding, and Lorenzo acting as interpreter." When she realized that Martínez was not translating her words accurately, she addressed the councilmen in Spanish. At first they declared they opposed any "American" stopping in their village, but after further discussion, they agreed that she might stay two or three weeks. Not caring to submit to Martínez's attempt at "extortion," she rented a two-room house for $5 per month in the nearby town.[9]

Her troubles were far from over, however. The governor of Taos Pueblo ordered tribal members not to go near her. Still, with her "faithful assistant" taking charge of meals and other chores, Stevenson spent her days attempting to make friends with the Indians who came to town. Eventually some overcame their fears of the governor and visited Tilly's house, where she treated them to coffee and other fare. In mid-March, she reported that "a fine fellow" had agreed to work with her—that he had said, "I think it is a great thing that the Government is willing to send you to write down our language and other things so that they will never die." Yet, he wanted his visits kept secret, and insisted that "the other American woman" keep watch and not let anyone in the house while he was there. A few days later, Tilly reported that Indians came to her every day, among them Ventura, "the greatest theurgist in the pueblo . . . venerated as the sage of his people." Hockenberry proved to be a vital asset. She "is good at every thing," Tilly avowed, "but especially is she good at playing watchman while I study with an Indian."[10]

Initially, Tilly received strong support from Clinton J. Crandall, superintendent of the Indian Industrial School near Santa Fe, who also supervised government teachers at Taos and other northern pueblos. He wrote to the Taos governor on her behalf, sending the letter to Tilly so that she might deliver it in person. But when the governor declined to meet with her, she sent a copy to Isaac W. Dwire, the government's resident farmer in Taos, requesting that he read the message to him. Crandall's letter read in part, "This will introduce to you Mrs. M. C. Stevenson, a representative of the Bureau of American Ethnology, from Washington, D.C. She comes among you with the full approval of Commissioner [of Indian Affairs] [Francis] Leupp and the Department at Washington. I ask that you show her kindness and courtesies, and permit her to go about her work uninterrupted."[11]

In subsequent correspondence describing her difficulties at Taos and other Rio Grande villages, Stevenson showed her willingness to use whatever methods were necessary to obtain information. The letters also reveal a great deal about her personality, underscoring her tenacity, dedication, imperiousness, patience, and quiet diplomacy.

On March 15, and again on March 18, Tilly requested that Holmes meet with the commissioner to inform him of the situation at Taos Pueblo. She had tried to reassure the Indians that she had come not to study their secret ceremonials, but to "write some of their language and to become better acquainted with them." She hoped that Leupp would "think of some means to frighten these fellows into not interfering with my work." Stevenson had learned a lesson from her recent experience with the press, however. She now advised Holmes to keep her affairs private; otherwise, "it might get into the papers and there are many here who would be only [too] pleased to inform the Indians. The Washington papers come here. The more quiet the matter is kept the better."[12]

Holmes subsequently met with the commissioner, and then informed Tilly that Leupp "has promised to do what he can to take the kinks out of your obstreperous governor." Still, the commissioner would not interfere directly with the affairs of the pueblo, but "will let the governor know that favors done him must be reciprocated in kind if he expects to ask additional concessions in the way of relief from taxes, etc." Leupp also promised to ask Crandall to look into the matter.[13]

By the first of May, Stevenson had achieved a modicum of success. She had made many "warm friends" among the Indians, including Ventura, who recently had dined twice with her and told her to have patience, that as the people came to love her, "things would be better after a time." She also became friends with "one of the great historians of the tribe," who visited her only at night to speak of Indian philosophy, and would remain nameless in her letters, at his request. "He is constantly watched that he does not come near me," Tilly told Holmes. "He throws his whole soul in his work with me." One night, she stayed up until 2:00 A.M. working through "a very knotty subject" with him. She was "touched" by his parting remarks, which she shared with Holmes:

> Senora [*sic*] Stevenson I am giving you the most sacred things of my life. When I am away from you I am always thinking how I can best make every thing plain to you and how to avoid all mistakes on your part. I wish you to have the best out of my life, but you will promise me that you will never tell my name to the President or any of the officials at Washington. I wish when I die to follow my road straight, and to reach my home, but I cannot if my people should chance to learn that I have told you of my home and the God I shall meet there. Will you promise me never to tell my name?[14]

During the second week of May, Superintendent Crandall visited briefly with Tilly before holding a council with Taos Pueblo officials. The ethnologist soon came to realize that the superintendent had no intention of advancing her cause among the Indians. Although at first he agreed to allow her to accompany him to the council meeting, he apparently reversed that decision, saying that the Indians might not wish her to be present. Several days after the meeting, she learned from Antonio Romero, the interpreter for Crandall, that he had failed to honor one of her requests: that he urge the governor to stop interfering with her work. According to Romero, "he only told the Council that they must treat Mrs. Stevenson well when she visited the pueblo, as she was a nice lady from Washington and the [commissioner] was interested in her." Deeply offended by Crandall's behavior, she vented her spleen in letters to Holmes, telling him also, however, that she would get on with her work despite Crandall's lack of cooperation.[15]

Stevenson's spirits soared, however, after Commissioner Leupp visited Taos Pueblo on May 27. He, too, held a council with Indian officials, but he called this meeting for the sole purpose of supporting her work. She learned details of the proceedings from an Indian interpreter who was present and from her friend Ventura.

Leupp had asked the governor if "he intended to cease interfering with Mrs. Stevenson's work." His determined manner, Tilly learned, had encouraged Ventura to speak up on her behalf. Two days after the council, the old man visited the ethnologist and announced that "he now had no fear in coming to see me. He remained to dinner," Tilly informed Holmes.[16]

Before leaving New Mexico, Leupp wrote to Tilly from Santa Fe, summarizing his recent meeting with the Indians. He thought the results would be "somewhat beneficial" to her work, though he admonished her to stay clear of reporters, and to be tactful in using the privileges now accorded her. He had worked out an arrangement with Taos officials, the details of which they insisted be placed in a memorandum, with copies given to Tilly and to the governor. It stated in part,

> [Mrs. Stevenson] will have the privilege of questioning and obtaining from the Taos Indians such information as they are able to give her concerning their language, history and social customs, and also such of their religious tradition and practices as they can properly communicate. She is to be treated with courtesy and consideration as long as she maintains the same course of conduct towards the Indians of the pueblo. The Governor will see that no unreasonable obstructions are thrown in the way of her obtaining the information she seeks which it is understood hereby is for the use of the Government of the United States in preserving the history and knowledge of the Taos Pueblo for posterity.

Leupp reminded Tilly, however, that Indians guarded well their religious knowledge, and nothing would change this. Moreover, he added, "You will have to bear in mind that your sex is in itself a handicap among these people."[17]

Just prior to the commissioner's visit, Tilly had moved into new quarters, a one-room house about a quarter of a mile outside of town and a bit closer to the pueblo. To make it more accessible to her Indian friends, she had a plank placed across the irrigating ditch behind her place so that they "could slip into the camp without coming over the highway." She also had a log shelter built nearby, where she (and presumably her assistant) would sleep, the house serving as her office and place to interview Indians. When the shelter proved untenable during high winds, however, she purchased a tent from a local merchant, and found that it provided better protection from the volatile weather. Her office had its own flaws, however. During one severe rainstorm, she spent an entire day and night "fighting water that came through the roof" to protect the boxes that contained her precious papers.[18]

For a brief period following Leupp's visit, more Indians turned up at Tilly's camp, although the historian continued to call only at night. Because her friend seemed in delicate health, she was grateful when Holmes approved her request to remain in the field beyond the close of the fiscal year. "I fear that I would never have another such opportunity of studying the Taos people," she told him. "The man with whom I am doing such fine work is not at all strong, and I fear he would not be here another year."[19]

Some of the villagers soon asked Stevenson why she did not fly the American flag over her camp like the government teachers did over their house. Did she not also work for the government? Tilly quickly secured a flag from the bureau—"to maintain my prestige," as she put it. Weeks later, she reported, "All the Indians are pleased to see the stars and stripes flying over my camp."[20]

By the end of June, the recent independence exhibited by the Indians had largely disappeared, and fewer felt free to talk to the ethnologist. Yet Tilly had faith that her loyal Indian friends would not desert her. "We will out-general the Governor," she declared optimistically. She continued to do her best work with the historian, and often praised him in letters to Holmes. On June 12 she wrote, "I am more than blessed in having a man not only willing to give me the history and philosophy of his people but [who] delights in the work of instructing me. It would be difficult to find another with whom I could accomplish so much, as these Indians are determined that their secrets shall be kept from all who do not belong to their tribe." She also worked to record the Taos language with various interpreters, one of whom had spent eight years at the Santa Fe Indian School.[21]

The need for secrecy remained throughout Tilly's stay at Taos. She said little about her work in her monthly reports, fearing that others besides Holmes might see their contents and leak news of her progress to the newspapers. It would be disastrous, she stated on more than one occasion, if it became known that she was learning the secrets of the Indians. In July she wrote, "If [the governor of Taos] supposed that I was getting any thing more than the language he would stop all coming to me."[22]

After her assistant Jessica Hockenberry left New Mexico in mid-July on the advice of her physician, Tilly continued to work surreptitiously with the historian, often without a sentinel to stand guard. In late August, her friend Emma Tyler (Senator Henry M. Teller's daughter) served in that capacity for several days while staying with the ethnologist. Later Tilly assessed the situation in a letter to Holmes:

> Now that Mrs. Tyler . . . has left me I have no one to act as guard while I am closeted with my historian and he jumps at every sound. I fully appreciate his anxiety for it means death to him should he be caught at work with me. We both know that Dr. Martin is spying upon me. Surely the gods have been with me that I have worked all these months without my historian having been caught. But I have given about as much of my brains to avoid detection as I have to my scientific work, and this has been most trying to me.[23]

It is easy to understand why tribal officials opposed the efforts of Stevenson, and later of Elsie Clews Parsons and other ethnologists, to record their sacred beliefs. To reveal religious knowledge to outsiders, many elders believed, would "weaken it." As one Taos Indian told Parsons, "People want to find out about this Pueblo; but they can't. Our ways would lose their power if they were known."[24]

Yet Stevenson persuaded some tribal members to reveal information about their philosophy and religious ceremonies. To secure the historian's assistance, she had told him he would "win the favor of his gods by allowing me to record their beliefs and so have them live always, for the gods would not wish the knowledge of their mysteries to die with his people while those of the Zuni gods will live forever because they have been recorded." Other anthropologists used similar arguments to entice Indians to talk about their culture. Washington Matthews, for example, persuaded Navajo singers that "it was their duty to future generations of Navajos to record oral traditions and knowledge in new media—pencil, brush, and paper." Elsie Clews Parsons told Pueblo Indians that the rules by which they lived were changing, "the old rules were passing away, they should be written down so that people would know how their grandfathers had lived." Such claims were effective. The Taos historian, in fact, took pains to insure that what Stevenson wrote down was accurate; when he corrected her work on one occasion, he stated, "What would my God in the undermost world do with me if you wrote lies from my talking, instead of truth."[25]

During this field season and the one to follow, Tilly acquired much information about the mythology and customs of the Taos people, as well as a list of their clan names. Her field notes, housed in the National Anthropological Archives, cover 318 pages and nearly one hundred cards and slips.[26] She accumulated this material from interviews with tribal members and from direct observation of public ceremonies. On September 30, 1906, for example, she and her friend Clara True were part of a large contingent of outsiders (the local press said more than two thousand people) who witnessed the annual harvest festival of San Geronimo, the patron saint of Taos Pueblo. After the Catholic priest held services, races took place between the kivas found on either side of the river that divides the village. Later Tilly reported to Holmes that although she had expected "to have many battles in my efforts to secure pictures . . . I had very little trouble." She used this incident to support her belief that her relations with the tribe were improving. Even though the assistant war chief ("one of my bitterest opponents") admonished her several times to stop taking photographs, "a twinkle in his eyes," she said, "told me to go on. Perhaps he knew that I would go on any way." Tilly also informed Holmes that "the purely Indian ceremonies begin the morning following this feast, and continue for several days." The tribe guarded these ceremonies so carefully, she added, that few outsiders knew anything about them.[27]

Throughout the summer, Stevenson focused her attention on the affairs of the Taos people, taking little time to socialize with members of the larger community. After receiving a visit from Virginia Couse, wife of the artist Irving Couse (one of several artists then living in Taos), she asked Holmes—a fine artist himself—if there was any reason for her to spend time with the couple. "My desire is to keep clear of all social obligations so as to be absolutely free to shut myself up at any time with an interpreter." During Emma Tyler's visit, however, she took Sundays off to drive with her guest and two or three other friends into the countryside, where they picnicked by a mountain stream. Clearly under the spell of the northern New Mexico landscape, Stevenson became almost lyrical in describing this "wonderfully beautiful country" to Holmes.

> The sunsets surpass any I have ever before seen. The Taos val-
> ley makes one forget that most of New Mexico appears like a
> desert. The vast valley is carpeted with green except where
> the golden wheat takes the place of the grass. The valley is
> surrounded by mountains which are green nearby, and all
> shades of blue and purple in the distance. My camp is on
> very high ground and I find it very restful after a hard day's
> work, to watch the ever varying sunsets.[28]

Tilly also apparently fell under the spell of Arthur R. Manby, whom she referred to in her letters as "my only friend in Taos" or the "only gentleman in Taos." Ten years younger than Tilly, the Englishman had arrived in New Mexico in 1883, and became a citizen of the United States sixteen years later. He seems to have spent most of his time scheming to amass wealth through mine and land speculation. By the time Stevenson met him in 1906, he had recently organized the Taos Valley Land Company, and filed a suit to quiet title to the Antonio Martínez grant of some 61,605 acres, one of the largest Spanish land grants in Taos County. He had spent years tracking down the Martínez heirs, and by harassment and other questionable means had induced most of them to sell their inherited shares in the grant to him at indecently low prices.[29]

Manby had grandiose plans for developing the grant. He would lay out towns, build a luxury resort hotel, and bring in colonists to cultivate the land. In order to finance his dream, he set out to sell one million shares in his land company, at par value of $1 per share. He named to his board of directors himself, his lawyer, and three of his eastern investors. Although Manby would later be discredited as a schemer and manipulator, he possessed sufficient charm and credibility to entice many worthy people, like Tilly and at least one of her relatives, to invest. Sometime that summer, Stevenson purchased twenty thousand shares in the company, apparently paying twenty-five cents per share. She must have dug deeply into her savings, for $5,000 was more than three times her annual salary. And this explains why she repeatedly asked the bureau that season to quickly settle her monthly expenses. On April 7, she wrote, "It is impossible at this time, for me to advance the money," and a month later, with her bills still unpaid, she moaned, "I do hate to owe money. I have certain obligations to meet besides the running expenses of my field work, and I shall be embarrassed if my accounts are not settled more promptly."[30]

Possibly Tilly introduced Manby to her niece Edith Prescott (the daughter of Tilly's sister Betty Kellogg) and Edith's husband, Alexander, of Rockville, Maryland; or perhaps the Prescotts introduced Stevenson to the land developer. At any rate, the Prescotts, Alexander's mother Mary R. Prescott, and Charles and Martha Hill of Chicago jointly bought two hundred thousand shares in the Taos Valley Land Company. In May 1907 (after Tilly had returned to Washington), the Hills and the Prescotts, accompanied by their sixteen-year-old daughter (also named Edith, but known as Pinkie to her family), visited Manby in Taos. After the briefest of courtships, Pinkie married the forty-eight-year-old Manby. It is not necessary to go into the sordid and complicated details of Manby's financial empire, but it eventually collapsed, a few years after Tilly died, leaving the Prescotts and other investors holding worthless paper. Although the ethnologist at one time had asked her lawyer to try to sell her twenty thousand shares, they remained in her possession at the time of her death. Pinkie Prescott Manby obtained a divorce from her husband two years after the marriage, and he lived out his final years in Taos as a recluse. His murder in 1929 remains one of New Mexico's unsolved mysteries.[31]

Stevenson left Taos on November 1, 1906, for Española, where she spent twelve days continuing her studies with the Santa Clara Indians. During this time, she lodged with the Trues—thirty-eight-year-old Clara D. True, her widowed mother Frances D. True, and Clara's widowed younger sister Elizabeth (Lizzie) Randall—paying $1.50 per day for her room and board.

The family's roots were in Kentucky, although in her late teens, Clara attended college in Missouri, and then taught in local schools there. She took up Indian reform work in the 1890s, and would serve six years as principal of the Bureau of Indian Affairs boarding school at the Lower Brule Agency on the Sioux Reservation in South Dakota. The Trues moved to New Mexico in 1902, when Clara received appointment as teacher at the Santa Clara day school and Frances became its housekeeper. Lizzie found work at a nearby pueblo as matron. After her difficulties at Taos, Tilly basked in the warm and comforting companionship she found in the True household; especially did she enjoy the company of Clara, whom she described as an "intelligent woman," one with "remarkable traits."[32]

During the time Tilly spent with the Santa Clara Indians, she obtained information about their clan system, religion, and "sociology." She also gained a clearer understanding of the division that had plagued the pueblo for more than twenty years, a split that Elsie Clews Parsons later described in *Pueblo Indian Religion* (1939). One party "adheres strictly to the old customs," Stevenson noted, "while the other believes in progress, and the abolishing of the dances." The old cacique whom she had met at the start of this field season controlled the conservatives, while another elder headed the progressives. She had established cordial relations with both men, and felt confident she could work with each faction, should she return for a prolonged visit.[33]

In mid-November, Stevenson left Española for Santa Fe, where she spent several days poring over old Spanish records (housed in the archives of the Historical Society of New Mexico), in search of material relating to the Taos Indians. Her work was eased by ex-governor Prince, president of the society and an avid collector of historical books and documents. She also made the acquaintance of New Mexico's current governor, Herbert J. Hagerman, whom she described as "a cultivated man." When she learned of Hagerman's plans to visit Washington, she suggested that Holmes introduce him to the Cosmos Club, as well as to several professional societies. Looking ahead, she noted, "there may be many ways in the near future in which he may be of service to us."[34]

Tilly planned to end her field season at Zuni Pueblo, where she would continue her studies of symbolism and of the Indians' use of medicinal and edible plants. To prepare for this leg of the journey, she had written to Douglas D. Graham, now serving as superintendent of the Zuni day school, to inquire about lodging. And she sent an urgent request to Holmes to forward her plant collection and the illustrations of symbolism used at the St. Louis World's Fair, items she needed to advance her work.[35]

Eager to reach Zuni, Stevenson soon boarded a train for Gallup, where she encountered Zuni Indians for the first time since leaving the pueblo two years before. On this and later occasions, the warmth of the Indians' welcome profoundly moved her. Her emotions, no doubt, were heightened by the stark contrast between the affectionate response of the Zunis and the tepid (if not hostile) reception she had received among the more secretive Taos people. She described what took place in a letter dated November 26:

> Two Zuni Indians came into a store in Gallup when I was making a purchase and when they saw me they could not speak for a moment. . . . They spoke only a few words. "My

mother, my mother has come back to us, thanks, thanks," and after shaking my hand in the most reverential manner they stood and gazed at me without saying another word. It was really dramatic. On reaching a ranch and trading station on the way to Zuni, I met three more Zuni and they met me in the same manner. It seemed impossible for them to speak more than the few words of thanks. I have had the same experience since reaching Zuni. They are all hurrying to see me as they learn of my arrival, and they continue to greet me in the same solemn manner. I am to them as one returned from the dead. Knowing that their book[,] as they call the Zuni book, was finished they thought that I would never come back to them. I have never witnessed such scenes before and while I knew that most of the Zuni loved me I never dreamed of the real depth of their affection for me. I have been deeply touched.[36]

She soon settled into a "comfortable room," which Graham had provided, at the Zuni school, and took meals with the teachers at their residence a short distance away. She would spend the next three months completing her studies of "certain phases" of native ritual and worship and of symbolism found on Zuni textiles and ceramics. She also revised her list of plants that the Zunis used for food and medicine. She took numerous photographs of Zuni ceremonies (after film for her camera belatedly arrived), and noted changes that had taken place since her earlier visits. Houses were now scattered over the plains in a "promiscuous" manner, she lamented; "all that remains to us of old Zuni are the early photographs by Mr. Hillers." She also observed "a dropping off" in the Sha'lako ritual and a "carelessness in the decoration of the masks." Nonetheless, she still found the ceremony "wonderful and picturesque."[37]

At the behest of several villagers, Tilly spent a good deal of time going over the Zuni book. "The Indian priests and theurgists," she reported, "are the happiest creatures you ever saw when looking at the illustrations and listening to me read from the book." She enjoyed even more working with a "remarkable woman," more than eighty years old, who assisted her with the study of symbolism. She "is as well if not better informed on this subject as any person in any tribe in the Southwest," Tilly avowed. "She goes down in Zuni history as the finest potter of whom there is definite knowledge, and she is the last person in whom the keeping of the knowledge of symbols as embodied in pictographs, ceramics, and fabrics was intrusted."[38]

Stevenson made only a few purchases this season for the National Museum, although Holmes told her not to hesitate to secure "interesting objects up to a reasonable amount." "Your judgment in such matters," he assured her, "can be implicitly relied upon." The object she apparently valued above all others was a rain priest's rattle, the one that had belonged to Nai'uchi. She paid $5 to Nai'uchi's son to obtain it, with the understanding that she would secure materials so that he might duplicate it as soon as possible, before others discovered that the rattle was missing. Emphasizing the urgency of her request, she asked Holmes to send her some sleigh bells and six small shells of light purple color. About the time the bells arrived, Tilly also received "an enormous amount of wild turkey feathers" from her sister-in-law, and distributed them to the priests and theurgists. "The Indians are crazy over [the feathers]," she reported. "Each god has his own particular plumes from some particular part of turkey and other birds, offered to him," she explained.[39]

Among the visitors to Zuni that winter was the president of Illinois's Wesleyan University, Dr. Francis (Frank) Barnes, who was anxious to learn "as much as possible" about the Zunis. Consequently he became Tilly's "shadow," and she obligingly took him to a late-night meeting of the Galaxy fraternity. He had arrived at the pueblo with a copy of the Zuni ethnography. And even though the Indians were well aware of the book by now, Tilly cautioned him to keep it out of sight; she still feared that seeing the book in the hands of outsiders would upset the Zunis.[40]

Barnes repaid Tilly's hospitality by supporting her efforts to join the eastern lecture circuit. By the turn of the century, attending public lectures had become something of a national pastime, for speakers often offered their audiences amusement as well as instruction. Tilly had submitted a proposal in November 1905 to Charles W. Fuergerson of the Chicago Lyceum Bureau to deliver a series of illustrated lectures on the Pueblo Indians. She claimed that her "lantern slides" would "charm the most intellectual as well as persons of ordinary attainments." She asked to be paid $125 per lecture, plus expenses. The unexpected extension of her field season, however, precluded any possibility that she would tour with her Indian talks in 1906.[41]

Nonetheless, Tilly enlisted Frank Barnes's aid as she continued to pursue a career as a public lecturer. Once he returned home, he dispatched identical letters, dated January 2, 1907, to four lecture agencies, including the Redpath Bureau in Boston, in which he extolled Tilly's virtues. He called her Zuni ethnography "the greatest ethnological work ever published in America," and described her as "the only real authority" on the Zunis. "Mrs. Stevenson is a refined, scholarly, and cultured lady," he declared, "and would not only instruct an audience, but would hold them with the most intense interest while telling the story of these strange and fascinating people." Their joint efforts came to nothing, however, for Tilly never did make her debut on the eastern lecture circuit.[42]

Before Tilly left Zuni for home, she became involved in an emotionally charged controversy involving the Catholic Church and Father Anselm Weber, a Franciscan missionary to the Navajos. On February 11, Weber poured out his side of the story in letters to Frederick W. Hodge, an acquaintance of his at the Bureau of American Ethnology, and to Reverend William H. Ketcham, director of the Bureau of Catholic Indian Missions in Washington. The Church had hopes of reestablishing its mission at Zuni, and had dispatched two missionaries in December to discuss the matter with the Zunis. According to Weber, the Indians at first approved having a mission in their midst. But later, they experienced a change of heart, allegedly after emissaries from Matilda Coxe Stevenson warned them not to accept missionaries, claiming that they would interfere with their ceremonies, force them to tithe and to pay for having their children baptized, and whip them for not attending mass.[43]

Weber himself had discussed the mission issue with Zuni officials on the evening of February 4, and then attended a large gathering of villagers on the plaza the following afternoon. "The meeting was an exciting one and lasted two hours," he told Reverend Ketcham. He tried "to refute the accusations brought against us [by Stevenson]," and then suggested that he and the governor go question her directly. According to Weber, an Indian went to fetch the ethnologist to the meeting, but she refused to attend, "under the plea that she was not well." In voicing his complaints to Hodge, the missionary asked if the bureau planned to sustain its ethnologists "in *directly* encouraging the Indians in their heathenism and their consequent superstitious practices, in opposing the progress and civilization and christianization [*sic*] of the Indians." In his letter to Reverend Ketcham, he denounced Stevenson's "sinister influence," and demanded her "immediate and permanent removal from Zuni."[44]

After Ketcham met with bureau officials in Washington, Holmes dispatched a letter to Stevenson asking for her side of the story. She immediately replied, denying emphatically that she had used any influence against the Catholic Church. She had stated repeatedly that she "did not care how many Catholics or Protestants they had here." Certainly the Zunis had the right, "as every citizen of the U.S. to worship as they please so long as they commit no offense against the law." But she also knew that there was "a *strong* opposition to the establishment of a mission here." She believed that a man named Jesus, whom she described as a "Mexican" married to a Zuni, had made all the trouble, convincing Weber that she controlled the Zunis.[45]

Tilly also told Holmes that shortly after his letter arrived, the governor of Zuni, Quicko Chaves, and his brother Lorenzo, the pueblo's official interpreter, paid her a visit. When the governor learned of the reports that Father Weber had sent to Washington, he became indignant, and asked that she write a statement for him setting the record straight. The ethnologist had not "used her influence in any way to prevent the Catholic Church from establishing a mission here at Zuni," he declared. All of the Zunis except Jesus opposed the mission. The governor went into great detail about what took place at the meeting with Father Weber, and denied that anyone had gone to fetch Tilly. Toward the end of this long disquisition, he said, "We came to Mrs. Stevenson because she is like our mother. We have known her since we were children, and we know she is our friend." He concluded with these words: "We wish to keep our own religion and be let alone by other religions. How can a man have two religions and be a man?"[46]

The fact that Tilly was due to leave Zuni within weeks seems to have assuaged Father Weber's sense of outrage. He returned to Zuni periodically thereafter through 1909 to offer mass in the home of the sacristan. In 1916, the Zunis would again oppose efforts to establish a Catholic mission. But a small Catholic contingent persisted, and in 1922, Saint Anthony's Mission Church was constructed, a move that led to a permanent division within the pueblo.[47]

By the time Stevenson left Zuni early in March 1907, she had been in the field for more than a year. Now she requested some time off. She planned to spend a day in Chicago to study collections in the Field Columbian Museum, and then linger somewhere en route to Washington and "give myself up to music, pictures—any thing but Indians." With Holmes's approval, she did not return to bureau headquarters until April 1.[48]

For the next four and one-half months, Tilly worked in her office preparing notes and reports on her recent field research. She also met with Edward S. Curtis, who was in the early stages of his career as photographer of North American Indians. His grandiose plan—to photograph and write about all the "vanishing Indians" in the United States and Alaska—had just been funded by J. Pierpont Morgan. Bureau ethnologists Holmes, Hodge, and Stevenson had written testimonials on Curtis's behalf. Tilly expressed her "high appreciation" for his "splendid work," and applauded his efforts to preserve "picture records of the North American Indian." He, in turn, valued her support. In a letter dated

May 5, 1907, he declared, "No words can express my appreciation of your help and encouragement."[49]

Still, the fact that Curtis paid cash to obtain information from Indians disturbed Stevenson. She had no qualms about purchasing religious artifacts, but she never paid Indians to reveal sacred knowledge. "I have always maintained," she wrote to Charles D. Walcott, the recently appointed secretary of the Smithsonian, "that the native peoples will not sell their religion and the beliefs sacred to them for money." The more money they receive, the more falsehoods they will tell. "Mr. E. S. Curtis declared to me," she continued, "that to reach the inner life of the Indian one must have his pocketbook over-flowing until the money runs out in a stream upon the ground. Had Mr. Curtis been an anthropologist I would have taken issue with him but I never argue for the mere sake of argument. Mr. Curtis [sic] work is beautiful as it is." Curtis eventually published his twenty-volume work, The North American Indian, between the years 1907 and 1930. Throughout the text dealing with tribes of the Southwest, he cited only sparingly the works of Stevenson and other researchers. Today his photographs are valued by collectors, treasured by descendants of his Indian subjects, and decried by scholars for his romantic portrayal of "the vanishing race."[50]

In mid-August, Holmes approved Tilly's plans to take her annual leave in New Mexico, where she planned to combine her holiday with some ethnological work. Shortly after reaching Española, she observed a ceremonial rabbit hunt at Santa Clara Pueblo, which she found quite similar to those at Zuni. She probably spent most of her time in the company of the True family, however, and in due time decided to purchase a ranch next to theirs, with funds she received from the sale of her Washington property on P Street. For many years she had dreamed of buying a place in New Mexico, where she would carry out her ethnological studies for as long as she remained with the bureau. This ranch seemed ideal; it was sufficiently remote from Taos that she could work with her Taos Indian friends unobserved, and when not busy with them, she could study with Santa Clara, San Juan, or San Ildefonso Indians.[51]

Tilly gladly accepted Clara True's offer to purchase the land from her neighbor, Charles E. Dagenett, after Clara convinced her that Dagenett would charge an outsider an extortionate price. Thus, Clara bought the property, which included buildings, livestock, farm equipment, and crops—with $4,700 of Tilly's money—in the name of Clara's mother, Frances, who quickly transferred the deed to Stevenson. The three women agreed that Tilly's ownership should be kept secret until she returned for an extended stay, for as Clara warned, "An absentee landlord is at a great disadvantage." The stage was now set for Tilly's heartbreaking and prolonged struggle with the Trues over land, money, and reputation, a struggle that disrupted her ethnological work, drained her finances, and sapped her emotional energy.[52]

Yet, blithely unaware, while on vacation, of the Trues' duplicitous temperaments, Tilly trusted the family implicitly, and discussed with them future plans for their adjoining properties. Before she left for home, Tilly gave Clara more than $100 for ranch expenses and $200 to purchase the "Blonger property," which lay in front of the spot where she planned to build a new house. If someone else were to build there, she avowed, it "would utterly destroy the beauty of my place."[53]

Tilly and Clara must have spent hours together discussing the younger woman's future. Convinced that her friend was too bright to waste her talents employed as a Bureau of Indian Affairs teacher, Stevenson dreamed of securing a spot for her on the staff of the Bureau of American Ethnology. Thus, she exacted a promise from Clara to visit her in Washington in January, for she felt sure "that with all I could say for you and with the impression you would make I could arrange something for you in the Ethnologic world." She also offered Clara's sister, Lizzie Randall, $40 per month to take charge of her government camp when she returned to the field.[54]

When the ethnologist left for Washington, she owned a cow, a calf, two horses, a field of hay, and an apple orchard, which she left in Clara and her mother's care, with the understanding that they would employ a neighbor to help on the ranch. Stevenson clearly intended to turn this into a profitable enterprise, believing that with hired help and the Trues' assistance, she could continue her ethnological studies without interruption. A letter from Clara dated November 6, 1907, was reassuring. She had a carload of Tilly's hay ready to send to Santa Fe, where it would sell for $12.75 per ton. Fences had been strengthened to keep herds of cattle out of Tilly's orchard and pasture. "I am treating your interests just as I should my own," Clara declared.[55]

Once back in Washington, Tilly again turned to her notes on the Rio Grande Pueblos and to her paper describing the medicinal and food plants of the Zuni Indians. For several weeks, she worked in the U.S. Agricultural Department, taking advantage of its many reference books on plants. She dined twice with Charles E. Dagenett (a one-eighth Indian, according to Tilly), when he came to town on business with the Department of the Interior. "I enjoyed so much seeing" him, she reported to Frances True. "We had such nice chats." Still, she did not reveal to him until several months later that she had purchased his former land from "Miss True." She did tell L. Bradford Prince, however, when he visited the capital, that she had bought one of Clara's orchards. Prince was delighted. He also owned property near Española, and congratulated Tilly "upon having secured one of the finest orchards in N. M." Clara True, he said, "had gotten hold of some of the best land in the territory."[56]

But Clara did not visit Tilly in Washington that winter as planned. Instead, she accepted a position in California as superintendent of the Malki Indian Agency at the Morongo Indian Reservation near Banning. The news of True's departure for the West Coast stunned the ethnologist. She had bought the ranch in the first place, she explained to Dagenett, because "I fell in love with the valley and thought it would be so pleasant to be near Mrs. and Miss True while pursuing my studies." She also expressed disappointment in letters to Clara. She had planned to make "her little ranch house as comfortable as possible, for all of us," she wrote, "and that you and I would do wonders in the way of development." She would indeed "miss the pleasure" of Clara's company.[57]

Foremost in Tilly's mind, besides her ethnographic work and her friendship with Clara, was the expense of running her ranch, which she named Ton'yo for the nearby Black Mesa. Even before Clara departed for California, Tilly seemed strapped for money. Writing from Washington on November 15, 1907, she told Clara, "I do not know where it has all gone but a great deal of money has slipped through my fingers since my return home. Living is so very expensive here. Every thing is double what it was a couple of years ago. Just think I am asked twenty-four dollars just for the making of a brown jacket to match the skirt I had west. I shall wait and have it made in Santa Fe." In the following weeks, she peppered the Trues with questions concerning her property; their slowness to reply added to Tilly's worries. She had no idea what it was costing to hire men to work on the ranch. She repeatedly asked whether the hay had been sold, and whether the Blonger property had been purchased. Early in January, she requested Frances True to clear any major expense with her before paying out cash. "I am compelled just now to count dollars and cents," she declared. "I will not go into debt." And on more than one occasion, she wrote of the need to realize some profit from the hay, for she had counted on this money to pay further expenses.[58]

Tilly received the first disheartening letter from Frances True in mid-April. Everything seemed to be going wrong. One horse had died, the barn was falling down, no water was available for irrigating the fields, workers had not been paid, and the hay was unsaleable. She would learn later that her fruit crop had failed—"not a dozen apples in this fine orchard." Through a lawyer's intervention, she did acquire the Blonger property—seemingly the only good news she received that spring pertaining to Ton'yo Ranch.[59]

Anxious to return to New Mexico, both to continue her work with the Indians and to check on her property, Stevenson gave up her apartment at the end of March, expecting to go almost immediately into the field. But "red tape" at the bureau delayed her departure until May 28. Her allotment of $800 was to cover travel and subsistence expenses and to pay for "indispensable" manual and clerical labor.[60]

She reached Santa Fe on June 1, 1908, and spent at least one night at the Palace Hotel. Lizzie Randall arrived soon after to present

Stevenson with an absurd bill of $300 for three months' salary and board, claiming that the ethnologist had hired her to take care of her ranch at $45 per month, starting on March 1. On Tilly's refusal to pay, Lizzie went to a lawyer to enter a lawsuit. Frances True soon claimed to have "hundreds of dollars in bills" that she allegedly had paid for Tilly, and more than $900 in debts to Indians for labor on Ton'yo Ranch. Shocked by their allegations, Stevenson quickly hired her own legal counsel, Alois (A. B.) Renehan, one of the best legal minds in Santa Fe, who was to remain her lawyer and trusted friend throughout the difficult days that lay ahead. Still, Tilly's lack of business acumen is apparent in her economic relationships with the Trues, as well as with Arthur R. Manby. By blindly trusting newly acquired friends, Tilly became entangled in endless litigation, and also lost a good deal of money.[61]

Stunned by Lizzie's demands, Stevenson went on to Española, and spent the next several days arranging her camp equipment and papers in a "shack" near the main house on her ranch. She reported to Holmes that her place was ideal for her studies, only three miles from San Ildefonso Pueblo and three and one-half miles from Santa Clara. The cacique of Santa Clara had greeted her warmly upon her arrival, as did other members of the pueblo. She stubbornly refused to let trouble with the Trues interfere with her fieldwork, although she admitted to Holmes that the shock of being treated so badly by people whom she had held in high esteem nearly caused a "break down." But, she told herself, "you are out here for the Government and you do not belong to yourself so brace up and be a man." "All the Evans are alike," she continued, "that the greater the trouble the greater their strength." With an American flag flying over her camp and her equilibrium somewhat restored, she asserted, "Were it not for the Trues I would be as happy as the mockingbirds that sing all the day long imitating all of the other birds."[62]

Tilly's field season would last until February 1910. She spent most of her time conducting research among the Tewa-speaking Pueblos of Santa Clara, San Ildefonso, San Juan, and Nambé, but she also continued her studies relating to Taos and Zuni Indians. Although her legal problems with the Trues escalated as the days went by, she remained steadfastly focused on her ethnological work.

A number of key individuals aided Stevenson that season, among them the old cacique of Santa Clara, who on occasion dined with her, and the governor of San Ildefonso, who called at Ton'yo Ranch to "pay his respects." "It was really refreshing to meet a man so very delightful," she reported to Holmes after the governor's visit. "I felt quite as if I were in the presence of an ambassador from a foreign country." He seemed pleased when she promised to send him some early Smithsonian photographs of his village.[63]

As a means of obtaining information, Stevenson often hired Indians to help around the camp or to serve as interpreters. An Indian comes to "make himself generally useful," she reported, "and invariably thinks he is in good luck to sit in the house and talk to me of the lore of other tribes [as well as his own] instead of doing the work he is paid to do." She also took Indians to isolated sites, where they would sit alone around a fire, and she would have them point out sacred mountains and other significant spots. "In this way we are brought into close companionship and they become greatly interested in talking with me." Indians often laughed when they told her "how they have always fooled students," she informed Secretary Walcott, "being determined that they should not know the truth." To assure the accuracy of her notes, she followed the guidelines established by her husband: never accept any information as fact until verified by three Indians, each unaware that the others had spoken to her.[64]

Tilly focused her studies primarily on the philosophy and religion of the Tewa Indians, although she recorded other aspects of their culture as well. She had to proceed with caution, she told Holmes, since these people, like the Taos Indians, were "extremely reticent regarding their inner life." Early on, she learned that many of the old customs were practiced in kivas and other ceremonial chambers, which she did not attempt to enter. She found that her Zuni book was a great help, however. When Indians became aware of her knowledge of other tribes' esoteric beliefs, they were more willing to talk to her. "The Governor of San Juan," she reported, "opened his heart at once after learning through the book what I knew of the Zuni."[65]

Through patience and diplomacy, she began to learn something of the Tewas' snake ceremonies, which they kept shielded from outsiders. In a long report to Walcott, she explained that the Indians spent four days and nights in a kiva holding ceremonies with snakes. They emerged briefly in the mornings to dance in the plaza "with rattlesnakes coiled around their throats and heads," offering prayers to the coming day. She made brief reference to a topic she would later explore in greater depth, much to the discomfort of Smithsonian officials: the alleged practice in olden days of sacrificing young infants to the snakes. This report was meant only for Walcott's eyes, she cautioned him. "It would be fatal to my work for it to be known that I had written of the snake worship."[66]

The ceremonies easiest for her to document were held in the plaza and open to the public. Two of the San Ildefonso ceremonies that impressed her the most were the Zuni dance, which she witnessed in December 1908, and the Buffalo dance, held on January 23 of the following year, in honor of the pueblo's patron saint. The Zuni dance, she explained, had been "stolen" long ago from the Zunis, and replicated one of their most sacred dances, with one major difference. The San Ildefonso dancers freely used the Spanish language, while the Zunis never allowed a Spanish word to be uttered "in the hearing of one personating a god" or anywhere near a Zuni mask. The Buffalo dance, which depicted hunters returning to the village with living game—buffalo, deer, and antelope—"was one of the most beautiful and interesting I have ever observed among Indians," she declared.[67]

Tilly was plagued that field season by scarcity of bureau funds to support her research. Although she tried to economize, she warned Walcott in November 1908 that she hardly had enough money to carry her through to the end of the year. She had long stressed the need to make "an exhaustive comparative study of the Pueblos." With her wealth of experience and success in becoming "close friends" with Tewa religious heads and others, the time seemed ripe for this work. To leave now would be a real catastrophe, she told the secretary, and urged him to find the means to keep her in the field. Should additional funds be unavailable, she vowed to pay for her own camp expenses. "I will make any sacrifice in order to go on with my field work," she declared.[68]

Stevenson's thoughts on comparative ethnography were quite similar to those that would be expressed by Alfred L. Kroeber in 1916, after he had spent his second summer at Zuni. "That the Pueblo civilization was substantially the same in every town, has always been assumed," he wrote, but "it begins to be evident that a great part of it has been borrowed back and forth in the most outright and traceable manner. The history of the cults and institutions of any one of these peoples therefore cannot be understood without a knowledge of the customs of the others: the problem is in its very nature a comparative one." Tilly would not live long enough to carry out her grand design, but Elsie Clews Parsons, who first visited Zuni in 1915, would complete the task with publication of her monumental *Pueblo Indian Religion* (1939).[69]

Even though Tilly went to great lengths to economize while in the field, a government auditor balked at paying some of the bills she submitted. He questioned whether such items as candy, tobacco, calico, axle grease, lumber, oilcloth, and a flagpole could properly be classified as "travel and subsistence" expenses. Tilly thereafter submitted a lengthy explanation, which apparently satisfied his objections. The candy, calico, and tobacco were purchased as gifts for Indians. "Tobacco is an especially necessary article in my connected studies," she wrote. "A few packs of tobacco and jokes . . . have often secured me entrance to a secret ceremonial." The axle grease, she explained, was necessary to lubricate the wheels of her wagon, which she used to travel over sandy roads to the various pueblos. She used the lumber to make tables and shelves for her office, thereby saving the bureau money by not buying manufactured articles. The oilcloth served as a covering for her office tables "and those upon which the Indians eat and food is placed." She gave the longest explanation for the purchase of the flagpole, "one of the most necessary articles about my camp." It was necessary, she said, to assure privacy for Indians who came to study with her. Too often, large numbers of Indians used a shortcut through her property; she found it advisable, therefore, to hoist the American flag and post signs, "A U.S. Government Camp—No Trespassing," to keep unexpected visitors away. "A few words of explanation was entirely satisfactory to the Indians," she continued, "who like the rest of the world have great respect for the flag." Had she taken any other means to protect her privacy, she would have created enemies.[70]

For several months, beginning in February 1909, Stevenson paid for most of her own field expenses, although Walcott allotted her an additional $150 in mid-March. This financial drain on her bank account forced her to resign from two professional organizations, the Washington Society of the Archaeological Institute and the Anthropological Society of Washington. "The sacrifice in leaving my studies at this time," she told Walcott, "would be far greater to me than the money involved in my paying my own expenses." One of her largest expenditures was for "entertaining my distinguished Indian friends." With a touch of wit, she wrote, "I am like you gentlemen in Washington. My dinner parties generally bring me great results. I get quite as much from Indians who simply visit me as from those I employ as interpreters but pretend to them they come for labor about camp." Despite her financial woes, Stevenson did continue to employ a camp helper—after a stint of doing her own household chores convinced her that she could not "do justice to my studies and look after camp too."[71]

She now regretted having turned down an invitation to lecture in Germany during the winter and spring of 1908, for the lectures would have brought in $4,000. Holmes had said she could take leave without pay, but, as she reported to Walcott, "I could not see my way clear to leave my work for four months, or even two." Her friend Dr. Sofie A. Nordhoff-Jung gently scolded her for this decision: "Do you know you missed a great deal by not accepting that position in Berlin. It would have opened up a new horizon to you and I should have been so glad to have had you show those Germans what a woman can do when she has brains and is in earnest about her work."[72]

Stevenson used part of the funds that Walcott provided to send for a Zuni priest, with whom she reviewed her manuscript on plants. A stickler for accuracy, she sought to justify the consequent delay in the publication of her work. "Perhaps I make the mistake of being too careful, and going too deeply into my subjects," she told Walcott, "but to me it seems as if we owe it to future generations to proceed with great caution and avoid error. There is no science in which error is so apt to occur as in anthropology, perhaps I should limit my expression more to ethnology." The Zuni priest stayed with her for nearly a month, during which time he made friends with San Ildefonso Indians. Thus, through his eyes, Tilly claimed, "I have been able to see into the kiva."[73]

Early in 1909, Stevenson resumed her work with the Taos historian— in her opinion, the most important facet of her fieldwork that season. He visited her camp periodically in secret, not even daring to tell his wife his destination, for fear his people would find out and suspect him of divulging information to the ethnologist. Nor would he stay longer than two weeks during any one visit. When he was unable to leave the pueblo later in the year, Stevenson traveled north to continue their studies together. "The nights were very cold camping out on my trip to Taos," she reported, "but I am Indian enough to have enjoyed it."[74]

With the start of the new fiscal year in July, Tilly received an allotment of $500, later augmented by an additional $75, to carry her through to the first of February, 1910. Her last major scientific work that season was with the Taos historian, who spent most of January at her Ton'yo camp. Despite the importance she attached to her Taos material, other projects took priority in later years. The only substantive result of her consultations with the historian and other Taos residents would be published posthumously. The tale of how this contribution to anthropology was almost erased from her record is worth retelling.[75]

In 1918, three years after Stevenson's death, the linguist-ethnologist John P. Harrington, of the Bureau of American Ethnology, began working with her Taos material. This included a detailed description of the Taos Blue Lake Ceremony, part of which she recorded in 1906. Anthropologist John P. Bodine, who discovered her manuscript among Harrington's voluminous records in 1965, states that Harrington "presumably intended to publish [her work] under his own authorship since the original . . . clearly shows that he scratched through Stevenson's name and put his own on the manuscript." Bodine calls her manuscript "one of the most valuable sets of documents that we have on Taos Pueblo."[76]

Bodine also identifies Stevenson's "principal informant" as Venturo Romero, "one of the most knowledgeable and politically influential people at Taos." Was Romero also Tilly's historian? Her letters indicate that more than one person supplied information about the Blue Lake Ceremony. In the twenty years following his discovery, Bodine checked the accuracy of Tilly's report on three separate occasions with his Taos consultants. In his estimation, "Stevenson received an accurate description of what transpired at Blue Lake at the turn of the century and still occurs today." In his final remarks on Tilly's "The Taos Blue Lake Ceremony," Bodine accurately assesses Tilly's strengths as an anthropologist: "She may not have been the equal of Elsie Clews Parsons in terms of analytical and evaluative skills, but as an ethnographer she was excellent and properly joins the ranks of those few women in the early days of American anthropology who truly contributed to the advancement of the discipline."[77]

Ironically, in light of his appropriation of Stevenson's Taos manuscript, John P. Harrington would spend his entire career fearing that colleagues might steal his data. Stevenson, on the other hand, generously shared results of her research with other scholars, and often encouraged them in their work. She befriended the twenty-four-year-old Harrington, for example, during his first visit to New Mexico in 1908. That summer, at his own expense, he began work at San Ildefonso Pueblo on the Tewa language. When smallpox subsequently hit the village, Tilly invited the young man to stay at her ranch. After a week or more in his company, she became his "ardent supporter," and described him in a letter to Holmes as "a most remarkable young man," "a fine scholar," "a most cultured fellow." Since Harrington seemed to have the attributes of a first-rate ethnologist, Stevenson suggested that Holmes hire him before another institution "picks him up."[78]

Harrington was only one of many students of anthropology to descend upon New Mexico that year. Many had connections with Edgar Lee Hewett, a self-taught archaeologist selected by the Archaeological Institute of America (AIA) in December 1907 to direct its newly created School of American Archaeology. An astute politician and promoter of Southwestern archaeology, Hewett spearheaded the drive to locate the school in Santa Fe. As part of his promotional activities, he opened a six-week field school in Canyon de los Frijoles in August 1908, an event extensively covered in the *Santa Fe Daily New Mexican*. Hewett's field assistants were John P. Harrington, Sylvanus G. Morley (a Harvard graduate student), and Harvard professors Roland B. Dixon and Alfred M. Tozzer, all of whom would become eminent scholars.[79]

Stevenson very likely met most, if not all, of these men at San Ildefonso Pueblo in September, during a dance held on the plaza. Hewett, Dixon, "and others from Harvard" were there and took pictures, she reported to Holmes. Possibly she also met Alice Fletcher later in November when Fletcher traveled to New Mexico in her capacity as an official of the AIA. A longtime friend of Hewett's, Fletcher backed his efforts to locate the school of archaeology in Santa Fe. Stevenson and Fletcher apparently never became intimate friends, however, despite their professional association in Washington. Nor did Tilly establish close ties with Hewett. Knowing of his friendship with Holmes, Stevenson may even have tempered her assessments of Hewett in her correspondence with bureau and Smithsonian officials. The nearest she came to criticizing him is in a letter to Secretary Walcott dated November 17, 1908: "Mr. Hewitt [*sic*] of the School of American Archaeology, said to me a few weeks since that the study of the Pueblo Indians was archaeology[,] that their present ceremonies were simply celebrations of saints days with remnants of their [old] dances," a position which she obviously did not support.[80]

During the course of the summer, Stevenson grew skeptical of the large number of neophytes who were in New Mexico. The issue was not one of turf, but of experience. "Most of these students imagine that a short stay among the Pueblos is sufficient to give them a thorough knowledge of these people," she reported, "and the literature ethnologic is not improved by such conditions." She later encountered a gentleman sent out by the American Museum of Natural History "to work up Taos." "I am not afraid of his duplicating my work," she assured Holmes, but feared that he would "publish a long paper on the Taos Indians after a few weeks visit with them." In a reflective mood, she wrote, "He reminds me so much of myself after my first year at Zuni. I thought I knew it all but returned to the pueblo to learn how little I did know."[81]

Given Stevenson's singular devotion to ethnology, it is painful to read of her acrimonious legal struggle with the True family. She and her lawyer tried to settle the Trues' financial claims out of court so that she could concentrate fully on her studies. Although willing to pay a reasonable sum, she balked at paying the several hundreds of dollars they continued to demand. Clara True, ensconced in California, exhibited little sympathy for her erstwhile friend, and advised her to pay her mother and the Indian laborers their just fees. A lawsuit of only a few hundred dollars, she wrote, was not good business. She bluntly pointed out that Stevenson had more to lose than the Trues. "On account of your greater importance to the government it would be harder upon you. If you lost, you would have costs to pay and if you won I should appeal and you would only have the reputation of escaping your bills to Indians and to Mrs. Randall and my mother."[82]

Stevenson soon discovered an unlikely ally in Superintendent Clinton J. Crandall, who was not surprised by the Trues' conduct. He, too, had earned Clara's enmity after reporting "her to the Indian Bureau for not paying back moneys she borrowed from teachers or matrons." Another ally was C. L. Pollard, a leading merchant in Española, who called Clara True "a small edition of Cassie Chadwick," the notorious Cleveland, Ohio, con artist whose trial in 1905 for fraud drew worldwide attention. The president of the First National Bank in Santa Fe, Rufus J. Palen, also regarded Clara "as decidedly crooked." As events unfolded, Tilly came to realize just how devious the schoolteacher could be.[83]

Later Tilly admitted that she had failed to look carefully at the deed transferring the Dagenett property to her at the time it was purchased. Imagine her shock when she discovered, in August 1908, that Clara had failed to include in the deed several parcels of land that had been purchased with Tilly's money. Outraged by this attempted swindle, Stevenson entered suit to recover her land. As it turned out, her lawyer had firsthand knowledge of Clara's deception, for she had hired him to draw up the papers transferring the land from Frances True to the ethnologist. Clara had specifically instructed him "to leave out certain parcels of land which were included in the deed from Dagenette [sic] to Frances D. True." "I knew nothing about the reasons why or wherefore," he later declared. But "the more investigation I have made, the more convinced I am that a great wrong has been done to Mrs. Stevenson, and that by chicanery, cunning and shrewdness, her confidence has been betrayed."[84]

Tilly also received sympathetic support from her friend Sofie Nordhoff-Jung, who expressed as well as anyone the sense of outrage one feels when betrayed by a friend. "What an awful experience to have a woman cheat you!" the physician wrote. "Aside from the pecuniary loss it is so depressing to find a person whom one has trusted not worthy of it. I am glad you have a good lawyer to defend your cause."[85]

The suit would not be settled until after Tilly left the territory. A sense of what the fifty-nine-year-old ethnologist was up against is gleaned from a letter Clara True sent to Stevenson's lawyer, A. B. Renehan, in December 1908, with a request that it be sent on to his client. After calling Tilly a "coarse, dictatorial, uncertain, appoplectic [sic] old woman," True rejected her proposal for settling the land issue. "I do not see how I can be simple enough to allow the old lady to walk over me even if she has pressed the soil of the Holy City of

Washington with her generous sole," she wrote. "Please for me tell Matilda to go hang. You will do me a personal favor by remarking that litigation is a thing I have no wish to escape. In fact I have a most unholy glee in looking forward to it with Matilda at the bat." One of True's friends once said that "evidently [Clara] loves power more than money," an assessment borne out in this battle with Stevenson.[86]

Indeed, the craving for power and authority is what drove Clara True in her assault on Tilly and other adversaries. On the one hand, True disliked being proved wrong in any situation; on the other, Stevenson's rapport with the Santa Clara Indians threatened Clara's influence with the tribe. As historian Margaret Jacobs points out, True was among the reformers (first as a schoolteacher and later as a private citizen) who attempted to impose their value systems upon the Indians—reformers, it might be added, who relished the power they held over a cluster of people they perceived as powerless. Stevenson, who maintained an open mind about cultural differences, clearly challenged True's hegemony.[87]

Despite Clara's caustic wit and vindictive nature, she had the uncanny ability to ingratiate herself with community and national leaders. She had made a favorable impression on Indian Commissioner Francis Leupp, for example, who, according to Jacobs, "passed over many men to elevate True" to the position of superintendent of the Malki Agency. "I gave her a man's work," he later declared, "and she has done it better than any man who has been in there for thirty years." He particularly applauded her efforts to rid the Morongo Reservation of whiskey dealers.[88] It is unlikely, then, that Stevenson's account of Clara's misdeeds would find an appreciative audience in the commissioner.

Still, when Leupp asked Stevenson to respond to a Miss Engle's complaint against True, Tilly took the opportunity, in letters dated December 23 and 29, 1908, to inform him in detail of the Trues' illegal maneuvers regarding her land, enclosing a copy of Clara's vituperative missive to Renehan for good measure. She added the further information that the Trues had entered two suits against her (on November 17), one by Frances True to recover the $1,500 she allegedly had expended on Tilly's behalf, and one by Lizzie Randall for $137 to pay for her "services." Commissioner Leupp, however, never acknowledged Tilly's communications.[89]

In March 1909, Tilly traveled to Santa Fe in expectation that her case against the Trues would be argued in court no later than the fifteenth. Disappointed when the judge postponed it, she nonetheless found satisfaction in her visit, for it coincided with the arrival of U.S. Chief Forester Gifford Pinchot, a close friend of ex-governor Prince and his wife. Santa Fe treated Pinchot royally during his overnight stop. Prince and other officials met him at the train depot on March 13, and then escorted him to the Capitol, where New Mexico's governor George Curry extended a cordial welcome. That afternoon, the Princes hosted a luncheon for him at their home (where he would spend the night), and Tilly was among the invited guests, as were Governor Curry, historian Ralph E. Twitchell, and three others. Stevenson clearly enjoyed the occasion. Days later, she wrote to Holmes, "It was a genuine pleasure to meet some one from Washington especially one for whom I have such respect."[90]

District Court Judge John R. McFie finally opened Tilly's case on April 20. Stevenson, who had taken two weeks of annual leave to attend to court matters, testified on her own behalf. The Trues also were on hand, including Clara, who came from Banning to testify. Several other witnesses took the stand in this nonjury trial, including more than a dozen Indians. Interruptions were numerous; court recessed for a week early in the proceedings, and then adjourned at the end of the month to allow McFie to hold court in Taos. Although final arguments were expected to be heard after his return, delays continued.[91]

With the case still unsettled, Tilly returned to Santa Fe in late June for a reunion with Edith and Alexander Prescott, their young son Stedman (who was to have a distinguished career in Maryland as lawyer and judge), and perhaps other of the Prescott children. Possibly the Prescotts also sought legal counsel in Santa Fe, prior to joining Martha and Charles Hill in a lawsuit against Arthur R. Manby's Taos Valley Land Company.[92]

Throughout the long, insufferable delays that plagued her case, Stevenson remained devoted to her ethnological studies—work that, in fact, reinforced her identity as a professional woman and kept her balanced during this troublesome time. She continued to be strapped for money, however, due in part to expending funds earlier in the year to run her camp, and to her ongoing efforts to place the ranch on a paying basis. To see her through, she had borrowed $200 from the First National Bank, the first time in her life, she avowed, that she had owed "any one a cent." But she never regretted having spent her own funds to stay in the field, for as she told her lawyer, "My whole heart is in the work my husband left me to do—to complete his unfinished work as far as possible." Indeed, the bond that had united Tilly and Jim Stevenson during their years of marriage remained strong long after his death. To carry out his work had become for her a vital motivating force. And she never published a major ethnological report without acknowledging her debt to the one who had taught her the "rudiments of ethnographic technique."[93]

On February 18, 1910, three days after Tilly left New Mexico for the East, Judge McFie signed a decree awarding Stevenson the three tracts of land that had been at the center of the controversy. He ruled in Tilly's favor also in the suits that Frances True and Lizzie Randall brought against her, and decreed that in all three cases, Tilly was to recoup court costs. Yet Stevenson did not consider this a complete victory, for she recovered only a small portion of the funds she accused the Trues of having mismanaged or stolen from her. And, as she was to find out, McFie's ruling did not bring an end to her troubles with the pugnacious Clara True.[94]

CHAPTER 7

Trouble at Ton'yo

Matilda Coxe Stevenson left Ton'yo Ranch on February 9, 1910, planning to spend a day in Denver visiting her sister Nina Zevely before returning to Washington. A severe attack of rheumatism, however, compelled her to remain in the mile-high city several days before she felt capable of continuing the trip. In a letter to Frederick W. Hodge, the new head of the Bureau of American Ethnology, she explained, "I am quite helpless and suffer considerable pain, otherwise I am very well. I am sure the trouble is caused by a little overexertion during my last days in camp, and [after] a few days rest, and care from my sister I will be myself again." And she added, "I am very anxious to get back and get my papers ready for publication."[1]

Sometime later that month, Tilly took up residence in the Cairo, an apartment building located in the capital's Dupont Circle area. On work days, she traveled into the Smithsonian's red-stone castle on the mall, where the bureau recently had moved from the Adams Building on F Street. Despite the poor lighting (due to the narrowness of the castle's windows), Hodge considered these facilities "far better" than the old.[2]

Tilly was delighted to be back "in civilization." On March 17, she attended the opening (by invitation) of the National Gallery of Fine Art (now housed in the new National Museum building), where her old friend, William H. Holmes, was director of the Anthropology Department. The opening "was fine in every respect," she reported. She enjoyed reestablishing her friendship with Sofie Nordhoff-Jung and meeting the wife of Vice President James S. Sherman at a reception. And she quickly scheduled meetings with the newly appointed commissioner of Indian Affairs, Robert G. Valentine, to inform him of Clara True's machinations. At the conclusion of their first session, he remarked, "I have a very slight acquaintance with Miss True, but she is certainly most convincing upon slight acquaintance"— to which Tilly responded, "most certainly or Mrs. Stevenson would never have taken a deed from her without even looking at it."[3]

Early in the spring, the ethnologist learned that Clara True had resigned her position with the Indian bureau, thus ending Tilly's efforts to force her removal. "She was dishonest and the Government is not supposed to harbor dishonest people," Tilly explained to a friend. She heaped praise upon Valentine, since he appeared sympathetic to her cause. "The present Commissioner is altogether different from Mr. Leupp," she wrote. "He is a most intelligent, level minded cultured gentleman and would not conceal any crookedness in his department."[4]

Stevenson spent most of her days at bureau headquarters, where she transcribed her recent field notes and prepared two papers for publication, one on the "Dress and Adornment of the Pueblo Indians," and the other on Zuni plants and their uses. Sometimes she worked in the Agricultural Department to be close to reference books. She meticulously checked the botanical and Indian names that would appear in the plant paper, and spent much time going over materials with Paul C. Standley, a botanist with the National Museum.[5]

Tilly also kept up a steady correspondence with Henry Pollard, the son of the Española businessman who had leased her ranch. Still determined to make it a success, she sent young Pollard advice and reports on fruit trees and other farm matters, which she obtained from the Agricultural Department. She had hoped to set out additional fruit trees in the spring, but told him that "the dreadful Trues have left me too cramped financially to venture this year." She did obtain some Kentucky bluegrass seed, and asked Pollard to have it sown on her property. If the experiment worked, she would plant it on the grounds of her new house "when that times comes."[6]

Other New Mexico matters preyed on Stevenson's mind, including Edgar L. Hewett's growing prominence within scientific circles. On May 26, she asked Hodge to arrange for a conference with Hewett during his visit to the capital, to discuss "his plans and mine, for work among the Tewa and other Pueblos." This discussion, to include Hodge and possibly Secretary Walcott, was of "vital necessity," she said, "so that the School of American Archaeology and the Bureau of American Ethnology may each find its path smooth and free from obstacles."[7] Recently Hodge and Hewett had announced a cooperative interdisciplinary research study of the upper Rio Grande Valley, and Tilly may have felt uneasy about the role she was to play. According to Don Fowler, the program was to include linguistic and ethnographic studies of the Rio Grande Pueblos, as well as "a comprehensive program of archaeological research focusing on the Pajarito Plateau."[8]

Hewett had moved rapidly to consolidate his control of archaeological and anthropological studies in the Southwest. Late in 1908, the Archaeological Institute of America had selected Santa Fe as the site of the School of American Archaeology. In February of the following year, the New Mexico legislature granted the school the use of the Palace of the Governors "as its permanent facility," and established the Museum of New Mexico, stipulating that it also be housed in the palace with Hewett as its director. He quickly set about hiring staff: John P. Harrington and Sylvanus G. Morley for the school, and two young associates, Jesse Nusbaum and Kenneth Chapman, for the museum. By establishing a proprietary claim to the palace, Hewett made enemies of Tilly's longtime friends ex-governor L. Bradford Prince and his wife, Mary, who had lived in the palace during Prince's four-year term as governor. Although the building no longer housed territorial governors, its east end was home to the Historical Society of New Mexico, over which Prince presided. And even though the society was to retain use of this space, the Princes resented having to share the premises with Hewett's crowd.[9]

Years later, some of Hewett's young colleagues would describe Tilly as a cantankerous old woman, yet documents in her papers often belie this image. At age sixty-one and suffering from rheumatism, she still retained the ability to smooth ruffled feathers, a talent recognized by Aleš Hrdlička, a physical anthropologist with the National Museum. In October 1910, he sought Stevenson's help in resolving a delicate issue that involved a distinguished visitor from France, Professor L. Capitan, and Tilly's friend, a Dr. Vaughn. On the day that Professor Capitan was to lecture at the museum, he slipped on the stairs in his hotel and dislocated a shoulder. The hotel physician called in Dr. Vaughn, who quickly set the shoulder. The next day, he submitted a bill for $50, a sum that embarrassed the physical anthropologist. He hoped that Tilly would persuade Vaughn to accept a more "favorable" amount. "I know this is an unpleasant matter to bother you with," he wrote, "but I, as well as Doctor [J. Walter] Fewkes and all the others of us who are equally concerned in the case, know that there is no one more diplomatic and whom we could more trust in such a matter than Mrs. Stevenson."[10]

Tilly's work was interrupted in November when she came down with pneumonia. She blamed her illness on the two days she worked in her office when it was without heat. Although "exceedingly annoyed" by this setback, she continued writing while propped up in bed. She also moved to "a suburban place in preference to a hospital," adding in a note to friends, "the pure air here is just the place for me."[11]

While convalescing, she expressed a desire to return to New Mexico by early March to observe Tewa ceremonials. She assured Hodge, "When I do get out of this climate I will enjoy my work the more because I will be free from pain and the cough." With characteristic optimism, she outlined how scholars would share work in the Southwest. "With Mr. Harrington to work on the Pueblo languages, Dr. Standley on the botany, I to plod along in my investigations, Dr. Fewkes and Mr. Hewett in their excavations there will be something worth while accomplished in the land of the Pueblos." She reminded Hodge that time was growing short to find "the aged [Pueblo] people who alone can be depended upon," and she promised—if allowed to continue her fieldwork—to "do my utmost to make as clear a record as possible of the beliefs and history of the Pueblos and of their relations with one another."[12]

Delays were inevitable, however; Tilly did not start west until April 12, 1911. By this date, she had submitted her paper on "Dress and Adornment of the Pueblo Indians," and Hodge in turn forwarded it to Secretary Walcott on April 28, with the request that it be referred to the Smithsonian's Advisory Committee on Printing and Publication. In former days, John Wesley Powell had decided what manuscripts were published in the annual reports. But after his death, the Smithsonian gradually assumed control for all publication decisions. Walter Hough, a curator of ethnology at the National Museum, quickly read Tilly's paper, and told his boss, William H. Holmes, "[I] think you would have no difficulty in recommending it for publication. . . . The paper is full of very good material and I believe that the statements and observations are accurate."[13]

Despite Hough's favorable review, the committee returned the manuscript, calling for extensive revisions: "The introductory portion covering the dress and adornment of the non-Pueblo tribes, together with the illustrations pertaining thereto, [should] be omitted, and . . . the entire paper . . . revised from a literary point of view; after which the paper can be submitted for final recommendation." Hodge forwarded this information to Stevenson, adding, "under the circumstances, I shall hold the paper until your return." He also advised her to paraphrase portions of Washington Matthews's account of Navajo weaving rather than incorporating so much of his paper verbatim.[14]

Dismayed by the committee's decision, Tilly shot right back that she regretted the manuscript would not be published immediately.

"I have a great deal of original matter in the paper which required years of investigation for me to secure," she told Hodge. She then asked for the names of the gentlemen on the advisory committee, apparently intending to quiz them about their ruling. Although Hodge willingly identified its eight members (which included himself), he would not reveal the names of the subcommittee—usually composed of persons not members of the main committee—that had undertaken a critical examination of her manuscript. "The proceedings of the [subcommittee] are confidential," he explained.[15]

Tilly remained continuously in the field from mid-April 1911 to mid-March 1915, and never revised her dress and adornment manuscript. It was rescued from near oblivion, however, by scholars Richard V. N. Ahlstrom and Nancy J. Parezo, who edited it for publication in 1987 in *The Kiva.* They followed the advice of Hodge and the advisory committee, and excised discussions of non-Pueblo groups and long passages from Matthews's paper on Navajo weavers, as well as other material that seemed irrelevant. The edited manuscript is a gem, for, as they point out, it contains "useful information on the production of textiles, on dress, and on adornment in pueblo villages, particularly Zuni, in the late nineteenth and early twentieth centuries."[16]

In the longest and most interesting section, "Manufacture of Fabrics," Stevenson described the preparation and weaving of cotton, milkweed, yucca fiber, and wool. She also praised the ingenuity of Indian artisans. "Think of the invention of the preparation of *Yucca baccata* leaf fiber, which must be submitted not only to the microscope, but to chemical analyses, to an understanding that it is not cotton. Think of the spinning and weaving of milkweed into cloth." In closing, she documented some of the changes that had occurred in Indian dress since she first ventured into Zuni territory. Schoolgirls now, she said, were clad "in blue and white check ginghams and the boys in khaki or overalls." Moccasins or bare feet had been supplanted "by the unyielding leather shoe." Soon, she predicted, the "picturesque Pueblo dress" would vanish, along with Indian arts and crafts. She ended her essay by calling for further ethnological studies. "Let all men with brains and hearts come to the rescue while it is yet time, to those who could with the proper means complete the records of the 'Vanishing Race.'"[17]

As Stevenson prepared to return to New Mexico, the *Washington Star* carried a long article that heralded her career as a government scientist, and publicized her views on American Indians. "Of the many distinguished women connected with the government service in every line of science, industry and art," wrote author Margaret B. Downing, "Mrs. Mathilda [*sic*] Coxe Stevenson holds an honored place, not only because of the reverence in which her husband's memory is held, but because of her own faithful and successful work in the field of American ethnology." She then summarized Tilly's early life, her work with her husband, and her later career as an ethnologist. She also spotlighted Stevenson's high regard for the Zuni Indians. "The Zunis are among the most fascinating of the pueblo Indians, and they possess the noblest qualities," she quoted Tilly as saying. Although some scientists took issue with her for having placed "this crude race of red men on the same high spiritual plane as the ancient Greeks," Tilly replied that "I have placed them just where I found them." Still, she confessed, "the similarity of the religious poetry of the Zunis and the Greeks made a deep impression on me throughout my researches. Any one who has read [John] Ruskin's exquisite book 'The Athena of the Air' cannot fail to see that the isolated red man of the American forest has as high and poetical a concept of the deity as the noble race of Hellenes." Downing's article reached New Mexico before Stevenson, and much of it was reprinted in the March 4 issue of the *Santa Fe Daily New Mexican.*[18]

Tilly left the capital on April 12, and proceeded to Santa Fe, where she spent several days purchasing camp supplies and making inquiries about Pueblo Indian history. She also met with Archbishop John B. Pitaval, having been given a letter of introduction to him from her erstwhile critic, Father William H. Ketcham, director of the Bureau of Catholic Indian Missions. It was a delightful meeting,

Tilly reported to Hodge. "He laughingly informed me that he had expected to find me with horns but he had a better opinion of me since meeting me." They parted "in good humor."[19]

From Santa Fe, Stevenson went directly to Ton'yo Ranch, where she found much to enjoy. "This climate is perfect beyond expression," she exclaimed. "The days are balmy at the same time bracing." It was "hard to realize," she wrote, "that I was so great a sufferer with my lungs and rheumatism for a year. I am in splendid health here." Nor were her spirits dampened by the fact that the renter (presumably Henry Pollard and his wife) occupied the main house, limiting her to the use of one room for sleeping. Although she planned to use a nearby structure for her government camp, its rickety roof forced her to erect a tent for that purpose. "I am quite comfortable . . . with the addition of the tent," she reported. Moreover, she had an excellent camp helper, a Miss Deeble—"a most superior woman," who "can assist me in many ways aside from the mere camp work."[20]

Best of all, her Indian friends seemed "very happy to have me back with them," she exulted. The old cacique of Santa Clara and her "best man" from San Ildefonso spent the first Sunday she was in camp talking to the ethnologist. She wrote cheerfully of her desire to continue her comparative studies, which would necessitate returning to Zuni as well as visiting other distant pueblos. Her elaborate plans for the coming fiscal year, which would cost an estimated $1,516, failed to win Hodge's approval, however. "I believe that better, more lasting, and certainly more immediate results can be obtained by concentrating attention on a single tribe or group of affiliated tribes, such, for example, as the Tewa," he wrote. "To extend your work from Taos to Zuni would seem to me to lead to scattered results, with nothing sufficiently intensive to afford the basis of a publication except in the indefinite future." He reminded her that her Tewa work had already cost the bureau $12,000, with little to show for it. Thus, he advised her to concentrate on one subject, such as the material culture of the Tewa, so that "we may publish some results in the reasonably immediate future." Her allotment for the new fiscal year of $400 was much less than she had requested, but, he wrote, "with economy you will have little difficulty in carrying on your work for several months."[21]

Hodge had little understanding of what it took to conduct fieldwork among the Rio Grande Pueblo Indians. In earlier years, he had participated in archaeological digs controlled by other scientists, and had edited numerous reports of other individuals' field projects. But, in the words of Don Fowler, he "had never organized, directed, collected, analyzed, and published a major project to call his own." To cut down on expenses, he advised Stevenson to take a room in San Ildefonso or Santa Clara, surround herself with Pueblo life, and become "part of the native life." He held Barbara Freire-Marreco up as an example for Stevenson to emulate. "After a very few months in Santa Clara," he reported, she "so ingratiated herself with the Tewa as to be appointed a kind of secretary to the council of the pueblo."[22]

Hodge had met Barbara Freire-Marreco, an Oxford University graduate student, the previous summer at Hewett's field school at the Rito de los Frijoles. She had reached Santa Fe on June 24, 1910, and Hewett took her to Santa Clara Pueblo, where he left her "with an Indian family for a short visit." A few days later, she joined Hewett in Frijoles Canyon, where she and Maude Woy, a history teacher from Denver, would be the only women in attendance. Freire-Marreco hoped to study the social structure of some Pueblo village, and although Hewett's school focused on archaeology, he saw to it that Santiago Naranjo, a workman on the project from Santa Clara, stayed with her to teach her about the Tewa language and give other information. Later in the season, she returned to Santa Clara for short visits. At the end of August, she spent a month living in a tent at the edge of the pueblo, and then moved into an Indian house. Before she left New Mexico, she traveled with a Santa Clara delegation to a general council of all the Pueblos at Santo Domingo.[23]

Once home in England, the ethnologist wrote "a little paper on Indian dances in relation to Indian social organization," which she mailed to Hewett in November 1911, requesting that he keep it out of the school's library, "where Indians might see it," and out of the local papers. Days after he received it, Stevenson was in Santa Fe, and "had just a peep at Miss Freire-Marreco's paper." Apparently impressed by what she read, she asked Hodge to secure a copy for her. The Englishwoman returned to New Mexico in the fall of 1912, and would spend a month at Santa Clara Pueblo, but the records fail to reveal whether she and Stevenson ever met to discuss their mutual interests.[24]

Tilly always responded to Hodge's instructions with respect, but she was not about to give up her comparative studies, even for the ethnologist-in-charge. In a report to him dated July 1, 1911, she wrote, "By your direction I am giving special study to the material culture of the Tewa. I am also continuing my investigations into their esoteric life in order to complete as fully as possible, the comparative study of the philosophy and religion of the Pueblo Indians." As if to meet Hodge's objections, she elaborated: "The material culture of any tribe could not be fully studied without including to a considerable extent, the esoteric side. The whole life of the Indian is so woven together that no side can be profoundly studied without touching upon many sides."[25]

For the remainder of the year, Stevenson worked primarily with San Ildefonso and Santa Clara Indians. In her monthly reports, she often offered tentative observations about their apparent similarities with and differences from other Pueblo Indians. She believed that the calendric ceremonials of San Ildefonso Pueblo, for example, were not as elaborate as those of Zuni, although some features of their religions were alike. Her work among Santa Clara Indians was made more difficult, however, by the continued influence of their former teacher. "I have had to pursue my studies among these people with the greatest care and diplomacy because of the Clara True faction," she reported. Nonetheless, Tilly succeeded in making many friends within the pueblo. Several, in fact, were anxious to receive copies of the pictures she had taken of one of their dances, and she urged Hodge to see that they were quickly sent. She was especially anxious to receive those of a little girl in her dance costume. "Her parents are very important people to me," Tilly explained, "and they are about to start to Oklahoma for a visit and very much want the pictures."[26]

Stevenson occasionally took time away from her studies to visit Santa Fe on ranch business. On one occasion, her friends persuaded her to stay over for the opening of the Democratic State Convention; "they thought as I had been coming to N.M. since 1879 I should give my presence here for this important occasion." Patriotic pennants and banners welcomed the three hundred or so delegates who crowded into the town's hotels, where Republicans and Democrats mingled and exchanged friendly banter. On opening night, October 2, 1911, an arch erected on one corner of the plaza spelled out in blazing electric lights, "Welcome to the Capital City." U.S. Congressman William Sulzer, "the fiery New York orator," gave the keynote address. Later that evening, Tilly attended a small dinner in his honor, and took the opportunity to discuss ethnology at length with him. "He declared himself ready to do every thing in his power for the cause," she reported to Hodge.[27]

In following weeks, Stevenson continued to work on her Zuni plant paper, and took it with her when she traveled to Santa Fe in late November to oversee a big shipment of apples from her orchard. During her stay in the capital, she had long talks with John P. Harrington, who convinced her to change the arrangement of the plant names, so that the Indian name would precede the Latin name "to avoid much confusion and repetition." These were tedious changes, she told Hodge, but the "main point is to do such work in the Bureau that it will stand for all time." Too much of a perfectionist to submit substandard work, she did not send the bulk of her manuscript to Hodge until July of 1912, with the promise that the rest would soon follow.[28]

Stevenson's "Ethnobotany of the Zuni Indians" would appear in the *Thirtieth Annual Report of the Bureau of American Ethnology, 1908–1909*, published in 1915. This is one of two monographs devoted to the subject of ethnobotany that the bureau published in a two-year span. In the introduction to her sixty-five-page account, Tilly stressed the importance of plants in the daily life of the Zunis.

"The Zuni live with their plants," she stated; "the latter are a part of themselves. The initiated can talk with their plants, and the plants can talk with them. Plants are sacred to the Zuni."[29]

She also referred to her research at the pueblo in 1879 with her husband, "the late Mr. James Stevenson." She then listed some of the changes that had taken place during the intervening years, including a decline in young people's knowledge of tribal religion. She acknowledged her debt to others who had helped with her study—Frederick W. Hodge, William H. Holmes, Walter Hough, Paul C. Standley, and John P. Harrington among them. She listed a number of Zunis who had aided her over the years: the late Nai'uchi, his son Ha'lian, Zuni Nick, Tsi'nahe and his wife, and others. She singled out Me'she, the late younger brother Bow priest, for special praise. He had helped her collect the specimens of plants that went into the study, and "gave his heart . . . to their classification according to the Zuni system and to their use by his people." Her technique, she explained, was to verify the information she received from Me'she with others, "both men and women, especially versed in plant lore." She considered this a preliminary report, however, since the plants she described probably were only "a portion of those employed by the Zuni." Thus, she called for "more extended comparative ethnobotanical researches among the Pueblo tribes of the Southwest."[30]

In the first and longest section of Stevenson's report, "Medicinal Practices and Medicinal Plants," she spent much time discussing plants that were used as antiseptics and narcotics. *Datura meteloides*, she stated, was used to render a patient unconscious while a doctor performed a simple operation. Several plants, including gum from the piñon pine tree, were used as antiseptics. A mixture of blossoms and roots from another plant, commonly called cold leaf, was used to smear over the bodies of those who danced in beds of coals. She described plants that were used to treat a host of ailments, including colds, bullet or arrow wounds, headaches, syphilis, fatigue, rheumatism, toothache, constipation, and hemorrhoids. In summary, she stated, "it is evident that for a long period the Zuni Indians have extensively employed legitimate medicines for healing the sick," and their use of narcotics and antiseptics predated by centuries the introduction of these drugs into the western world.[31]

In a shorter section, devoted to edible plants, Stevenson described how plants were prepared, including dishes made from corn and wheat. She then discussed the use of plants in weaving, dyeing, basketry, and pottery decoration, as well as in grooming, folklore, clan names, and ceremonies.[32]

As the new year of 1912 got under way, New Mexicans prepared to celebrate President William H. Taft's proclamation admitting New Mexico into the Union as the forty-seventh state. Tilly had expected to attend the inauguration of the state's first governor, William C. McDonald, in Santa Fe on January 15. But the death of her cousin Rear Admiral Robley D. Evans earlier in the month meant that she would stay at home, out of respect for his memory. Newspapers throughout the nation, including the *Santa Fe Daily New Mexican*, paid tribute to "fighting Bob," the *New York Times* calling him "the most famous American naval officer since David Glasgow Farragut [of Civil War fame]."[33]

Despite Evans's death, Tilly soon resumed her ethnological studies. On January 22 and 23, she observed the Eagle and Buffalo dances at San Ildefonso, along with Governor and Mrs. McDonald and some of Hewett's clique, John P. Harrington, Kenneth Chapman, and Karl Fleischer, the artist of the School of American Archaeology. Tilly found both dances attractive, the costumes "most elaborate." Still, "the most graceful figures" that she ever had observed, she declared, were those of the Eagle dance. She took photographs of both ceremonies, but later reported that she had "never experienced such opposition to my camera." The elderly Pueblo men seemed pleased to have her make pictures, with "the English speaking 'educated' Indians" opposing her photography. "I had earth thrown at me with orders not to make pictures," she reported to Hodge, "and when the orders were not obeyed many threats were made, one fellow taking position beside me, with a club threatening to strike, but intelligence dominated brute force."[34]

The acceptance/opposition reactions to her camera work continued. In October, she had no trouble taking photographs of dances in Santa Clara, where residents often requested copies of her pictures. But opposition surfaced again in San Ildefonso, this time from a member of the Bow priesthood who objected to her use of a Kodak. The governor of the pueblo, however, came to her rescue, "declaring that as long as he was Governor his word should be obeyed." Tilly not only secured pictures of the San Ildefonso Harvest dance, but also contributed to the gifts that the dancers threw to the populace "as evidence of the prosperity of the people." "My donation of tobacco, candy, and apples from my camp orchard was highly appreciated," she told Hodge.[35]

In late March of that same year, Tilly's sister Nina Zevely arrived in Santa Fe from Colorado, followed shortly thereafter by her sister Betty Kellogg (and Betty's son) from Japan. Tilly advised Hodge after Betty's arrival that she was "taking a couple days leave to show them Indians and ruins." She evidently maintained close relations with all the Evans sisters. Sometime earlier, after learning that Tilly had been ill, Betty had written, "I do hope Tilly dear you are feeling quite well again but I do wish you would leave the West to go back to Washington where you would be near Edith [Betty's daughter]; it seems so weird to think of you being alone there. . . . I hope [one day] we sisters can live near each other."[36]

Tilly returned to Santa Fe in late May to deliver one of her rare public addresses at an event sponsored by the Historical Society of New Mexico. On the evening of the 27th, she and two other speakers were introduced by the society's president, L. Bradford Prince. Later, the local press declared that Stevenson, "the celebrated ethnologist of the American Bureau of Ethnology," had "presented the subject of the Zuni Indians in a new and interesting way."[37]

Throughout the year, Tilly focused most of her attention on the Tewa Indians, sometimes working far into the night with an Indian. The cacique of Santa Clara continued to render valuable aid, and the ethnologist reciprocated by providing photos of the old gentleman, which he wished to hang in his house. She worked well also with "the old governor" of San Ildefonso, who along with other Tewas had been made unhappy by Clinton J. Crandall's recent transfer to South Dakota. She passed along to Hodge an example of the old man's humor, occasioned by the arrival of Crandall's replacement. "He said to the new superintendent who appeared in the village armed with a Winchester, 'Why do you wear your Winchester when you come here? We are not deer, we are men. You will find no game here.'"[38]

In mid-May 1912, in answer to Hodge's inquiry about her future research plans, Stevenson told him that she expected to have her Tewa material "ready for publication before very long." "I know that I am more tardy than other students in completing work for publication," she acknowledged, "but I also know that when my work is published neither the Bureau or myself can be called upon to correct errors of statement regarding the Pueblos." She then described a technique she used to avoid making mistakes, which was "to write out my notes among the people so that whenever a doubt enters my mind it can be settled without delay."[39]

But delays in submitting the Tewa manuscript kept occurring. When she was late with her annual report for the fiscal year, she pinpointed another reason for her tardiness, the need to entertain Indian visitors. "I have not had a minute for several days," she explained to Hodge, "owing to the coming of Indians to the camp. Some have brought their friends who are here for the great dance at Santa Clara next monday [sic]. My visitors are those with whom I am doing important work and when they desire their far away friends to meet me and bring them to the camp I hardly like to refuse to see them and when once admitted they stay, and stay, and stay." To complicate matters, her camp helper was away, forcing Tilly to fix the meals she served to guests.[40]

Nonetheless, in August, Stevenson wrote an extensive synopsis of the results of her investigations during the previous fiscal year, which Hodge later incorporated into his annual report. She had worked primarily with the San Ildefonso and Santa Clara Indians, but also had studied with the San Juan and Nambé peoples. Each of the Tewa Pueblos was divided into clans with patrilineal descent, she reported, and also into the Sun and Ice peoples, each with its

own kiva, where the sacred fraternities met. She described ceremonies that occurred in the kivas, information she apparently
gleaned from Indian friends rather than through direct observation. She wrote of their cosmogony and religious beliefs, as well as
ceremonies involving snakes. "From birth to death the life of these
people is a vast ceremonial," she avowed. She concluded with a
brief account of Tewa material culture.[41]

Stevenson planned to spend the new fiscal year pursuing her
comparative studies among the Taos, Picuris, and Isleta Indians.
Most of the residents of Taos who had opposed her during her
first visit, she assured Hodge, "are warm friends now." And she
promised to complete her Tewa work before embarking on other
research. In summary, she requested a new allotment of $800, to
cover the costs of a camp helper, interpreters and assistants, rations
for the camp helper, rations and tobacco for Indians, and other
incidental expenses.[42]

A mid-July rain and hailstorm in the Española Valley, however,
would take Tilly temporarily away from her work, and would lead
to unexpected difficulties with Clara True. These were distress-
ingly prolonged difficulties, as it turned out, still unresolved at the
time of Stevenson's death. Nonetheless, on February 15, 1913, she
sent to Hodge the first of three brief reports, "Studies of the Tewa
Indians of the Rio Grande Valley," which appeared later that year
in the *Smithsonian Miscellaneous Collections.* More importantly, Tilly
submitted on February 23 a detailed table of contents for her
Tewa manuscript. Like her Zuni book, the major part of this new
ethnography would be devoted to philosophy and religion, with
shorter sections on social customs, material culture, and changes
in arts and industries. Hodge was duly impressed. In the bureau's
annual report, he asserted, "A preliminary table of contents of the
proposed memoir indicates that her studies of the customs and
beliefs of the Tewa will be as comprehensive as the published results
of her investigation of the Sia and the Zuni tribe [*sic*]."[43]

Tilly was pleased by Hodge's response, yet she would not say
when the ethnography would be finished. She assured him, however, that she had assembled all the information needed for writing

it, each statement verified "by at least three aged Indians," none knowing that the others had talked to her. But the delays continued, partly due to her thoroughness. She insisted on gathering new material and then reviewing it with her Indian helpers.[44]

Exasperated by her tardiness, Hodge recommended to Secretary Walcott that Stevenson be recalled to Washington to finish writing the ethnography. In the face of her escalating troubles with Clara True, however, he relented and allowed her to remain in the field. But he urged her to submit the manuscript for publication as quickly as possible, before John P. Harrington and Herbert J. Spinden (a recent Harvard Ph.D. graduate) published their works on the Tewa Indians. "It would hardly be possible for three people working in the same field not to duplicate each others's [sic] work in some degree," he warned her, "hence the one whose paper first appears would have the credit of priority for much of the work." And he did not want to see her or the bureau "'left out in the cold' in the matter of priority."[45]

Although Tilly assured him that she would submit the manuscript by the close of 1913, she failed to meet this deadline, mainly because of her legal problems with Clara True. Still, on July 16, 1914, Stevenson reported that her manuscript now consisted of some four hundred pages. Throughout this difficult time, she continued to revise her work and to gather photographs of Tewa activities, with the help of photographer W. M. Gray and San Ildefonso Governor Juan Gonzales.[46]

Amidst the pressure to complete the Tewa manuscript, Stevenson struggled to turn Ton'yo Ranch into a profitable enterprise. Since returning to New Mexico in 1911, she invested all of her surplus funds in its operation. Just prior to leaving Washington, she had applied for a Civil War widow's pension on the basis of her late husband's service record. During a lengthy routine investigation, Tilly told a special examiner that after she entered government service she had "an income sufficient for my needs," implying that the pension of $12 per month, which she eventually received, would help finance her fruit ranch. Later, in March 1912, she mortgaged her property to secure a $2,500 loan from the First National Bank of Santa Fe, the money doubtless put into her business.[47]

Water to irrigate her fields and orchard was absolutely essential to the success of her venture, however, a fact that Clara True hoped to turn to her own advantage. The trouble started when the Española area was inundated with floodwaters during July 1912. The local press recorded the severity of the storm: "The rain came down in certain places in sheets of water and carried away everything before it. The railroad track was washed out in more than a dozen places between Santa Clara and San Ildefonso, so that no train could pass for two days." Tilly described her own ordeal in a letter to Hodge dated July 22. She had carried her manuscript on Zuni plants to the railroad station near her ranch to mail it to Hodge. While waiting for the train, she became drenched in the great cloudburst; "my only escape was to wade knee deep in water across the country to my camp." She kept the manuscript dry "by carrying it under my rain coat—nothing ever seemed so heavy to me as the small package as I held on to it while I waded and was almost beaten down by the sheet of water from the heavens." Water rose to the doors of her house, but "did not get in." Once the train was running again, she went into Santa Fe, "representing the San Ildefonso Indians, my Mexican neighbors and myself, to secure assistance to have the ditch repaired."[48]

The ditch she referred to was the Acequia de San Ildefonso, which carried water from the Rio Grande to irrigate San Ildefonso farmlands, as well as those of Stevenson and Clara True. True had returned to New Mexico in 1910 to take up ranching on her property next to Tilly's. Accompanying her from California was the wealthy Mary Bryan of Redlands, who allegedly paid off True's debts and financed improvements on her ranch. The two women were to remain lifelong companions.[49]

Once back in New Mexico, True took up several causes that not only increased her stature as a public figure, but also demonstrated a resoluteness of character, a trait she shared with Tilly, that was to cause the latter so much misery in the future. In June 1911, for example, she drummed up support for the defense of

Juan Cruz, a Santa Clara policeman who had shot and killed a San Juan Indian when he (Cruz) attempted to arrest the latter for having whiskey unlawfully in his possession. Among those who contributed to Cruz's defense fund at Clara's behest were Elsie Clews Parsons, who had met Clara in 1910 during her first visit to New Mexico, and Barbara Freire-Marreco. True also contributed money in the spring of 1912 to the Santa Fe Mothers' Club, to support its efforts to encourage schoolchildren to plant backyard gardens. True's letter to a club official, in which she praised the project, was printed in the *Santa Fe Daily New Mexican*, along with the statement that "Miss True has shown a laudable public spirit in presenting this fund to the club."[50]

Then, on August 19, 1912, the newspaper carried a long article describing True's efforts on behalf of the Women's Christian Temperance Union (WCTU) during its convention in Santa Fe. She had arranged for thirty-five delegates to witness Indian dances at Santa Clara Pueblo, after which she and Bryan conveyed them in wagons to the True ranch. Here the two women helped Frances True prepare and serve dinner to the delegates, seated at tables under apple trees, which had been decorated with lanterns. Soon a delegation of Santa Clara Indians rode in—"gorgeously attired and [wearing] war-bonnets"—to perform still more dances. At midnight, the delegates retired to the guesthouse and to two large tents fitted out with beds. On their departure the next day, they agreed that they had had the "time of their life."[51]

True also won the approval of several prominent Santa Fe leaders, including Edgar L. Hewett and Judge John R. McFie, for backing the statewide drive to preserve Indian ruins, and for soliciting funds for the Museum of New Mexico. In return, Hewett appointed her to a local committee coordinating plans for an upcoming meeting in Santa Fe of the International Congress of Americanists.[52]

Yet, the *Santa Fe Daily New Mexican* also carried articles that harshly criticized Clara True. On August 23, 1912, for example, it printed a long report from the head of the South Dakota WCTU, which castigated True and William E. Johnson, an Indian bureau

official, for spreading false rumors that had led to Clinton J. Crandall's transfer to that state. The report attributed this miscarriage of
justice to True and Johnson's "personal vindictiveness and hatred"
for the superintendent. Five months later, the same newspaper
headlined a story about a complex issue that divided the Santa
Clara people: "Proceedings Were Instituted by Clara D. True, Long
a Meddler with Matters Connected with the Santa Clara Indians."[53]

Clara True's vindictiveness surfaced again after floodwaters of
the Rio Grande destroyed part of the Acequia de San Ildefonso.
As events unfolded, it became clear that Tilly's nemesis meant to
drive her not only off her property, but out of New Mexico as
well. In the face of True's relentless and prolonged campaign, the
wonder is that Stevenson accomplished as much as she did on her
Tewa manuscript.

Following the July 1912 storm, local ditch officials entered into
negotiations with Santa Clara Indians for permission to build a ditch
across their lands. True, in the meantime, constructed her own mile-
long ditch, and then secured approval from the *mayordomo* (steward)
of the Acequia de San Ildefonso to connect her ditch with that portion of the San Ildefonso ditch that remained intact. At a December
meeting of the shareholders of the San Ildefonso acequia, True
offered to donate the ditch she constructed to the shareholders, on
condition that Stevenson pay $32 into the treasury, to be used to
maintain the entire ditch during the coming irrigation season. Other
shareholders would pay nothing, she explained, since they were very
poor. All the shareholders at the meeting, including Tilly's representative, Julio Roybal, agreed to the proposition, although Stevenson
had no prior knowledge that such action was to be taken. Either at
this meeting or a little later, Clara became one of the commissioners
of the acequia, and soon was elected mayordomo.[54]

During the spring 1913 irrigation season, True, acting in her
capacity as mayordomo, delivered water to all the shareholders
except Stevenson, on the grounds that Tilly had failed to pay the $32
fee. And on April 28, she entered Stevenson's land and tore down a
headgate that Tilly had constructed to control waters flowing in the

acequia. In letters to Stevenson and to the Smithsonian, True craftily referred to Tilly's ranch as a government operation. She addressed one to "Manager Smithsonian Institute Farm," clearly intending to make trouble for the ethnologist with Washington officials. Indeed, after receiving one such letter from True, Hodge asked Tilly for an explanation. With some irritation, he wrote, "It is very annoying to receive letters of this kind, on account of the reflection that it tends to cast on the Bureau's name."[55]

Tilly stubbornly refused to accede to Clara's demands. Instead, during the first week in May, she filed a petition in district court before Judge Edmund C. Abbott for a writ of mandamus to prevent True from shutting off irrigation water to her property. In her petition, Tilly stated that part of her land was planted in alfalfa, another part in apple trees, and other parts she had intended to plant in corn and oats. Because of True's failure to furnish water, the orchard and alfalfa fields were suffering, and the corn and oats had not been planted. "Unless water is immediately furnished," she avowed, the crops will be "destroyed and lost to the great damage of the petitioner." The ensuing court battle received full coverage in the *Santa Fe Daily New Mexican*.[56]

In this weeklong nonjury trial, Abbott heard testimony from a large number of witnesses, starting on May 21. Many prominent Santa Feans were in the courtroom to enjoy the repartee between the opposing counsels. Tilly's lawyer, A. B. Renehan, kept her on the stand the entire first day. True's lawyer, J. H. Crist, later asked Stevenson questions to which he wanted only yes-or-no answers. But, the press reported, she was determined "to reply as she saw fit." After an exasperated Crist raised his voice to ask another question, she replied "that she was not deaf[,] whereupon there was a ripple of laughter."[57]

The day that True took the stand in her own defense, the press headlined its story, "Nervous on Stand is Miss True." Although outwardly calm, Clara showed her nervousness "by the constant use of her hands"—pulling a ring off her finger and then putting it back, rubbing a pencil between her palms, "twisting one finger about the other." During the course of the trial, the press reported in full on Tilly's earlier successful case against the Trues to recover her land. On May 27, Judge Abbott rendered a decision in Stevenson's favor, and subsequently ordered True to furnish Tilly with her due share of water from the acequia.[58]

As it turned out, True ignored or evaded the court's order by resigning her position as mayordomo. At a quickly called meeting of acequia shareholders, which only a few attended, new officers were elected, including Mary Bryan as mayordomo. Thereafter, with True essentially controlling the acequia, Tilly's fields remained without water.[59]

Clara now began in earnest her campaign to drive Stevenson from the region. Mary Bryan, with Clara's support, sent a letter to the Bureau of American Ethnology in June of 1913, in which she lodged several serious charges against the ethnologist, among them misappropriation of government funds, drunkenness, use of obscene language, and mistreatment of a child (apparently a young Indian girl who had stayed briefly with Tilly). Although Stevenson absolutely denied these accusations, Hodge's response emotionally devastated her. In a letter to her friend the California writer George Wharton James, Tilly explained her reaction: "The whole thing is so disgusting. Mr. Hodge sent me a copy of the charges requesting me to answer. The shock which I experienced when I was requested to take notice of such charges, or that the Bureau of American Ethnology could take notice of such charges, nearly killed me." Several gentlemen, including James, had visited her ranch, and "no one," she avowed, ever saw liquor on her table or saw her drunk.[60]

To place Tilly's reaction to Bryan's charges in perspective, it must be remembered that, despite her unconventional life as a field ethnologist, she had been raised as a Victorian woman who valued certain social conventions. Like any respectable woman of her era, she was deeply shocked that anyone would claim that she was less than an upright, highly principled, professional woman whose family background placed her above the likes of Mary Bryan and Clara True.

Shortly after receiving Hodge's letter, Stevenson moved to Santa Fe, possibly to be closer to loyal friends who supported her and away from "those dreadful women." She also demanded an immediate investigation "here on the spot where all data could be had." Hodge arrived in Santa Fe on August 12 to combine visits to ancient ruins in Frijoles Canyon and elsewhere with a thorough probe into Bryan's charges. Before he left New Mexico, Tilly initiated a lawsuit, on September 3, against the two women for $32,000 in damages for defamation of character and slander. As she explained to James, "[Hodge] agreed with my [attorney] that a libel suit was necessary in order to be rid of these women."[61]

Although Stevenson expected the suit to come up in January, long delays prevented any immediate resolution of the issue. Hodge's slowness to exonerate Stevenson (which he eventually would do) is difficult to understand. Soon after the start of the new year, he informed her that the matter of the charges had "been held completely in abeyance since my return to Washington. I think it desirable that nothing further be done until the termination of your approaching suit which is brought for the purpose of your personal vindication. Any report made on the inquiry would be incomplete without that, it seems to me, and would certainly be far less satisfactory to yourself."[62]

Tilly's relocation to Santa Fe permitted her to make the acquaintance of Hughes and Florence Bryant of Kansas City, who arrived during the late summer of 1913 "to see America's unique city in all its summer glory." Florence's father, Judge J. M. Lowe, was president of the National Old Trails Association and vice president of the National Highways Association, two organizations contemplating the building of a highway through Santa Fe to the Grand Canyon and on to the West Coast. The Bryants brought with them a message to the people of Santa Fe from Judge Lowe, in which he predicted that this new continental road would infuse "new life" into the city.[63]

During the Bryants' stay in Santa Fe, Tilly and Florence became good friends, a friendship that the younger woman "treasured." Thereafter, the two women kept up a correspondence, which no doubt buoyed Tilly's spirits during her prolonged legal battles with Clara True. A recent letter from Tilly had made "Mr. Bryant and I [*sic*] homesick for Santa Fe," Florence wrote late in the year. "Sometimes when I'm overtired," she continued, "I picture the sweet rest I had in New Mexico, and always I remember you." She then requested that Tilly send a photograph of herself, preferably one showing her in a lovely dress that she had worn one evening in Santa Fe. A few months later, Florence sent another warm letter, thanking her for the picture and expressing her admiration for the older woman. "Really I just felt like talking to it [the photo]," she wrote. "Those happy hours of last summer spent in your charming company, all came back to me. . . . You are an aristocratic little lady, it shows in every line. . . . Your expression is perfect, your hair dressed so prettily, the pose splendid and your dress looks so beautifully [*sic*]. . . . I have seen you smile this expression many a time. If only pictures could talk back, when we want to see one so much."[64]

Sometime after the Bryants left New Mexico, Stevenson sought medical treatment from Dr. T. F. Tannus, whose card in the local press identified him as an eye, ear, nose, and throat specialist "late from Europe." Dr. Tannus diagnosed her ailments as rheumatism and heart disease brought on by a great shock. He promised to "bring me back to as fine health as I ever had," she reported to Hodge, "if I would only cease to worry over my trouble." She had tried to banish her "awful experience" from her mind, but found it difficult to "shut out the fact that the Bureau was waiting for the result of the libel case to vindicate me from those vile charges sent to the Bureau by the True and Bryan women." She had worked so hard "day and night" to learn all she could about the Indians, and then these women "came in to interfere." She then emotionally described the heartbreak of the situation:

> You know Mr. Hodge that my life has not been mixed up with low vulgar people but it has been the very extreme from a shadow of any thing vulgar. The Secretary of the Smithsonian knows the same for he was a frequent visitor at my home and knew my husband, my parents, and the people who frequented our home. He found only culture

and refinement there. No one ever found any thing but refinement there. No one ever found any thing but refinement at any camp I ever presided over. No living creature ever heard me use a coarse word, and to be mixed up in any way with the wretched women who dared write such charges against me, and that I was expected to take any notice of such charges has almost killed me. Nothing but the great constitution inherited from both parents has saved me.[65]

As Stevenson's slander case slowly made its way through the courts, she desperately worked to save her ranch. On March 25, 1914, she signed a lease with Douglass Walker, Judge Abbott's brother-in-law, to manage her Ton'yo property, the rent to be one-half the gross proceeds of all harvested crops. That same day, she filed a petition in district court to have a receiver appointed to take charge of the Acequia de San Ildefonso and distribute its waters to shareholders. She claimed that her one thousand fruit-bearing trees, valued at $8,000, had been endangered by Clara True's failure to furnish her with water. After Judge Abbott recused himself, Herbert F. Reynolds, judge of the Second Judicial District, appointed Walker as receiver.[66]

Renehan soon filed contempt-of-court proceedings on Stevenson's behalf against True and Bryan, avowing that the two women had ignored court orders by refusing to recognize Walker's authority. Moreover, Clara had threatened to horsewhip Walker if he took charge of the acequia, and vowed to "go to jail before she would permit [Stevenson] to have any water." Renehan also claimed that True and Bryan had secretly cut holes in the ditch to prevent water from reaching Tilly's fields. These are "desperate and unruly women," he continued, "totally lacking in respect for the court's receiver and the court's order and fully capable . . . to resort to violence again for the purpose of preventing water flowing in the . . . ditch." He therefore requested that a peace officer be assigned to assist the receiver. A few days later, however, on April 28, Judge Reynolds dismissed the contempt-of-court proceedings, and discharged the receiver, citing a recent opinion of the state supreme court that irrigation ditches were public, or quasipublic, corporations, and consequently a receiver could not be appointed.[67]

Sympathetic to his client's predicament, Renehan kept Hodge informed of the difficulties she faced. On May 12, he wrote,

> We are still compelled to fight every inch of the way with our recalcitrant, intelligent, resourceful and daring female opponents. They are shrewd enough to ingratiate themselves where publicity favorable to them will result, such as the Archaeological School here, of which Miss True has become a life member by the payment of $100.00; such as the Womans Club, of which she has become a member; and by employing as associate counsel the husband of the president of the Womans Club, she draws to herself more attention. In the Archaeological School, with reference to the expected visit here in October of the Americanists, she attracted further attention to herself by offering to furnish wagons, teams, camp and tenting outfit for the scientists on their way to the Rito de los Frijoles, and by an actual subscription of money in addition.[68]

Because the slander case again had been delayed, Renehan urged Hodge to exonerate Stevenson of the charges preferred by Mary Bryan, "charges the untruth of which you learned during your investigations of them." In a statement that challenges a later generation's opinion that Tilly had become an alcoholic as she grew older, Renehan declared, "The outrageous character of the accusations alone stamps them with falsity and viciousness. The class of people with whom Mrs. Stevenson associates here is refutation enough to the reasonable mind." He concluded, "I trust that a sense of justice alone will convince you of the propriety of this request on my part."[69]

And, in fact, Hodge complied with Renehan's request, if somewhat begrudgingly, for he continued to justify his tardiness in issuing such a report. Nonetheless, he did emphatically declare that all of

Bryan's charges were false. His inquiries had resulted "in testimony in support of Mrs. Stevenson's good name," he noted, and "people of the highest standing" believed "it impossible for Mrs. Stevenson to have been guilty of any of the charges brought against her." He also reported that during the investigation, True and Bryan had asserted that they had made up their minds "to drive Mrs. Stevenson out of the country." Hodge had never established a comfortable relationship with Tilly, however, and consequently he could not, or would not, absolve her of all blame in the circumstances leading to her troubles. "During the course of my inquiry," he told Renehan, "I could not satisfy myself that Mrs. Stevenson has always been discreet in her criticism of others, and that this tendency, and to the extreme forcefulness of her character, some of her difficulties have been due."[70]

It was this perceived "extreme forcefulness" of character that possibly accounts for Stevenson's tenuous ties with Edgar L. Hewett's School of American Archaeology and its staff, the younger members of whom (all male) seemed to delight in telling disparaging stories about her after she died. Occasionally, she expressed in writing her sense of alienation from the other Santa Fe scientists. On September 15, 1914, for example, she wrote to a friend, "I miss intellectual companionship here [in Santa Fe]. . . . Of course there are some cultured people here, but they are few and far between." And in a letter written the next day to Herman Schweizer, manager of Fred Harvey Company's Indian department, in which she conveyed a desire to help with exhibits at the forthcoming Panama-California Exposition in San Diego, she wrote, "Of course I know that there are some interested in the exposition that would not wish to have one as well posted as myself associated with it. This feeling has been shown most clearly during my recent stay in Santa Fe."[71]

Indeed, Tilly's primary social contacts in Santa Fe were with Mary and L. Bradford Prince and other community leaders. Her friendship with the Princes, in fact, must have placed her in an awkward position with Hewett, for late in 1913, the ex-governor sided with a vocal minority of Santa Feans (including Bronson M. Cutting, publisher of the *Santa Fe Daily New Mexican*, and Henry H. Dorman, president of the chamber of commerce), who staged a vigorous, but ultimately futile, campaign to have the archaeologist replaced as director of the School of American Archaeology. Splashed across the newspaper during this boisterous attack were letters written by eastern-establishment anthropologists Franz Boas, Alfred Tozzer, Roland B. Dixon, and Pliny Earle Goddard, disparaging Hewett's credentials as an archaeologist.

Tilly kept out of the fray, reporting to Hodge only that "the attack on the Director of the School of American Archaeology came like a bomb. I thought that the Chamber of Commerce and the School were like devoted brothers." She was quite aware, of course, that Hewett thought highly of her adversary, Clara True. And as the date for the libel trial approached, she told her boss, "I think every gentleman outside the School of American Archaeology, in New Mexico feels so incensed with the two women that they think only of my complete vindication."[72]

Tilly could take some small comfort in knowing that she was not the only target of Clara True's vindictiveness. Besides Clara's role in forcing Crandall's transfer, she and Bryan also sent in charges of graft against Francis Wilson, U.S. attorney for the Pueblo Indians. "What pleasure can these women find in endeavoring to ruin the characters of others!" Stevenson exclaimed after talking to Wilson. She might even have felt some satisfaction upon learning of Clara's own legal problems. In the summer of 1914, the U.S. government entered a lawsuit to recover more than $3,000 that True failed to account for while in the Indian service in California, and in November two major mercantile firms sued her for recovery of debts.[73]

Still, the unresolved libel suit took its toll on Stevenson both emotionally and physically. The trial "has hung over me like a sword," she wrote to Hodge in August, "not that I fear the result but that I must come in contact with those dreadful women and their coarse attorney." With heartfelt honesty, she confessed that she had "been ill and unhappy during the past year, more so than words can express." She suffered from rheumatism, and frequently took a powerful heart stimulant to maintain her strength. When informed in October that her lawsuit had been postponed until the following March (1915), "it seemed that I must surely die," she exclaimed. She felt strongly, however, that no matter what the cost to her financially and emotionally, she must remain for the trial to clear her good name for the sake of the bureau. "I could not rest in my grave without a complete vindication through the courts, to file in the Smithsonian Institution. I must not die until this is accomplished. I owe it to the man who gave his life for the benefit of science, to my parents and to myself, and to all those with whom I have been associated in the scientific world, including, of course, my friends in the Smithsonian Institution."[74]

Throughout this difficult time, Stevenson struggled to carry on her professional work. On August 7, 1914, her brief article on "The Galaxy Fraternity of the Pueblo Indians of New Mexico" appeared in the *Santa Fe Daily New Mexican*, and later that same month she reported that her Tewa manuscript was "virtually completed, all to finishing two chapters."[75] She also took the time to support a drive by the Santa Fe Chamber of Commerce and New Mexico's congressional delegation to push through Congress a bill to create a National Park of the Cliff Cities (also called the Pajarito National Park), which would preserve Indian antiquities northwest of Santa Fe. She wrote letters to the chamber of commerce and to personal friends in support of the bill. She also sent plans for the park to Rudolph Kauffman of the *Washington Star*—"a friend of many years"—and the *Star* subsequently carried an article backing the bill. These efforts by local supporters eventually led to the establishment of Bandelier National Monument in 1916, but Congress failed to grant "national park status" for a much larger surrounding area.[76]

By the close of 1914, Stevenson had decided to sell her ranch and establish a home elsewhere, possibly in Denver, where her sister lived, and where she had several good friends. Here she would continue to write and pursue her studies, traveling to Washington "only occasionally to see about the publication" of her work. To a friend she confessed that she would prefer living in Denver (rather than in the nation's capital), where "I could be more quiet. People will not let me be to myself in Washington and I have been so long out here I would find it tedious I fear, to enter into the old world of Washington as delightful as it is."[77]

The sixty-five–year-old ethnologist concealed the seriousness of her illness from family and friends, however. Her lawyer finally convinced her to drop the libel suit and to leave New Mexico, for he feared that the stress of a trial "would bring collapse, if not demise." He later reported to Hodge that he had been concerned about her health for some time, and he gave a graphic picture of the extent of her decline. "It was quite apparent to me that her circulation was bad. I feared, and indeed anticipated, apoplexy. She was really an invalid, and for a large part of the time was confined to her bed or her room. Her color was purplish. It seemed as if the blood would burst out of her cheeks and lips. She had numerous fainting and falling spells, due to syncope, heart failure, heart weakness, or whatever it may be called. Her heart was not doing its work in anything like orderly fashion."[78]

On March 14, 1915, Matilda Coxe Stevenson left New Mexico, a land she had come to love and wherein she had spent most of her professional career. Local newspapers noted her departure, the *Santa Fe Daily New Mexican* referring to her as "the well known ethnologist," and the *Santa Fe State Recorder* declaring that she had "won recognition as one of the most accomplished students of Indian life in the country."[79]

Shortly after Tilly departed, she was elected in absentia to the committee of research of the newly organized Southwestern Anthropological Society, a society dedicated to "the study of the Indians of the Southwest and the folklore and customs of the early Spanish colonists." At an organizational meeting held in Santa Fe on March 27, 1915, Dr. Livingston Farrand, president of the University of Colorado and formerly professor of anthropology at Columbia University, was elected president, and Paul Radin, one of Franz Boas's former students, was elected secretary. A stellar cast of anthropologists joined Tilly on the research committee: Pliny Earle Goddard and Nels C. Nelson of the American Museum of Natural History, Franz Boas of Columbia University, A. L. Kroeber of the University of

California, and Alfred M. Tozzer of Harvard University.[80] Stevenson's declining health, however, must have dampened any pleasure she derived from this special honor.

Tilly stopped over in Denver on her way east to stay several days with her sister and to consult a heart specialist, "the celebrated Doctor C. E. Edson." He found her to be in a "worse condition" than she had anticipated, and ordered complete rest for a week; he "would neither allow me to open my manuscript or . . . even write a letter," she reported to Hodge. Upon Edson's recommendation to move to a lower elevation, she continued her travels, and, on March 29, reached Rockville, Maryland, where she would spend several weeks with her niece Edith Prescott. Although a physician urged her not to do any work for at least three or four weeks, she optimistically informed Hodge on April 2 that she felt "quite sure that I can have my Tewa work done and ready to turn over to the Bureau by the end of June."[81]

In late May, a doctor pronounced her "decidedly improved"; still, she thought it prudent to make out a new will. "Hearts some times give out when least expected to do so," she wrote to her legal adviser Herman E. Gasch on the thirty-first. Since she had destroyed an earlier will years ago, and "while I am as poor as a church mouse," she made known her wishes in case she died unexpectedly before she could execute a formal will. All of her personal property, with the exception of a sewing machine and a few boxes left with her sister in Denver, was now stored at the Prescott residence. This included personal and official papers, as well as a deed to four catacombs in a vault at Rock Creek Cemetery in Washington, where her husband, father, and mother were buried. "The fourth remains for me," and she asked Gasch to have someone see that her name was placed on the slab in the event of her death. She left all of her worldly goods to her sister Nina Zevely, including her property in New Mexico and twenty thousand shares in the Taos Valley Land Company, although she doubted the latter was worth anything.[82]

Despite Tilly's precarious health, she courageously attempted to deal with the hornet's nest stirred up when her statements about Tewa human sacrifice appeared in national newspapers. As historian

Cheryl Foote points out, Stevenson "was not the first ethnologist to suggest that the Pueblos practiced human sacrifice." While at Zuni in 1881, Frank Cushing had confided to John Bourke his belief "that human sacrifices were still kept up, altho, in the deepest secrecy and at rare intervals." Stevenson first mentioned her discovery of the Tewa ceremonies in a brief report to Hodge dated April 5, 1913. A year later, she expanded on the topic in a report that was published late in 1914 in *Smithsonian Miscellaneous Collections* and titled "Strange Rites of the Tewa Indians." "The most shocking ceremony associated with the zooic worship of the Tewa," she wrote, "is the propitiation of the rattlesnake with human sacrifice to prevent further destruction from the venomous bites of the reptile. The greatest secrecy is observed and the ceremonies are performed without the knowledge of the people except those directly associated with the rite which is performed quadrennially."[83]

In following months, in letters to Hodge, she graphically described the ceremonies, and although admitting to one inaccuracy in her first account, she staunchly defended the rest of her report after naturalists challenged her assertions. Still, as Hodge continued to ask for more details, she begged him to keep the Smithsonian report from New Mexico. "Should those terrible women get hold of it . . . they could cause me unlimited annoyance." But she insisted that she had been given accurate information. "I have had very long years of experience in studying the native peoples," she asserted. "I *know them* and they *know me*. If they wished to deceive me they would surely tell a far different story and not allow themselves through desire to fool—[to] be associated with such a dark spot in their lives."[84]

Tilly should have known from her long experience, however, that such volatile information would eventually reach New Mexico. The *Washington Post*, on April 17, 1915, carried a brief story titled "Human Sacrifices by Indians, Tewas Offer up Women and Children in Rites, Says Mrs. Stevenson." Almost immediately, Commissioner of Indian Affairs Cato Sells quizzed Hodge about Stevenson's report. She in turn phoned Sells, and invited him to call so they could "fully discuss the matter." But the damage had been done.

Newspapers around the country picked up the story, which led to protests by a plethora of officials and Indians who ridiculed Stevenson's assertions.[85]

The *Santa Fe Daily New Mexican* carried the Washington story on April 19. Within days, it also printed statements by J. H. Crist, U.S. attorney for the Pueblos; Francis C. Wilson, former U.S. attorney for the Pueblos; Clinton J. Crandall, former superintendent of the Santa Fe Industrial School; and S. F. Naranjo, a Santa Clara Indian, attacking Stevenson's findings. They believed that the ethnologist had been deceived, that Indians had deliberately told her sensational stories. This, of course, is entirely possible; it is also likely that she misinterpreted tribal legends she heard about rattlesnakes and the sacrifice of infants. The Bureau of Indian Affairs and the Bureau of American Ethnology gladly let the matter drop after Stevenson's death. No ethnologist thereafter followed up on her allegations.[86]

Tilly finally succumbed to heart disease on June 24, at the age of sixty-six. Shortly before her demise, she had moved to a Mr. and Mrs. J. E. Powell's residence near Oxon Hill, Maryland, possibly a boarding house or rest home, to continue her recuperation. Herman E. Gasch sent a brief message to notify Secretary Walcott of Tilly's death: "Mrs. Stevenson died this morning at the residence of Mr. Powell, near Oxen [*sic*] Hill, Maryland. She has been failing for some time but died without suffering. She had every care."[87]

That evening, the *Washington Star* carried an announcement of Stevenson's death, describing her as "late of the bureau of American ethnology and widow of the late Col. James Stevenson." The *New York Times* carried a lengthy obituary on June 25, and the *Santa Fe Daily New Mexican* followed on the twenty-eighth. After listing her professional accomplishments and alluding briefly to the recent controversy concerning human sacrifice, the *New Mexican* concluded, "Mrs. Stevenson was especially well known here because of the fact that she had a ranch near here for years and was frequently a visitor to this city."[88]

The most puzzling factor connected with Tilly's death was the subsequent disappearance of her Tewa manuscript. The Bureau of American Ethnology moved quickly to claim ownership to it and to the other professional papers in her possession at the time she died. But inevitably the courts were slow to process her estate. A year after her death, Secretary Walcott appealed to the U.S. attorney general to help recover this "large body of valuable manuscripts and notes, drawings, and photographs." On January 17, 18, and 19, 1917, her private belongings were auctioned off in Washington by C. G. Sloan and Company, while her professional papers were set aside in a trunk to be returned to the bureau. Yet it took another year of legal maneuvers before Hodge sent a courier to the auction house, on January 16, 1918, to pick up the material.[89]

The mystery only deepens thereafter. In his annual report for 1914–1915, Hodge had stated that declining health had prevented Stevenson from completing the final revisions of the manuscript before she died. But he added, "It is believed . . . that when an opportunity of fully examining Mrs. Stevenson's completed manuscript and notes is afforded it will be found in condition for publication after the customary editorial treatment."[90] Neither he nor his successors at the bureau, however, ever again mentioned Stevenson's Tewa ethnography in their published reports.

We do know, however, that Stevenson's professional papers were turned over to bureau staff member John P. Harrington to examine, edit, and publish. On April 2, 1918, he reported that Tilly's Tewa material amounted to 973 pages of manuscript, 243 prints, and 277 films. But his linguistic work among the Mission Indians of California took precedence over the editing of her Tewa ethnography. And although he never did publish any of Stevenson's papers, he absolutely refused to allow Elsie Clews Parsons access to the Tewa manuscript, a document that would have assisted her in writing a comparative study of the Pueblo Indians.[91]

Recognized today as one of the premier early-twentieth-century Pueblo ethnologists, Parsons made at least four requests between 1918 and 1924 to study Stevenson's unpublished materials, even offering to edit the Tewa manuscript herself. Early on, she had learned that Harrington had it in his possession, and she argued forcefully that their roles should be reversed. In a 1922 letter to J. Walter Fewkes, Hodge's successor at the bureau, she pointed out that Harrington was "too much engrossed in his linguistic work to edit the Stevenson ms." Besides, she added, "I have been Mrs. Stevenson's successor, so to speak, at Zuni and am familiar with her methods of work." Two years later, in the midst of her comparative study, she again inquired about the Stevenson manuscript, telling Fewkes that "it seems a pity that between the Stevenson material and mine no correlation should be made." Because of Harrington's strong objections to sharing Tilly's work, however, Parsons concluded her study of the Tewa Indians without ever having seen any of her predecessor's unpublished material. In the preface to *The Social Organization of the Tewa of New Mexico* (1929), she listed the few ethnologists who had visited the Tewas: Harrington, Stevenson, Herbert J. Spinden, and Barbara Freire-Marreco. The reason she had embarked upon her own study of the Tewas, she explained, was because "no publication was in prospect and no material available even in manuscript." To undertake a comparative study of the Pueblos, which she intended to do, "more knowledge of the Tewa" was absolutely "indispensable."[92]

Today most of Tilly's Tewa material, including the four-hundred-page ethnography, is missing from the National Anthropological Archives.[93] Given Harrington's appropriation of her "Taos Blue Lake Ceremony," possibly the manuscript became submerged in his own voluminous papers, or perhaps it was dismantled to support whatever he was working on. The hope is, however, that one day Stevenson's Tewa ethnography will surface intact.

CHAPTER 8

"Every Moment Is Golden for the Ethnologist"

Matilda Coxe Stevenson was a strong, determined woman, dedicated to the task of preserving for posterity the traditions and beliefs of Pueblo Indians, a task that she and her husband had set out to accomplish together after their marriage. Tilly carried on with this work for nearly three decades after James Stevenson died; indeed, the deep bond that had united them in life bolstered and fed her determination to complete their work. Tilly's unflagging passion for anthropology and her strength of character stood her in good stead, for these traits allowed her to surmount major crises that threatened to derail her career.

Stevenson had many other admirable qualities, both as an ethnologist and as a human being. In her studies, she cared most about getting at the truth, figuring out how another society worked and unraveling the intricacies of its religion. She became emotionally engaged with Indian people, especially with the Zunis, many counting her as a true friend. She also treasured her husband, family, and friends; in their eyes, she was generous, warmhearted, and caring. Other acquaintances found her pleasant and engaging as well. She had limitations, of course. The very personality traits that led to her success, traits often admired in men—ambition, assertiveness, tenacity—generated antagonism among some people, especially those who expected women to be subservient and retiring. At times she was obstinate, difficult, outspoken, and domineering. But surely these less-attractive qualities stemmed in part from her fight to gain respect and recognition within the male scientific community.

Stevenson made several important contributions to anthropology during her remarkable career. Like her contemporaries Frank Hamilton Cushing and Franz Boas, she initiated participant observation as a primary method for obtaining information about Indian societies. And like Boas, she believed that only prolonged fieldwork would allow outsiders like herself to understand Pueblo culture. Between 1879 and 1906, she made approximately twelve field trips to Zuni, during which time she collected detailed and valuable information about the Zunis' religion, ceremonies, and everyday life. Often this required that she undertake long and arduous trips to examine shrines, and labor far into the night with her Indian friends. She showed marvelous adaptability to local conditions, and rarely complained of inconveniences.

Stevenson's work for the Bureau of American Ethnology was more than a mere job. It was a calling, a mission. She passionately believed that the task of preserving indigenous culture for the historical record was a moral duty, both for herself and her Indian friends. Like many other anthropologists, she believed that Indian cultures would inevitably vanish as indigenous peoples assimilated into mainstream America. Although single-minded in her pursuit of knowledge, she never presented herself as "the omniscient scientist." Her greatest wish, she once remarked, was "to erect a foundation upon which students may build." Her Zuni book, in fact, set a standard for future ethnographers, and became a prime reference for scholars and Zunis alike, all the more remarkable because she had no models. There were no precedents.[1]

Although modern-day critics decry Stevenson's aggressive field techniques (common to her generation of ethnologists), they rarely note the reciprocal nature of her relationships with Indian people or herald her diplomatic skills. Certainly some Indians benefited from her presence, among them individuals she rescued from persecution as alleged witches and those she supplied with medical help. She also intervened on Indians' behalf in Washington, and performed lesser services as well. She treated their beliefs with respect, showed compassion for her Indian collaborators, and evinced a willingness to listen carefully to what was most important to them. In this way, over months and years, she developed rapport and trust with members of each group with whom she worked. And to her credit, she allowed their voices to be heard in her published reports, and noted many of the changes taking place within their communities. By bringing herself into her narrative, she also told readers something of the complex relations that are a part of fieldwork.[2]

Not only was Stevenson a pioneering ethnologist, she also was a pioneer for women's rights. By her example, she made it easier for other women to follow in her footsteps. As the founder of the Women's Anthropological Society of America, she helped women reinforce their identities as professional scientists. At times it was a difficult and lonely path. For most of her career, she dealt professionally mainly with male anthropologists; only during the early years of the WASA did she share feedback and camaraderie with other female ethnologists. And she constantly had to fight for prestige, recognition, and equality within a male-dominated discipline.

Among anthropologists of her generation, Stevenson was noted for her rigorous research and thorough collecting of data. John Wesley Powell admired the dedication and energy she brought to her Zia work. W J McGee judged her fieldwork as excellent. William H. Holmes, in his memoriam to Stevenson, called her Zuni ethnography "a monument to her energy, ability, and perseverance." Holmes also held Tilly's indomitable spirit in high regard, describing her as "able, self-reliant, and fearless, generous, helpful, and self-sacrificing."[3]

Younger anthropologists who followed Stevenson to the Southwest were less kind in their appraisals of her work and character. Undoubtedly her increasing alienation from the young men who descended upon Santa Fe, as well as her forceful personality, accounts for a later generation's lack of appreciation for her accomplishments. For some male anthropologists, her unconventional lifestyle and personality loomed larger than her professional accomplishments.[4]

For Matilda Coxe Stevenson, every moment indeed was golden for the ethnologist. "I have endeavored to live the life of these people, think as they think, see nature as they see it," she stated in 1912, "and by so doing I have secured a close insight into the religious and social life of these people."[5] Although speaking of the Tewas, her remarks apply equally well to her relations with other Pueblo Indians. Should her missing manuscript ever be located, it will present as revealing a picture of the Tewas as they lived in the early twentieth century as her Zuni ethnography did for the Zunis in the late nineteenth and early twentieth centuries. As it stands, Stevenson's legacy to the American people—Indians and non-Indians alike—is the detailed ethnographic descriptions of Pueblo Indians that she painstakingly recorded over a lifetime.

Abbreviations Used
In the Notes

AR	Annual Report
BAE	Bureau of American Ethnology
BE	Bureau of Ethnology
BIA	Bureau of Indian Affairs
ECP	Elsie Clews Parsons
GPO	Government Printing Office
JS	James Stevenson
LR	Letters Received
MCS	Matilda Coxe Stevenson
NA	National Archives
NAA	National Anthropological Archives
NMFJD	New Mexico First Judicial District
NMSRCA	New Mexico State Records Center and Archive
RG	Record Group
SIA	Smithsonian Institution Archives

Notes

Preface

1. Woodbury, "Past is Present," 3–4.
2. Field, Stamm, and Ewing, *The Castle*, 122, 151.
3. On charges of alcoholism, see, for example, Lurie, "Women in Early American Anthropology," 64.
4. McFeely, *Zuni and the American Imagination*, 54.

Chapter 1

1. Hogan, *The Texas Republic*, 29, 123, 125, 149, 152, 217. Quotation is found on 153. See also Crocket, *Two Centuries in East Texas*, 118, 218, 268; Winchester, *James Pinckney Henderson*, 51–52.
2. The year of Matilda Coxe Stevenson's birth is often listed as 1850. But the correct date of 1849 is verified by Texas Census, 1850, RG 29, NA, and MCS, "The Zuni Scalp Ceremonial," 484. Information about the Evans family comes from Texas Census, 1850, and undated family documents in MCS Papers, MS4689, NAA.
3. Crocket, *Two Centuries in East Texas*, 288–89.
4. Ibid., 245–46.
5. Alexander Evans to Sam Houston, December 14, 1853, and undated family document, MCS Papers, MS4689, NAA.
6. Clay-Clopton, *A Belle of the Fifties*, 26–29, 58, 138, 142; Vedder, *Reminiscences of the District of Columbia*, 84; *Historical Statistics of the United States*, 26; Hurd, *Washington Cavalcade*, 102; Green, *Washington, Village and Capital, 1800–1878*, 228.

7. *Washington Post,* July 30, 1893.

8. Undated family document, MCS Papers, MS4689, NAA; Evans, *A Sailor's Log,* 9–11; Blessing, "Robley Dunglison Evans," 210.

9. MCS to William H. Holmes, April 7 and November 19, 1906, MCS to Francis Leupp, December 29, 1908, MCS to Frederick W. Hodge, May 28, 1914, BAE, LR, MCS, NAA; MCS to George Wharton James, October 14, 1914, MCS Correspondence, P-E 211, Bancroft Library.

10. Joy McPherson, "Matilda Coxe-Stevenson Papers," NAA; District of Columbia Census, 1860, RG 29, NA; MCS to Charles D. Walcott, January 29, 1907, Charles D. Walcott Collection, SIA.

11. The Evanses' address is recorded on a letter sent to Alexander H. Evans, dated October 23, 1858, MCS Papers, MS4689, NAA.

12. Evans, *A Sailor's Log,* 11; *Washington Post,* July 30, 1893; *Congressional Directory for the Second Session of the Thirty-fifth Congress,* 26; *Congressional Directory for the First Session of the Thirty-sixth Congress,* 23.

13. Evans, *A Sailor's Log,* 46, 50–51.

14. Mary Henry's diary is located in the archives of the Smithsonian Institution. I consulted the diary via the Internet at http://www.si.edu/archives/documents/mary.htm. I have retained Henry's spelling.

15. Crocket, *Two Centuries in East Texas,* 246. Crocket relied on the reminiscences of old-time Texas residents for this information. Archivists at the National Archives, however, have failed to locate Confederate service records for Alexander H. Evans.

16. James Stevenson, Pension Application Files, RG 15, NA; Joy McPherson, "Matilda Coxe-Stevenson Papers," NAA; Parezo, "Matilda Coxe Stevenson," 39; clipping from *Washington Post,* November 23, 1894, undated family document, and Theodosia to My Dearest Sister, June 14, 1894, MCS Papers, MS4689, NAA.

17. Seitter, "Union City," http://www.gdg.org/seiter.htm.

18. Tillie Pierce's diary, quoted in "The Battle of Gettysburg, 1863," http://www.eyewitnesstohistory.com/gtburg.htm. See also Alleman, *At Gettysburg.*

19. Seitter, "Union City"; Nash, *First City,* 242.

20. James Stevenson, Compiled Military Service Records, RG 94, NA.

21. Nash, *First City,* 225, 231.

22. Gallman, *Mastering Wartime,* 170–73; Shankman, *The Pennsylvania Antiwar Movement,* 64–69, 82, 108, 117–19, 168.

23. Woloch, *Women and the American Experience,* 126–27; Woody, *A History of Women's Education in the United States,* 329.

24. Mulhern, *A History of Secondary Education in Pennsylvania,* 407, 428.

25. *McElroy's Philadelphia City Directory for 1863,* 896; Wickersham, *A History of Education in Pennsylvania,* 484–85.

26. Pennsylvania Census, 1880, RG 29, NA; Anna Anable to MCS, March 13, 1877, MCS Papers, MS4689, NAA.

27. *Compendium of the Tenth Census, Part 1*, 20; Whyte, *The Uncivil War*, 13–17, 31–32.

28. Whyte, *The Uncivil War*, 13–14.

29. Ibid., 70–72, 92, 174–76, 279.

30. *Washington Post*, July 30, 1893; District of Columbia Census, 1870, RG 29, NA.

31. Joy McPherson, "Matilda Coxe-Stevenson Papers," NAA. See also Parezo, "Matilda Coxe Stevenson," 39.

32. Lamb, "William Manuel Mew," 401–402. For several years Mew served as acting assistant surgeon in the U.S. Army.

33. Joy McPherson, "Matilda Coxe-Stevenson Papers," NAA; Parezo, "Matilda Coxe Stevenson," 39, 41; Kohlstedt, "In from the Periphery," 90; Wilson, *The American Woman in Transition*, 3–7, 20–21; Degler, *At Odds*, 8, 26, 154; Rossiter, *Women Scientists in America*, xvi.

34. Kohlstedt, "In from the Periphery," 83–88; Rossiter, *Women Scientists in America*, 2–12, 52.

35. Powell, "James Stevenson," 42–44; James Stevenson, Pension Application Files, RG 15, NA; James Stevenson, Compiled Military Service Records, RG 94, NA; *Washington Post*, July 26, 1888; *Washington National Tribune*, August 2, 1888; Foster, *Strange Genius*, 43–53, 73–75, 153–58; Bartlett, *Great Surveys of the American West*, 11–12.

36. Powell, "James Stevenson," 42–44; *Washington Post*, July 26, 1888; *Washington National Tribune*, August 2, 1888; Goode, "Biographical Notice of James Stevenson," 187–90. Logan, Hayden, and Stevenson had once lived in the same Washington boarding house. Boyd, *Boyd's Directory of Washington*, 1870.

37. J. Stevenson to My dear Tilly, December 30, 1871, MCS Papers, MS4689, NAA; *Washington Evening Star*, April 19, 1872; Degler, *At Odds*, 8; Rothman, *Hands and Hearts*, 4.

Chapter 2

1. MCS to James Stevenson, August 22, 1872, MCS Papers, MS4689, NAA.

2. Ibid.; Bonney, *The Grand Controversy*, 20–37; Rodgers, *John Merle Coulter*, 15, 17; U.S. Geological Survey of the Territories, *Sixth AR*, 1872, 231.

3. Parezo, "Matilda Coxe Stevenson," 40; Powell, "James Stevenson," 44; "James Stevenson," 556–57; Hough, "James Stevenson," 631–32.

4. Among the best works examining post–Civil War America's fascination with the West are White, *"It's Your Misfortune and None of My Own,"* and Truettner, ed., *The West as America*.

5. Bartlett's *Great Surveys of the American West* remains the best, most comprehensive history of the four surveys. See especially ix–xv, 11; Foster, *Strange Genius*, 4, 155–58, 230.

6. Cassidy, *Ferdinand V. Hayden*, 170–71, 183; Merrill, ed., *Yellowstone and the Great West*, 19.

7. U.S. Geological Survey of the Territories, *Third AR*, 1869, 5.

8. Chittenden, *The Yellowstone National Park*, 309.

9. Foster, *Strange Genius*, 4; Bartlett, *Great Surveys*, 22; Henry W. Elliott to Ferdinand V. Hayden, August 23, 1875, Hayden Survey, LR, RG 57, M623, roll 7, NA; Goode, "Biographical Notice of James Stevenson," 189.

10. Foster, *Strange Genius*, 221.

11. U.S. Geological Survey of the Territories, *Fifth AR*, 1871, 3; Merrill, *Yellowstone and the Great West*, 5, 15–18; Cassidy, *Ferdinand V. Hayden*, 128, 143, 155; Lincoln, "Robert Adams," 94–95. Cyrus Thomas had married Logan's sister, Dorothy, who died in 1864.

12. Jackson, *Time Exposure*, 194, 204; Merrill, *Yellowstone and the Great West*, 58, 68, 244n11.

13. Bartlett, *Great Surveys*, 43–56; Merrill, *Yellowstone and the Great West*, 19–20, 72, 121–41, 224.

14. Bartlett, *Great Surveys*, 51–52; Merrill, *Yellowstone and the Great West*, 22, 141, 264n14; U.S. Geological Survey of the Territories, *Fifth AR*, 1871, 5.

15. U.S. Geological Survey of the Territories, *Fifth AR*, 1871, 4; Bartlett, *Great Surveys*, 56. Hayden states in his AR that the party disbanded at Evanston. Merrill asserts, however, that survey members continued on the Union Pacific east to Fort Bridger, where the survey "officially disbanded on Monday, October 2." Merrill, *Yellowstone and the Great West*, 200.

16. Boyd, *Boyd's Directory of Washington*, 1871; Boyd, *Boyd's Directory of the District of Columbia*, 1872.

17. Foster, *Strange Genius*, 217, 221–23, 383n4; Merrill, *Yellowstone and the Great West*, 207–208; Bartlett, *Great Surveys*, 57–59; Haines, *The Yellowstone Story*, 1:164–72.

18. Powell, "James Stevenson," 43; "James Stevenson," 558.

19. Foster, *Strange Genius*, 228–30; Bartlett, *Great Surveys*, 59.

20. Foster, *Strange Genius*, 237–38; E. R. Beadle to Hayden, September 11, 1872, Hayden Survey, LR, RG 57, M623, roll 2, NA.

21. Quoted in Wilkins, *Thomas Moran*, 83; Bartlett, *Great Surveys*, 43.

22. Fernlund, *William Henry Holmes*, 19; Haines, *The Yellowstone Story*, 1:185; Brayer, ed., "Exploring the Yellowstone with Hayden," 279; Bartlett, *Great Surveys*, 70.

23. Thompson and Thompson, *Beaver Dick*, 3–4, 9, 19–20, 25–26, 32, 37, 72. A good summary of the 1872 expedition can be found in U.S. Geological Survey of the Territories, *Sixth AR*, 1872, 1–10.

24. Annie P. Cope to Hayden, September 20 and 22, 1872, Hayden Survey, LR, RG 57, M623, roll 2, NA; Osborn, *Cope: Master Naturalist*, 182.

25. Bonney, *The Grand Controversy*, 32–33, 45–46; Langford, "The Ascent of Mount Hayden," 129–57 (see especially 143). In later years, some writers and mountaineers raised doubts about the claim that Stevenson and Langford had reached the top of the Grand Teton (which Langford referred to as Mount Hayden).

Bonney's book explores the controversy in detail, and presents conclusive evidence that they did indeed reach the summit.

26. Bonney, *The Grand Controversy*, 94.

27. Charles D. Walcott to MCS, September 2, 1888, MCS Papers, MS4689, NAA.

28. MCS to James Stevenson, August 22, 1872, MCS Papers, MS4689, NAA.

29. Lystra, *Searching the Heart*, 9, 13, 21.

30. Paul, *Mining Frontiers of the Far West*, 123–27.

31. Ibid., 126; Bird, *A Lady's Life in the Rocky Mountains*, 138.

32. *Denver Rocky Mountain News*, May 14, 1873; Paul, *Mining Frontiers*, 125; Bartlett, *Great Surveys*, 80.

33. Hafen and Hafen, eds., *The Diaries of William Henry Jackson*, 216.

34. U.S. Geological and Geographical Survey of the Territories, *Seventh AR*, 1873, 1–2.

35. Hafen and Hafen, *The Diaries of William H. Jackson*, 217, 223–24, 228; Jackson, *Time Exposure*, 210.

36. Boyd, *Boyd's Directory of the District of Columbia*, 1873; Bartlett, *Great Surveys*, 100; Foster, *Strange Genius*, 260.

37. C. Thomas to Hayden, July 31, 1873, Hayden Survey, LR, RG 57, M623, roll 3, NA; Foster, *Strange Genius*, 251. For an extract from Rawlinson's address, see *Denver Rocky Mountain News*, September 2, 1873.

38. Hafen and Hafen, *The Diaries of William H. Jackson*, 259–60; *Denver Rocky Mountain News*, July 14, 15, and 19, 1874; U.S. Geological and Geographical Survey of the Territories, *Eighth AR*, 1874, 9.

39. Wilkins, *Thomas Moran*, 136–37, 346n4; Jackson, *Time Exposure*, 216–18.

40. Wilkins, *Thomas Moran*, 137; see Thomas Moran to Hayden, November 24, 1872, Hayden Survey, LR, RG 57, M623, roll 2, NA.

41. Bassford and Fryxell, eds., *Home-Thoughts*, 45.

42. Wilkins, *Thomas Moran*, 137–41; *Denver Rocky Mountain News*, September 1, 1874.

43. Hafen and Hafen, *The Diaries of William H. Jackson*, 332; U.S. Geological and Geographical Survey of the Territories, *Eighth AR*, 1874, 11–12. Jackson's diary shows that he met the Stevensons on October 2; the editors note, however, that the correct date should be October 3. See Hafen and Hafen, *The Diaries of William H. Jackson*, 331.

44. Hafen and Hafen, *The Diaries of William H. Jackson*, 333.

45. Trenholm, *The Arapahoes*, 158–60; Hughes, *American Indians in Colorado*, 57.

46. Trenholm, *The Arapahoes*, 229, 236, 254; Rockwell, *The Utes*, 72, 81, 96–99; Hughes, *American Indians in Colorado*, 61–66.

47. Rockwell, *The Utes*, 81; Pettit, *The Utes*, 22.

48. Hafen and Hafen, *The Diaries of William H. Jackson*, 333; Rockwell, *The Utes*, 45, 81; Hughes, *American Indians in Colorado*, 115n12.

49. Parezo, "Matilda Coxe Stevenson," 40. Although some scholars state that Stevenson's first ethnographic studies were made among the Utes and Arapahos, I have been unable to document her presence near any Arapaho camp. See Parezo, ibid.; Joy McPherson, "Matilda Coxe-Stevenson Papers," NAA. Still, it is possible that she encountered some Arapahos on her 1878 trip to Cheyenne, Wyoming. In late 1877, the government moved about one thousand Northern Arapahos from Dakota Territory to the Shoshone Wind River Reservation in west-central Wyoming. See Larson, *History of Wyoming*, 106.

50. Robert Adams to Hayden, March 8, 1875, Hayden Survey, LR, RG 57, M623, roll 5, NA; see also Ernest Ingersoll to Sullivan, January 5, 1875, Hayden Survey, LR, RG 57, M623, roll 8, NA.

51. U.S. Geological and Geographical Survey of the Territories, *Eighth AR*, 1874, 16–17; Henry W. Elliott to Hayden, August 23, 1875, Hayden Survey, LR, RG 57, M623, roll 7, NA. See also Miers Fisher to Stevenson, February 28, 1876, Hayden Survey, LR, RG 57, M623, roll 7, NA, which shows that Stevenson had returned to Hayden's survey by at least February 21, 1876.

52. U.S. Geological and Geographical Survey of the Territories, *Twelfth AR*, 1878, xiii–xviii (quote is on xiv).

53. *Cheyenne Daily Leader*, July 16, 18, and 20, and August 9, 1878.

54. *Cheyenne Daily Leader*, October 16, 1878; Stevenson to [name unclear], September 26, 1878, Hayden Survey, LR, RG 57, M623, roll 12, NA.

55. Stevenson to [name unclear], September 26, 1878, Stevenson to Dr., October 29, 1878, and Stevenson to Hayden, November 8, 1878, Hayden Survey, LR, RG 57, M623, roll 12, NA.

56. Powell, "James Stevenson," 44; Hough, "James Stevenson," 632; *Washington National Tribune*, August 2, 1888; Parezo, "Matilda Coxe Stevenson," 40; Parezo and Hardin, "In the Realm of the Muses," 270.

57. U.S. Geological and Geographical Survey of the Territories, *Twelfth AR*, 1878, xiii, xviii; Foster, *Strange Genius*, 155, 327.

Chapter 3

1. Fowler, *A Laboratory for Anthropology*, 106–107; Green, ed., *Cushing at Zuni*, 32. "Pueblo" refers to one of several Indian tribes living in the Southwest; "pueblo" refers to the village in which the Pueblo people live.

2. Worster, *A River Running West*, 216–17, 258, 273–77, 286–91, 397.

3. Ibid., 397–98, 600n24; Fowler, *A Laboratory for Anthropology*, 92.

4. Fowler, *A Laboratory for Anthropology*, 95–99; Worster, *A River Running West*, 442–43.

5. See Parezo, "Matilda Coxe Stevenson," 45.

6. John W. Powell to JS, August 4, 1879, MCS Papers, MS4689, NAA.

7. Powell to Henry M. Teller, January 21, 1902, BAE, LR, MCS, NAA.

8. See a series of letters of introduction, mainly dated July 1879, found in MCS Papers, MS4689, NAA. See also M. C. Meigs to Stephenson [*sic*], July 25, 1879, MCS Papers, MS4689, NAA, and Lawson, "Baskets, Pots, and Prayer Plumes," Ph.D. diss., 11.

9. Green, *Cushing at Zuni*, 32–34.

10. MCS, "Zuni and the Zunians," 1–2; Edward Hatch to all officers of the army serving in the district of New Mexico, September 5, 1879, MCS Papers, MS4689, NAA.

11. Green, *Cushing at Zuni*, 34–35.

12. Ibid., 35; Green, ed., *Zuni, Selected Writings*, 59, 78.

13. MCS, "The Zuni Indians," 16; JS to Powell, September 16, 1879, BAE, LR, JS, NAA.

14. Graves, *Thomas Varker Keam*, 45, 62, 68, 93; Hieb, personal communication.

15. Green, *Cushing at Zuni*, 38; Ealy, *Water in a Thirsty Land*, 180.

16. Green, *Zuni, Selected Writings*, 53–54; Bender, ed., *Missionaries, Outlaws, and Indians*, 123; Hart, *Pedro Pino*, 69.

17. Camp, ed., *George C. Yount and His Chronicles of the West*, 38; Crampton, *The Zunis of Cibola*, 60–64. See also Hart, *Pedro Pino*, 15.

18. Crampton, *The Zunis of Cibola*, 103–106, 114–15; Lawson, "Baskets, Pots, and Prayer Plumes," 18–20. Fort Defiance was established in 1851 within country claimed by the Navajo Indians, traditional enemies of the Zunis.

19. For information about the Ealys, Jennie Hammaker, and Graham, see Bender, *Missionaries, Outlaws, and Indians*, and Ruth R. Ealy (their daughter), *Water in a Thirsty Land*. For Graham, see also Green, *Cushing at Zuni*, 364n62. For the complex history of the railroad line built from the Rio Grande through the region north of Zuni, see Bryant, Jr., *History of the Atchison, Topeka and Santa Fe Railway*, 84–90.

20. See B. M. Thomas to Commissioner of Indian Affairs, August 14, 1879, in Fay, *Treaties, Land Cessions, and Other U.S. Congressional Documents*, part II, 99.

21. MCS, "Zuni and the Zunians," 8–9. Lieutenant A. W. Whipple, who visited Zuni in 1853, said it resembled "an immense ant hill." See Crampton, *The Zunis of Cibola*, 104.

22. Ferguson and Mills, "Settlement and Growth of Zuni Pueblo," 247, 251; Hart, "Historic Zuni Land Use," 10–11; MCS, "Zuni and the Zunians," 9.

23. Green, *Zuni, Selected Writings*, 59; MCS, "The Zuni Indians," 16.

24. Green, *Zuni, Selected Writings*, 59; Ealy, *Water in a Thirsty Land*, 181; Bender, *Missionaries, Outlaws, and Indians*, 123–24. In a speech given in 1890, Cushing said that Stevenson had rented two rooms from the governor; in an earlier account, he mentioned only one. Part of his talk is reproduced in Green, *Cushing at Zuni*, 38–41.

25. Worster, *A River Running West*, 403–404; BE, *Third AR*, 1881–82, xx.

26. Parezo, "The Formation of Ethnographic Collections," 36–37; JS, "Illustrated Catalogue of the Collections Obtained from the Indians of New Mexico and Arizona in 1879," 313, 319, 322. Stevenson states that on this 1879 trip the

expedition collected 1,500 objects from Zuni (322). Parezo, after making a careful study of the items collected that year in Zuni and later accessioned into the Smithsonian, lists 2,243 (37). See also Parezo, "Cushing as Part of the Team," 763–74.

27. JS to James Pilling, October 12, 1879, BAE, LR, JS, NAA.

28. MCS, "The Zuni Indians," 379; Parezo, "Matilda Coxe Stevenson," 46; Green, *Cushing at Zuni*, 93; Taylor F. Ealy to Pueblo Indian Agent, July 17, 1879, in Fay, *Treaties, Land Cessions, and Other U.S. Congressional Documents*, part II, 104. On window glass at Zuni, see Ferguson and Mills, "Settlement and Growth of Zuni Pueblo," 252–54.

29. Bender, *Missionaries, Outlaws, and Indians*, 84–93, 197n22. Until their house was built, the Ealys had living quarters in the home of former governor Pedro Pino (Patricio Pino's father). They also rented a room in Zuni for their school. Ibid., 84–89, 198n27.

30. In an unfinished letter dated October 7, Cushing wrote that the Stevensons planned to leave Zuni the next day. Ealy noted in his diary that the Stevensons left on October 10. See Green, *Cushing at Zuni*, 42; Bender, *Missionaries, Outlaws, and Indians*, 124.

31. JS to Pilling, October 12, 1879, BAE, LR, JS, NAA; Thomas V. Keam to George M. Lockwood, November 14, 1879, and JS to Commissioner of Indian Affairs, November 21, 1879, copies of letters, courtesy of Louis A. Hieb (originals are in LR, Commissioner of Indian Affairs, microfilm edition).

32. JS to Pilling, October 18, 1879, BAE, LR, JS, NAA; Parezo, "The Formation of Ethnographic Collections," 36–37; JS, "Illustrated Catalogue of the Collections Obtained from the Indians of New Mexico and Arizona in 1879," 313–15.

33. Green, *Cushing at Zuni*, 62–63; Green, *Zuni, Selected Writings*, 75–77; Ealy, *Water in a Thirsty Land*, 188–89; JS to Pilling, November 21, 1879, BAE, LR, JS, NAA.

34. Green, *Zuni, Selected Writings*, 56–60.

35. MCS, "The Zuni Indians," 17, 240–46; Green, *Zuni, Selected Writings*, 83–84; Roscoe, *The Zuni Man-Woman*, 1–2.

36. MCS, "Zuni and the Zunians," 24.

37. Roscoe, *The Zuni Man-Woman*, 2, 29, 44–52; Ealy, *Water in a Thirsty Land*, 211.

38. MCS, "The Zuni Indians," 380. I follow Stevenson's example in referring to We'wha as female.

39. See Roscoe, *The Zuni Man-Woman*, 50; Green, *Cushing at Zuni*, 58.

40. Green, *Cushing at Zuni*, 58.

41. Lurie, "Women in Early American Anthropology," 55, 59; Parezo, "Matilda Coxe Stevenson," 46–47.

42. McFeely, *Zuni and the American Imagination*, 94; Green, *Cushing at Zuni*, 7–8, 10, 61, 110, 140.

43. MCS, "The Zuni Indians," 17, 245.

44. Green, *Cushing at Zuni*, 2–3, 7, 44, 61, 65; McFeely, *Zuni and the American Imagination*, 85; Flack, *Desideratum in Washington*, 92.

45. Green, *Cushing at Zuni*, 7, 44, 61–62, 65, 93, 310, 351–52n36; Judd, *The Bureau of American Ethnology*, 59.

46. Green, *Cushing at Zuni*, 7, 43, 62. See Parezo, ed., *Hidden Scholars*, 6, 15, 33–34, 339–42; Foote, *Women of the New Mexico Frontier*, 127.

47. Green, *Zuni, Selected Writings*, 24n4, 43, 61–68; Green, *Cushing at Zuni*, 32–40, 351n31; McFeely, *Zuni and the American Imagination*, 89, 115, and photograph following 112. Jesse Green pictures Tilly Stevenson as a domineering woman, best known for her Zuni ethnography (1904) and "for her aggressive ways with Indians and whites alike." *Cushing at Zuni*, 350–51n31. The competition between Cushing and Stevenson, he states, "seems to have been sharp and ill-natured from the beginning." Much of his characterization of Stevenson, however, is based largely on Smithsonian anecdotes and Cushing's assessments of her. *Zuni, Selected Writings*, 24–25n4.

48. Cushing, "Outlines of Zuni Creation Myths," 337–38; Bandelier, *The Southwestern Journals of Adolph F. Bandelier, 1883–1884*, 40; MCS, "The Zuni Indians," 17; Ealy, *Water in a Thirsty Land*, 190; Fowler, *A Laboratory for Anthropology*, 107–109; Merrill and Ahlborn, "Zuni Archangels and Ahayu:da," 177, 184–86, 202n24. Recently the Smithsonian Institution returned one statue to the pueblo.

49. JS to Pilling, November 15 and 21, 1879, BAE, LR, JS, NAA; Green, *Zuni, Selected Writings*, 61, 90; Green, *Cushing at Zuni*, 42–43, 58–59, 63, 218.

50. JS to Powell, July 27, 1880, and JS to Pilling, July 10 and August 6, 1880, BAE, LR, JS, NAA.

51. JS to Powell, December 17, 1879, BAE, LR, JS, NAA; Boyd, *Boyd's Directory of the District of Columbia*, 1880; District of Columbia Census, 1880, RG 29, NA; James Stevenson, Pension Application Files, RG 15, NA. See photographs of the Stevensons' house in this book.

52. Worster, *A River Running West*, 437–40; Flack, *Desideratum in Washington*, 58–60, 80–86, 107–14, 143; Rossiter, *Women Scientists in America*, 73–99.

53. JS, "Illustrated Catalogue of the Collections Obtained from the Indians of New Mexico and Arizona in 1879."

54. MCS, "Zuni and the Zunians," 1–2.

55. Ibid., 3–30; see McFeely, *Zuni and the American Imagination*, 50–53.

56. Morgan, *Houses and House-Life of the American Aborigines*, 137–40.

57. Moore, *Picturesque Washington*, 242–43; Keim, *Keim's Illustrated Hand-Book*, xv–xvi; Hinman, *The Washington Sketch Book*, 41.

58. *Washington Post*, January 24, 1886; Logan, *Reminiscences of a Soldier's Wife*, 424; Roscoe, *The Zuni Man-Woman*, 58–59.

59. Powell to JS, September 8, 1880, MCS Papers, MS4689, NAA.

60. Samuel B. Holabird to Orlando B. Willcox, July 3, 1880, and Holabird to Alexander McCook, July 31, 1883, MCS Papers, MS4689, NAA.

61. JS to Pilling, September 18, 1880, BAE, LR, JS, NAA; *Santa Fe Daily New Mexican*, September 21, 1880; Bryant, *History of the Atchison, Topeka and Santa Fe Railway*, 62; Lawson, "Baskets, Pots, and Prayer Plumes," 51–56.

62. Tobias and Woodhouse, *Santa Fe,* 14–25.

63. Ibid., 7, 23–24; Wilson, *The Myth of Santa Fe,* 58–60, 66–67; Morand, *Santa Fe,* 10–11, 13, 22, 24–25; Noble, ed., *Santa Fe,* 78, 85, 125, 129, 141–44.

64. Wilson, *The Myth of Santa Fe,* 64–65; Tobias and Woodhouse, *Santa Fe,* 21–23, 69.

65. Fowler, *A Laboratory for Anthropology,* 99–102, 172–73; Bandelier, *The Southwestern Journals of Adolph F. Bandelier, 1880–1882,* 89–90, 178.

66. JS to Pilling, September 22, 1880, and JS to Powell, September [*sic,* should be October] 2, 1880, BAE, LR, JS, NAA; Lawson, "Baskets, Pots, and Prayer Plumes," 20, 60. By the early 1880s, Pueblo Indian women often visited Santa Fe to sell their pottery on the plaza, some of their wares being purchased by the town's early curio dealers. See Batkin, "Tourism is Overrated," 282–83, 286–87, and Lawson, "Baskets, Pots, and Prayer Plumes," 91, 93.

67. JS to Powell, September [*sic,* should be October] 2 and October 16, 1880, BAE, LR, JS, NAA; JS, "Illustrated Catalogue of the Collections Obtained from the Indians of New Mexico in 1880," 426, 429–30; Parezo, "The Formation of Ethnographic Collections," 37–38.

68. JS, "Illustrated Catalogue, 1880," 430; Parezo, "The Formation of Ethnographic Collections," 37; Lawson, "Baskets, Pots, and Prayer Plumes," 65.

69. JS, "Illustrated Catalogue, 1880," 430–32; Parezo, "The Formation of Ethnographic Collections," 37; JS to Powell, October 27, 1880, BAE, LR, JS, NAA; Lawson, "Baskets, Pots, and Prayer Plumes," 68.

70. JS to Pilling, October 15 and 16, 1880, BAE, LR, JS, NAA.

71. JS to Powell, October 27, 1880, and JS to Pilling, October 27, 1880, BAE, JS, LR, NAA; Bandelier, *Journals, 1880–1882,* 178. Jim Stevenson later enlisted Bandelier to purchase Indian artifacts on his behalf (91).

72. JS to Pilling, October 27, 1880, BAE, LR, JS, NAA; JS, "Illustrated Catalogue, 1880," 433; JS, "Report of Explorations in New Mexico and Arizona," 138; Lawson, "Baskets, Pots, and Prayer Plumes," 63, 68, 73, 81. Stevenson reported he had collected twenty-eight hundred objects; Parezo, in "The Formation of Ethnographic Collections," 12, puts the number at two thousand.

73. Bandelier, *Journals, 1880–1882,* 164–65, 169, 181; Bandelier, *The Southwestern Journals of Adolph F. Bandelier, 1889–1892,* 252.

74. Bandelier, *Journals, 1889–1892,* 252. See Green, *Cushing at Zuni,* 305, 317–18.

75. On March 7, 1881, James Stevenson was appointed general assistant in the geological survey at a salary of $3,000; on April 3, 1883, he was named as the survey's executive officer, with no change in salary. Powell's salary, in 1880, as director of the Bureau of Ethnology was $3,600. See document dated May 26, 1911, James Stevenson, Pension Application Files, RG 15, NA. See also Worster, *A River Running West,* 393–94, 419–20; Judd, *The Bureau of American Ethnology,* 13.

76. Lawson, "Baskets, Pots, and Prayer Plumes," 116–20.

77. Powell to JS, July 20, 1881, MCS Papers, MS4689, NAA; Green, *Cushing at Zuni*, 175; Fowler, *A Laboratory for Anthropology*, 140.

78. JS to Powell, November 3, 1881, BAE, LR, JS, NAA; Green, *Cushing at Zuni*, 175.

79. Osborn, *Cope: Master Naturalist*, 295–96.

80. Ibid; JS to Powell, October 12 and November 3, 1881, BAE, LR, JS, NAA; Holmes, "In Memoriam, Matilda Coxe Stevenson," 553.

81. JS to Powell, October 12, 1881, and November 3, 1881, BAE, LR, JS, NAA; BE, *Third AR*, 1881–82, xx–xxi; McNitt, *The Indian Traders*, 178.

82. Undated newspaper clipping entitled "The Cliff Dwellers and Their Descendants," found in James Stevenson Scrapbook, Museum of Indian Arts and Culture/Laboratory of Anthropology [hereafter, James Stevenson Scrapbook]. For a detailed account of factionalism at Oraibi and Oraibi responses to outsiders, see Whiteley, *Deliberate Acts*.

83. JS to Powell, November 10, 1881, BAE, LR, JS, NAA; BE, *Third AR*, 1881–82, xx–xxi; JS, "Illustrated Catalogue of the Collections Obtained from the Pueblos of Zuni, New Mexico, and Wolpi, Arizona, in 1881," 517.

84. Hart, "Protection of Kolhu/wala:wa ('Zuni Heaven')," 199–201; Green, *Cushing at Zuni*, 140, 343–44. See also Wilson, "Cushing at Zuni: Another View," 141–46.

85. MCS, "The Zuni Indians," 154–55. Tilly makes no mention of taking religious objects from the shrine, although E. Richard Hart asserts that she did. Hart, "Protection of Kolhu/wala:wa," 200.

86. Merrill and Ahlborn, "Zuni Archangels and Ahayu:da," 181–84, 194.

87. Ibid., 184–94. See also Cain, "God, Grace, and Government," Ph.D. diss., 182–92. In recent years the Zunis successfully campaigned to have these Ahayu:da returned to the pueblo.

88. Porter, *Paper Medicine Man*, 112–23; Green, *Cushing at Zuni*, 142, 183–85.

89. JS to Powell, December 3, 1881, BAE, LR, JS, NAA; Green, *Cushing at Zuni*, 200. Jim does not mention Tilly by name in his report to Powell. Because we know she accompanied him to Hopi during this expedition, it is safe to assume she was with him on both visits to Hopi during this field season.

90. It is not known when Jim Stevenson joined the Anthropological Society of Washington. However, his name appears on a membership list dated September 18, 1882. *Transactions of the Anthropological Society of Washington*, 19. See also Lamb, "The Story of the Anthropological Society of Washington," 564–79.

91. Undated newspaper clipping written by "Miss Grundy," James Stevenson Scrapbook; Hart, *Pedro Pino*, 119–22; Green, *Cushing at Zuni*, 218, 264.

92. Undated newspaper clipping written by "Miss Grundy," James Stevenson Scrapbook.

93. BE, *Fourth AR*, 1882–83, xxxiv; JS to Spencer F. Baird, August 24, 1882, BAE, LR, JS, NAA; R. S. Mackenzie to C. O., Fort Wingate, September 2, 1882, MCS Papers, MS4689, NAA; *Santa Fe New Mexican*, August 25 and September 10 and 19, 1882; Jones, *John A. Logan*, 147, 154, 158–60.

94. *Santa Fe New Mexican*, September 10 and 19, 1882; *Eureka Herald* (Kansas), September 28, 1882. The Santa Fe newspaper and dates on photographs taken by Ben Wittick of the Logan party show that the Logans stayed at Zuni September 14–19. Hieb, personal communication. Documents pertaining to the so-called Logan land-grab scheme can be found in Fay, *Treaties, Land Cessions, and Other U.S. Congressional Documents*, part I, 18–55. See also Green, *Cushing at Zuni*, 261–334. Although Tilly Stevenson had little to do with the land-grab scheme, James Stevenson, in a rare lapse of judgment, sided with the Logan party and against the best interests of the Zunis. In reporting on water issues on the Zuni reservation at the request of Secretary of the Interior Henry Teller, Jim suggested, in a letter written in April 1884, that the land in question be taken from the Zunis and a dam be erected a few miles above the pueblo on the Zuni River to make up for the loss of Nutria Spring. Teller concluded from Jim's report that the Zunis made no use of water from Nutria Spring—a preposterous supposition. Fay, *Treaties, Land Cessions, and Other U.S. Congressional Documents*, part I, 22–25, 48.

One of Logan's accusers, W. E. Curtis, a Chicago newspaperman friendly to Frank H. Cushing, asserted in the Chicago *Inter-Ocean* that the senator's interpreter had "understood little if any of [the Zuni] language." Given his antipathy to Logan and given Tilly's determination to understand the Zunis, it seems likely that by 1882 she had acquired a working knowledge of the language. According to her husband, by the end of 1884 she had become fluent in both Zuni and Spanish. Green, *Cushing at Zuni*, 283, 327. A more accurate description might be that of a Washington reporter, who in 1886 avowed that "Mrs. Stevenson speaks the Zuni language well enough to make herself understood." *Washington National Tribune*, May 20, 1886.

95. *Eureka Herald*, November 2, 1882; JS, AR, 1882, located in the John P. Harrington Papers, NAA; Hieb, personal communication. For the best account of James Stevenson's exploration of Canyon de Chelly, see Hieb, "'The Flavor of Adventure Now Rare,'" 205–48. I am indebted to Lou Hieb for allowing me to read his essay before it was published. Since chronologies of the Canyon de Chelly expedition, as found in the accounts by James Stevenson and Rizer, are sometimes at odds, I have relied on the one that Hieb believes is correct.

96. *Eureka Herald*, November 2, 1882; JS, AR, 1882, John P. Harrington Papers, NAA. Stevenson's report for 1882 was published as "Ancient Habitations of the Southwest."

97. *Eureka Herald*, November 2, 1882; JS, AR, 1882, John P. Harrington Papers, NAA.

98. *Eureka Herald,* November 2, 1882. The Navajo guide named George received two dollars a day for his services from October 7 to October 27. Lawson, "Baskets, Pots, and Prayer Plumes," 167.

99. JS, AR, 1882, John P. Harrington Papers, NAA; *Eureka Herald,* November 2, 1882.

100. JS, AR, 1882, John P. Harrington Papers, NAA; *Eureka Herald,* November 9 and 16, 1882.

101. JS, AR, 1882, John P. Harrington Papers, NAA.

102. BE, *Fourth AR,* 1882–83, xxxvi; JS, AR, 1882, John P. Harrington Papers, NAA; *Eureka Herald,* November 23, 1882.

103. JS, AR, 1882, John P. Harrington Papers, NAA; BE, *Fourth AR,* 1882–83, xxxvi; Bandelier, *Journals, 1880–1882,* 358; Green, *Cushing at Zuni,* 247–48; clipping, *Denver Daily Times,* December 12, 1882, James Stevenson Scrapbook.

104. Ten Kate, *Travels and Researches in Native North America,* 261.

105. BE, *Fifth AR,* 1883–84, xxiii–xxiv; JS to Powell, September 20, 1883, BAE, LR, JS, NAA; "Washington's Women of Science," William H. Holmes, LR, MS4745, NAA (copy, courtesy of Nancy J. Parezo); Foote, *Women of the New Mexico Frontier,* 128; Lawson, "Baskets, Pots, and Prayer Plumes," 196, 202.

106. BE, *Fifth AR,* 1883–84, l–li; MCS, "The Religious Life of the Zuni Child," 533–55; Mead and Bunzel, eds., *The Golden Age of American Anthropology,* 205.

107. Clarence E. Dutton to JS, September 30, [1884], MCS Papers, MS4689, NAA; JS to Powell, October 1, 1884, BAE, LR, JS, NAA; MCS, "The Religious Life of the Zuni Child," 539–40; Parezo, "Matilda Coxe Stevenson," 54.

108. Tylor, "How the Problems of American Anthropology Present Themselves to the English Mind," 550.

109. MCS, "The Religious Life of the Zuni Child," 542; MCS, "The Zuni Indians," 354–58; *New York Times,* January 3, 1885.

110. MCS, "The Zuni Indians," 358; BE, *Sixth AR,* 1884–85, xxix, xlix. The bureau planned to exhibit the Stevensons' collection at the World's Industrial and Cotton Exposition in New Orleans (1884–85). But the collection did not arrive in Washington in time, and items already in the National Museum were forwarded to New Orleans instead. BE, *Sixth AR,* 1884–85, xlix. The number of artifacts collected at Zuni is from Parezo, "The Formation of Ethnographic Collections," 38–39 (see also 13).

111. *Santa Fe New Mexican,* September 13 and 20, and December 9, 1884. The identity of these children is not known. Tilly later stated that she enrolled Nina, the granddaughter of Nai'uchi, in the government school at Zuni, "exacting a promise from Nai'uchi that he would compel her regular attendance." MCS, "The Zuni Indians," 314, 382. See Simmons, *Albuquerque,* 309.

112. For more about changes brought about in Indian groups by anthropologists, see Parezo, "Now Is the Time to Collect," 11–18; Parezo, "The Formation of Ethnographic Collections," 1–47.

113. Faris, *The Nightway*, 40; Parezo, "Matthews and the Discovery of Navajo Drypaintings," 53–54, 57, 71n8.

114. I am grateful to Nancy J. Parezo for providing me a copy of James Stevenson's lecture, entitled "Zuni Sand Altars." The original is in the John P. Harrington Papers, NAA. See also Parezo, "Matilda Coxe Stevenson," 54–55.

115. BE, *Seventh AR*, 1885–86, xviii–xxiv; *Albuquerque Morning Journal*, August 30, 1885.

116. BE, *Seventh AR*, 1885–86, xxv; JS, "Ceremonial of Hasjelti Dailjis and Mythical Sand Painting of the Navajo Indians," 229–85 [quote is on 235]; Powell to Teller, January 21, 1902, BAE, LR, MCS, NAA; Hieb, "Alexander M. Stephen and the Navajos," 365–66; Hieb, personal communication. I am indebted to Louis A. Hieb for sharing his research materials and insight into Tilly Stevenson's authorship of the Nightway article.

117. Hinsley, *Savages and Scientists*, 197; Faris, *The Nightway*, 8, 40–42. See also Parezo, "Matthews and the Discovery of Navajo Drypaintings," 71n8.

118. Hieb, personal communication; Alexander M. Stephen to Jesse W. Fewkes, October 11, 1893, MS4408, NAA, courtesy of Louis A. Hieb; Faris, *The Nightway*, 42.

119. Catalogue of Ethnological and Archaeological Collections from Hopi Pueblos, October–November 1885, MS 775, NAA. The ornate handwriting in this catalogue appears to be Tilly Stevenson's. See similar ornately written captions in the James Stevenson Scrapbook, which Tilly must have kept, rather than Jim— known as a man of action, not a man who bothered with scrapbooks.

120. Parezo, "Cushing as Part of the Team," 768–71.

121. *Washington Post*, February 15, 1886; *New York Times*, February 15, 1886.

122. Cushing, Fewkes, and Parsons, "Contributions to Hopi History," 273. The caricature of the Stevensons is reproduced in Babcock and Parezo, *Daughters of the Desert*, 11. See also Lurie, "Women in Early American Anthropology," 59–60; Parezo, "Matilda Coxe Stevenson," 46–47.

123. See Parezo, "Matilda Coxe Stevenson," 53–57; Rossiter, *Women Scientists in America*, 80–82.

Chapter 4

1. Roscoe, *The Zuni Man-Woman*, 2, 53–62, 236n2; *Washington Evening Star*, March 27, 1885; *Albuquerque Morning Journal*, December 5, 1885; Boyd, *Boyd's Directory of the District of Columbia*, 1886. Roscoe presents the most comprehensive and sensitive account of We'wha's life.

2. Parezo, "Matilda Coxe Stevenson," 55. Rossiter points out that numerous "all-women scientific clubs" existed from the 1840s to the end of the century, but members appear mainly to have been women pursuing hobbies "outside the home" and not professional women. Rossiter, *Women Scientists in America*, 75.

3. Lurie, "Women in Early American Anthropology," 36; "Women Who Serve Science, the Minervas of Washington," *Washington Evening Star,* July 6, 1889.

4. *Washington Post,* January 31, 1886; *Washington Evening Star,* February 13, 1886; McGee, "The Women's Anthropological Society of America," 240–42; "Women Who Serve Science," *Washington Evening Star,* July 6, 1889; Moldow, *Women Doctors in Gilded-Age Washington,* 148–49.

5. *Washington Post,* January 31, 1886; *Washington Evening Star,* February 13, 1886.

6. Dr. D. Willard Bliss was the chief physician who attended President James A. Garfield after he had been shot. William J. McGee signed all of his letters and was known professionally as W J McGee (without periods behind the initials). "Women Who Serve Science," *Washington Evening Star,* July 6, 1889; Moldow, *Women Doctors in Gilded-Age Washington,* 127, 148–49; Hinsley, *Savages and Scientists,* 233; "The Sofie Nordhoff-Jung Papers," Special Collections, Georgetown University; May, "The Women's Anthropological Society," M.A. thesis, 41.

7. *Organization and Historical Sketch of the Women's Anthropological Society of America,* 13–15; *Washington Post,* January 31, 1886; Moldow, *Women Doctors in Gilded-Age Washington,* 11, 148–49; May, "The Women's Anthropological Society," 40–47; Kate Field to MCS, February 6, 1887, MCS Papers, MS4689, NAA; Moss, ed., *Kate Field, Selected Letters,* xi, xvii–xxx. Some sources state that WASA member Emma Hammond Ward was wife of Lester Frank Ward, a scientist with the U.S. Geological Survey who became one of the nation's leading sociologists. This assertion is incorrect. Ward's first wife died in 1872, and his second, Rose Simons Pierce, whom he married soon after the death of his first wife, was still alive in 1908. See Scott, *Lester Frank Ward,* 25–26, 38.

8. McGee, "The Women's Anthropological Society of America," 240–42; *Washington Post,* January 24, 1886; *Washington Evening Star,* February 13, 1886.

9. *Washington Evening Star,* March 31, 1886; *Washington Post,* April 1, 1886; Roscoe, *The Zuni Man-Woman,* 61.

10. Lurie, "Women in Early American Anthropology," 36–37; McGee, "The Women's Anthropological Society of America," 240–42; May, "The Women's Anthropological Society," 45–48; Parezo, "Matilda Coxe Stevenson," 55–56, 61n14.

11. Jayanti, "Erminnie Adelle Platt Smith (1836–1886)," 327–30; BE, *First AR,* 1879–80, xxii; Lurie, "Women in Early American Anthropology," 40–43; Hough, "Erminnie Adelle Platt Smith," 262.

12. Mark, *A Stranger in Her Native Land,* 3–4, 34–39, 45–73; Temkin, "Alice Cunningham Fletcher (1838–1923)," 95–101.

13. Roscoe, *The Zuni Man-Woman,* 56, 59; *Washington Evening Star,* June 12, 1886; MCS, "The Zuni Indians," 130, 312.

14. As quoted in Roscoe, *The Zuni Man-Woman,* 56. See also 54.

15. *Washington Evening Star,* June 12, 1886.

16. Roscoe, *The Zuni Man-Woman,* 61–62; Mason, "The Planting and Exhuming of a Prayer," 24–25; *Washington Evening Star,* June 12, 1886.

17. MCS, "The Zuni Indians," 20, 310; *Washington National Tribune,* May 20, 1886.

18. *Washington National Tribune,* May 20, 1886; Roscoe, *The Zuni Man-Woman,* 69, 90. Unlike Tilly Stevenson, Roscoe uses the masculine pronoun when referring to We'wha. Mason, "Planting and Exhuming of a Prayer," 24–25.

19. *Washington National Tribune,* May 20, 1886.

20. Ibid.; *Washington Post,* May 30, 1886.

21. *Washington Post,* May 9 and 14, 1886; *Washington Evening Star,* May 14, 1886.

22. *Washington Post,* May 9 and 14, 1886; *Washington Evening Star,* May 14, 1886; McFeely, *Zuni and the American Imagination,* 70–71. The second performance of the Kirmes occurred the evening of May 14, followed by a matinee the next day. The event raised $5,000 for the hospital. *Washington Post,* May 15 and 30, 1886.

23. Lurie, "Women in Early American Anthropology," 57; Roscoe, *The Zuni Man-Woman,* 46, 52–54; Parezo, "Matilda Coxe Stevenson," 47.

24. MCS, "The Zuni Indians," 310; Roscoe, *The Zuni Man-Woman,* 235n67.

25. *Washington Evening Star,* June 12, 1886.

26. Will Roscoe reproduces Stevenson's letter to Cleveland's secretary in *The Zuni Man-Woman,* 70.

27. *Washington Post,* June 24, 1886.

28. Roscoe, *The Zuni Man-Woman,* 73.

29. *Washington Evening Star,* December 12, 1885, and February 9, 1886; *Washington Post,* January 24, 1886.

30. McNitt, *The Indian Traders,* 187, 192–97; Graves, *Thomas Varker Keam,* 145–46, 179–86, 289n47; "A Petition Signed by Twenty Hopi Indians," MS3967, NAA; Fowler, *A Laboratory for Anthropology,* 138–39; Hieb, "A Question of Authorship," 410–12.

31. JS, "Annual Report," [1886–87], MS4734, NAA. Tilly stated that she visited Zuni "about two months after" We'wha returned to her home, which would have occurred sometime in late summer or early fall, 1886. MCS, "The Zuni Indians," 130.

32. Untitled manuscript on Mission Indians, in box labeled M. C. Stevenson, located in the John P. Harrington Papers, NAA.

33. JS, "Annual Report," [1887–88], located in the J. P. Harrington Papers, NAA, copy courtesy of Nancy Parezo; BE, *Ninth AR,* 1887–88, xxvii–xxix; Worster, *A River Running West,* 409; Fernlund, *William Henry Holmes,* 124, 250n59. Jim did not mention Tilly in his annual report for 1887–88, but other documents place her at his side during their field season in New Mexico. With her experience on horseback, it is logical to assume that she went into the Jemez Mountains with Jim and Powell.

34. Fernlund, *William Henry Holmes,* 116, 124; Fernlund, personal communication; Holmes, "In Memoriam, Matilda Coxe Stevenson," 557.

35. JS, "Annual Report," [1887–88], J. P. Harrington Papers, NAA.

36. Ibid.; MCS, "The Sia," 9–12, 89–91. Anthropologists in Stevenson's era referred to Zia Pueblo as Sia.

37. *Washington National Tribune*, August 2, 1888; Powell, "James Stevenson," 44; Boyd, *Boyd's Directory of the District of Columbia*, 1888.

38. MCS, "Zuni Religion," 136–37.

39. Mark, *Stranger in Her Native Land*, 142–43; Parezo, "Matilda Coxe Stevenson," 60n5; Thompson, "Edgar Lee Hewett and the Political Process," 276; Fletcher, "On the Preservation of Archaeologic Monuments," 317; Fletcher and Stevenson, "Report of the Committee on the Preservation of Archaeologic Remains on the Public Lands," 35–37; MCS to G. H. Van Stone, June 15, 1914, MCS Papers, MS4689, NAA. Part of the proposed area for the National Park of the Cliff Cities later became what we know today as Bandelier National Monument.

40. *Washington Post*, July 26–28, 1888; *Washington National Tribune*, August 2, 1888; JS to "My dearest," June 21, 1888, MCS Papers, MS4689, NAA. Other pallbearers were Major William F. Tucker and Samuel F. Emmons.

41. Robert Adams to MCS, [no date], and Otto Gresham to MCS, August 15, 1888, MCS Papers, MS4689, NAA.

42. O. Mason to MCS, July 27, 1888, Charles Walcott to MCS, September 2, 1888, and Louis Sayre to MCS, August 6, 1888, MCS Papers, MS4689, NAA; James Stevenson, Pension Application Files, RG 15, NA. Dr. Sayre was related to Tilly Stevenson through her mother's family. Undated genealogy, MCS Papers, MS4689, NAA.

43. Boyd, *Boyd's Directory of the District of Columbia*, 1889, 1893. After her parents died in the 1890s, Tilly preferred living in boarding houses or hotels, although she retained ownership of the P Street residence for several years. On single women living in boarding houses or apartment-hotels around the turn of the twentieth century, see Wilson, *The American Woman in Transition*, 29.

44. Mason to Samuel P. Langley, November 14, 1888, G. Brown Goode to Langley, November 14, 1888, and Itemized bill of purchase, November 24, 1888, Accession 21664, U.S. National Museum, Accession Records, SIA; Mason, "Report on the Department of Ethnology in the U.S. National Museum, 1889," 281. In 1903, Stevenson sold nine Zuni and Navajo blankets to the National Museum for $550. She had collected these items before 1886. MCS to William H. Holmes, [June] 1903, and Memorandum to Registrar, June 29, 1903, Accession 41372, U.S. National Museum, Accession Records, SIA.

45. Anita McGee to MCS, November 18, 1891, MCS Papers, MS4689, NAA. John Wesley Powell had been out of town when the vote was taken.

46. In 1893, Tilly read a paper on the "Foundation of the Zuni Cult" before a joint meeting of the ASW and the WASA. May, "The Women's Anthropological Society," 49; Parezo, "Matilda Coxe Stevenson," 61n14; Moldow, *Women Doctors in Gilded-Age Washington*, 153. Possibly the ASW also welcomed the women's financial support to help revive its languishing publication program. See May, ibid., 6; Parezo, ibid., 56; and Rohde, "It was No 'Pink Tea,'" 283–86.

47. Certificate of Membership, August 17, 1892, and Stephen Peel to MCS, December 7, 1892, MCS Papers, MS4689, NAA; Mark, *Stranger in Her Native Land*, 19, 84. Several weeks after her election to the AAAS, Stevenson presented a paper at the society's meeting in Rochester, New York. See MCS, "Tusayan Legends of the Snake and Flute People," 258–70.

48. Moldow, *Women Doctors in Gilded-Age Washington*, 154–56; MCS to John E. Watkins, June 15, 1914, MCS Papers, MS4689, NAA.

49. MCS to A. B. Renehan, September 21, 1909, MCS Papers, MS4689, NAA; BE, *Eleventh AR*, 1889–90, xxxix–xli; John W. Powell to Langley, June 30, 1893, and Memorandum of Salaries for 1902–03, Records Relating to the Investigation of the Bureau of American Ethnology, 1903, NAA [hereafter, BAE, 1903 Investigation, NAA]; Powell to Henry M. Teller, January 21, 1902, and MCS to Holmes, June 10, 1904, BAE, LR, MCS, NAA. Other women ethnologists who were not permanent staff members worked for the bureau as collaborators—this included Alice Fletcher and later Frances Densmore. See Judd, *The Bureau of American Ethnology*, 56, and BAE, *Thirtieth AR*, 1908–1909, 10. During the early part of her career, Tilly Stevenson signed her reports as T. E. Stevenson, but soon after she was hired by the bureau, she began signing business letters as M. C. Stevenson or Matilda Coxe Stevenson. Her correspondents also addressed their letters to Mrs. Stevenson. Even such friends as Anita Newcomb McGee and Sofie Nordhoff-Jung addressed their letters to Mrs. Stevenson. Yet her aunt and sister Betty (and probably other relatives) continued to address her as Tilly. I have chosen to refer to her in this more familiar manner, as this is how many of her associates, I believe, continued to think of her.

50. Powell to MCS, March 15, 1890, BAE, LR, MCS, NAA.

51. MCS to Powell, April 29, 1890, BAE, LR, MCS, NAA. May Clark's story, as recounted by Matthew W. Stirling, who became chief of the bureau in 1928, when Clark still worked there, is found in Lurie, "Women in Early American Anthropology," 60–61. Clark related several Stevenson anecdotes to Stirling, but what she personally thought of the ethnologist is unknown.

52. MCS, "The Sia," 15.

53. Ibid., 130–31.

54. Ibid., 132–43; White, *Zia—The Sun Symbol Pueblo*, 5. White's book originally was titled *The Pueblo of Sia, New Mexico* (Washington, D.C.: GPO, 1962).

55. MCS, "The Sia," 97–101.

56. Ibid., 21–29, 78. Stevenson was grateful for Clark's assistance, especially in her efforts to take photographs by flashlight. "The writer is pleased to congratulate Miss Clark," Tilly wrote, "for having succeeded under the most trying circumstances." Ibid., 78.

57. MCS to Powell, July 7, 1890, BAE, LR, MCS, NAA.

58. Elsie Clews Parsons, an ethnologist who followed in Stevenson's footsteps, also used this technique when she worked among the Rio Grande pueblos in the 1920s. See Parsons, *Tewa Tales*, x–xi; Zumwalt, *Wealth and Rebellion*, 243–45.

59. BE, *Eleventh AR*, 1889–90, xxx; BE, *Twelfth AR*, 1890–91, xxix; MCS, "The Sia," 3–157; Powell to MCS, June 15, 1891, MCS Papers, MS4689, NAA.

60. BE, *Eleventh AR*, 1889–90, xl–xli; Powell to Robert Adams, January 25, 1902, Samuel P. Langley, Incoming Correspondence, SIA; MCS, "The Sia," 3–157; Parezo, "Matilda Coxe Stevenson," 43.

61. MCS, "The Sia," 3–157 (for direct quotations, see 9, 22); White, *Zia*, 2. On allowing Indian voices to appear in the text, see Lamphere's introduction to "Women, Anthropology, Tourism, and the Southwest," and "Gladys Reichard Among the Navajo," 8, 95–96.

62. MCS, "The Sia," 12–16, 67, 140–43.

63. Daniel G. Brinton to MCS, June 18, 1895, MCS Papers, MS4689, NAA.

64. Fowler, *A Laboratory for Anthropology*, 161–62; Fewkes, "A Comparison of Sia and Tusayan Snake Ceremonials," 118, 121, 129–35, 140–41; Hieb, personal communication.

65. MCS to J. Walter Fewkes, [no date], MCS Papers, MS4689, NAA; Fewkes, "Tusayan Snake Ceremonies," 305, 309. Leslie A. White, who studied at Zia periodically over several years, stated in his monograph on this pueblo, published in 1962, that to learn anything about its culture, it was necessary for him to interview informants away from the village—as Tilly had done years before. He also offered a balanced critique of Stevenson's "The Sia," calling it "an excellent work in many respects." He agreed with Fewkes that her account of the initiation ceremony of the Snake Society (which she obtained from an informant) was "quite incomprehensible." Yet "her description of the esoteric ceremonies which she witnessed are vivid and detailed; they have not been duplicated in studies of the Keres [Acoma, Cochiti, Laguna, San Felipe, Santa Ana, Santo Domingo, and Zia] and they probably never will be repeated." White, *Zia*, 2–7.

66. BE, *Thirteenth AR*, 1891–92, xxx–xxxi; MCS, "The Zuni Indians," 57, 180–81.

67. MCS, "The Zuni Indians," 204.

68. Cushing, Fewkes, and Parsons, "Contributions to Hopi History," 273; Bandelier, *The Southwestern Journals of Adolph F. Bandelier, 1880–1882*, 29–30; Lawson, "Baskets, Pots, and Prayer Plumes," 78; Parezo, "Matthews and the Discovery of Navajo Drypaintings," 58; Rohner, "Franz Boas, Ethnographer on the Northwest Coast," 164–67, 172; Lurie, "Relations Between Indians and Anthropologists," 548.

69. MCS, "The Zuni Indians," 579–86.

70. Ibid., 253, 256.

71. Ibid., 250–54, 256–83.

72. Ibid., 463; Roscoe, *The Zuni Man-Woman*, 48. For an interesting account of Stevenson's "pioneering" use of the camera to produce "detailed, almost film-like photographic sequences" of Indian activities, see Isaac, "Re-Observation and the Recognition of Change."

73. Hart, *Pedro Pino*, 177n351; Hinsley, *Savages and Scientists*, 199.

74. BE, *Thirteenth AR*, 1891–92, xxxviii.

75. MCS to L. Bradford Prince, December 28, 1892, and January 10, 1893, NMSRCA, L. Bradford Prince, LR, Territorial Archives of New Mexico, microfilm rolls 112–13; MCS, "The Zuni Indians," 392–406.

76. Dorchester, "Report of Superintendent of Indian Schools," 554–55; Green, *Zuni, Selected Writings*, 123–25.

77. MCS, "The Zuni Indians," 397–406.

78. MCS to Prince, December 28, 1892, and January 10, 1893, NMSRCA, L. Bradford Prince, LR, Territorial Archives of New Mexico, rolls 112–13; *Santa Fe Daily New Mexican*, December 21, 1892.

79. Roscoe, *The Zuni Man-Woman*, 98–110.

80. Fowler, *A Laboratory for Anthropology*, 206–207; U.S. National Museum, *AR*, June 30, 1893, 86–95, 333–34.

81. Fowler, *A Laboratory for Anthropology*, 204–209; Rydell, *All the World's a Fair*, 39–41, 46–47; U.S. National Museum, *AR*, June 30, 1893, 109.

82. U.S. National Museum, *AR*, June 30, 1893, 108–14; BE, *Fifteenth AR*, 1893–94, xxiv; MCS to Virginia Meredith, June 15, 1893, MCS Papers, MS4689, NAA.

83. Fowler, *A Laboratory for Anthropology*, 211; Sewall, ed., *The World's Congress of Representative Women*, v, xix, 6–7, 932; Mrs. James P. Eagle to MCS, April 18, 1893, MCS Papers, MS4689, NAA; MCS, "The Zuni Scalp Ceremonial," 484–87; Weimann, *The Fair Women*, 545–46.

84. *Washington Post*, July 30, 1893; Powell to Adams, January 25, 1902 (containing an extract of MCS to McGee, dated September 1, 1893), Samuel P. Langley, Incoming Correspondence, SIA; Wake, ed., *Memoirs of the International Congress of Anthropology*, vii, xv; MCS, "A Chapter of Zuni Mythology," 312–19; Fowler, *A Laboratory for Anthropology*, 212. Cushing himself often suffered debilitating illnesses, yet his death in April 1900 came after he choked on a fishbone. Green, *Cushing at Zuni*, 26.

85. BE, *Fifteenth AR*, 1893–94, xxii–lxxxvii.

86. *Washington Post*, June 23, 1893; Worster, *A River Running West*, 523–24, 534, 536–37.

87. Testimony of MCS, July 14, 1903, BAE, 1903 Investigation, NAA; Worster, *A River Running West*, 537–38; BAE, *Sixteenth AR*, 1894–95, lvi; BAE, *Seventeenth AR*, 1895–96, liv; W J McGee to Langley, February 21 and March 13, 1902, Samuel P. Langley, Incoming Correspondence, SIA.

88. Theodosia to Dearest Sister, June 14 and September 18, 1894, MCS Papers, MS4689, NAA; undated family documents, ibid.

89. Powell to Adams, January 25, 1902 (containing an extract of MCS to Powell, dated January 1, 1896), Samuel P. Langley, Incoming Correspondence, SIA.

90. Worster, *A River Running West*, 559–60, 564.

91. BAE, *Eighteenth AR*, 1896–97, xxvii–xxviii; Goode to MCS, June 26, 1896, U.S. National Museum, Accession Records, SIA; McGee to Powell, July 10, 1896,

and Testimony of MCS, July 14, 1903, BAE, 1903 Investigation, NAA; MCS, "The Zuni Indians," 19.

92. MCS, "The Zuni Indians," 116, 173; Merrill and Ahlborn, "Zuni Archangels and Ahayu:da," 191–93.

93. MCS, "The Zuni Indians," 297–303.

94. The following section on We'wha's illness and death is based on MCS, "The Zuni Indians," 310–13. See also Roscoe, *The Zuni Man-Woman,* 123.

95. MCS, "The Zuni Indians," 243; MCS to McGee, January 12 and 26, 1897, BAE, LR, MCS, NAA; BAE, *Eighteenth AR,* 1896–97, xxvii–xxviii, xxxii–xxxiii.

96. The best account of events that transpired at Zuni during 1897–98 is Roscoe's *The Zuni Man-Woman,* 111–20. Besides witchcraft, other issues disrupting Zuni society included the government's assimilation policies, forced enrollment of Indian children in schools, and attempts to stamp out Indian ceremonials that Euro-Americans found tasteless or lewd. On witchcraft, see Parezo, "Matilda Coxe Stevenson," 48–49; Foote, *Women of the New Mexico Frontier,* 132–35. See also MCS, "The Zuni Indians," 317, 406; Eggan and Pandey, "Zuni History, 1850–1970," 477.

97. MCS to McGee, January 20, 1897, February 18, 1897, and MCS to Powell, August 15, 1900, BAE, LR, MCS, NAA; Powell to Adams, January 25, 1902 (containing extracts of MCS to Powell, [February 1897], MCS to [name not given], March 1, 1897), Samuel P. Langley, Incoming Correspondence, SIA; BAE, *Nineteenth AR,* 1897–98, xxvii–xxviii.

98. MCS to McGee, July 17, 1898, BAE, LR, MCS, NAA; MCS to G. K. Gilbert, [1898], MCS Papers, MS4689, NAA; MCS, "Zuni Ancestral Gods and Masks," 33–40; BAE, *Twentieth AR,* 1898–99, xxii; BAE, *Twenty-first AR,* 1899–1900, xxx; BAE, *Twenty-second AR,* 1900–1901, xxxvi; Parezo, "Matilda Coxe Stevenson," 56.

99. Powell to Adams, January 25, 1902, Samuel P. Langley, Incoming Correspondence, SIA; Showalter, *The Female Malady,* 121–44; Haller, Jr., and Haller, *The Physician and Sexuality in Victorian America,* 5–11, 28–29.

100. MCS to Powell, August 15, 1900, BAE, LR, MCS, NAA.

101. Ibid.

102. Parezo, "Matilda Coxe Stevenson," 43. Parezo notes that "government employees had no paid sick leave at this time."

Chapter 5

1. MCS to John W. Powell, June 3, 1901, BAE, LR, MCS, NAA.

2. W J McGee to MCS, June 5, 1901, and MCS to McGee, June 6, 1901, BAE, LR, MCS, NAA; Frederick W. Hodge to Samuel P. Langley, November 28, 1901, Samuel P. Langley, Incoming Correspondence, SIA.

3. MCS to McGee, June 6, 1901, BAE, LR, MCS, NAA; Exhibit F, List of Manuscripts Purchased, BAE, 1903 Investigation, NAA; Parezo, "Matilda Coxe Stevenson," 44; Noelke, "The Origin and Early History of the Bureau of American Ethnology," Ph.D. diss., 75–78.

4. Powell to MCS, June 20, 1901, and Hodge to Langley, November 28, 1901, Samuel P. Langley, Incoming Correspondence, SIA.

5. MCS to Powell, June 23, 1901, BAE, LR, MCS, NAA.

6. Hodge to Langley, November 28, 1901, Samuel P. Langley, Incoming Correspondence, SIA; Testimony of Matilda Coxe Stevenson, July 14, 1903, BAE, 1903 Investigation, NAA.

7. R. Rathbun to McGee, July 24, 1901, and Rathbun to MCS, July 24, 1901, BAE, LR, MCS, NAA; Testimony of Matilda Coxe Stevenson, July 14, 1903, BAE, 1903 Investigation, NAA.

8. MCS to Director of the Bureau of Ethnology, July 31, 1901, BAE, LR, MCS, NAA.

9. Hodge to Langley, November 28, 1901, and MCS to Langley, December 24, 1901, Samuel P. Langley, Incoming Correspondence, SIA.

10. McGee to Langley, February 17, 1902, Samuel P. Langley, Incoming Correspondence, SIA; MCS to Director of the Bureau of Ethnology, January 9 and 13, 1902, BAE, LR, MCS, NAA.

11. Powell to MCS, January 21 and 25, 1902, and Langley to Powell, January 25, 1902, BAE, LR, MCS, NAA.

12. Powell to Henry M. Teller, January 21, 1902, BAE, LR, MCS, NAA; Powell to Robert Adams, January 25, 1902, Samuel P. Langley, Incoming Correspondence, SIA; Worster, *A River Running West*, 567–68. In his masterful biography of Powell, Worster does not explore in detail Powell's complex relationship with Stevenson.

13. Hinsley, *Savages and Scientists*, 237, 249; Fernlund, *William Henry Holmes*, 175–78. Twice in 1903, Langley's airplane was catapulted into the air, only to plunge directly into the Potomac. In December of that same year, the Wright brothers made history with the flight of their plane. According to Fernlund, "Langley was devastated [by his failure] and died three years later." Fernlund, *William Henry Holmes*, 176.

14. Langley to Adams, February 14, 1902, Samuel P. Langley, Incoming Correspondence, SIA.

15. McGee to Frank Russell, January 3, May 27, and October 18, 1901, and January 31, 1902, and Director of the Bureau of Ethnology to Langley, May 20, 1902, BAE, 1903 Investigation, NAA; BAE, *Twenty–third AR*, 1901–1902, xvii–xviii; Parezo, "Matilda Coxe Stevenson," 44; Fowler, *A Laboratory for Anthropology*, 321–22. Russell died in Kingman, Arizona (after having contracted tuberculosis), in November 1903. Fowler, 322. Russell's "The Pima Indians" appeared in BAE, *Twenty-sixth AR*, 1904–1905, 3–389.

16. McGee to MCS, March 14, 1902, and Testimony of Matilda Coxe Stevenson, July 14, 1903, BAE, 1903 Investigation, NAA.

17. MCS to Director of the Bureau of Ethnology, May 13, 1902, BAE, LR, MCS, NAA; Langley to McGee, May 17, 1902, Director of the Bureau of Ethnology

to Langley, May 20, 1902, and Rathbun to Teller, June 21 and 26, 1902, BAE, 1903 Investigation, NAA.

18. Teller to Langley, June 6, 1902 (with enclosures), and Langley to Teller, June [date missing], 1902, Samuel P. Langley, Incoming Correspondence, SIA; Rathbun to Teller, June 21 and 26, 1902, BAE, 1903 Investigation, NAA; Parezo, "Matilda Coxe Stevenson," 45.

19. Rossiter, *Women Scientists in America*, xv–xviii; Parezo, *Hidden Scholars*, 34, 339–42.

20. Washington Matthews to MCS, May 10, 1902, MCS Papers, MS4689, NAA.

21. MCS, "Studies of the Late Washington Matthews," 345; Fowler, *A Laboratory for Anthropology*, 128–32.

22. BAE, *Twenty-fourth AR*, 1902–1903, xiv–xvi. E. Richard Hart questions "whether the esoteric fraternities used different Indian languages." Rather, he writes, "in the kivas, and in important political discussions, the men often used archaic words and archaic phrases." Hart, personal communication.

23. MCS to Director, Bureau of American Ethnology, July 29, 1902, BAE, LR, MCS, NAA; MCS to McGee, August 18, 1902, and MCS to Frank M. Barnett, August 29, 1902, BAE, 1903 Investigation, NAA.

24. MCS to Director, BAE, July 29 and August 30, 1902, BAE, LR, MCS, NAA; MCS, "The Zuni Indians," 357.

25. MCS to Director, BAE, August 30, 1902, BAE, LR, MCS, NAA.

26. MCS to Chief of the Bureau of American Ethnology, [no date, probably November 1902], ibid.; MCS, "The Zuni Indians," 41–43.

27. MCS, "The Zuni Indians," 41–43.

28. Ibid., 390–91.

29. Ibid., 343, 385–86; BAE, *Twenty-fourth AR*, 1902–1903, xvi.

30. MCS to Chief of the Bureau of American Ethnology, [no date, probably November 1902], BAE, LR, MCS, NAA.

31. Worster, *A River Running West*, 537, 569–70; Hinsley, *Savages and Scientists*, 249–53; Fernlund, *William Henry Holmes*, 177–81; Statement of MCS, May 13, 1903, and Testimony of MCS, July 14, 1903, BAE, 1903 Investigation, NAA.

32. Trigger, *A History of Archaeological Thought*, 125; Hinsley, *Savages and Scientists*, 264–69; Fernlund, *William Henry Holmes*, 181–87; Noelke, "The Origin and Early History of the Bureau of American Ethnology," 221–28, 311–13, 322–23; Fowler, *A Laboratory for Anthropology*, 242; Woodbury and Woodbury, "The Rise and Fall of the Bureau of American Ethnology," 284–90.

33. Statement of MCS, May 13, 1903, and Testimony of MCS, July 14, 1903, BAE, 1903 Investigation, NAA; Hinsley, *Savages and Scientists*, 253; Fowler, *A Laboratory for Anthropology*, 145–46.

34. Hinsley, *Savages and Scientists*, 253, 265–74; Fowler, *A Laboratory for Anthropology*, 145–46.

35. Testimony of MCS, July 14, 1903, and Caroline B. Dinwiddie to MCS, February 21, 1902, BAE, 1903 Investigation, NAA.

36. Testimony of MCS, July 14, 1903, BAE, 1903 Investigation, NAA.
37. Ibid.
38. On Stevenson obtaining an office at the bureau, see ibid. See also Powell to MCS, December 5, 1901, Samuel P. Langley, Incoming Correspondence, SIA.
39. MCS, "Zuni Games," 468–97; Culin, "Games of North American Indians," 3–809; Fowler, *A Laboratory for Anthropology*, 228–29.
40. MCS to Langley, March 2, 1904, BAE, LR, MCS, NAA; BAE, *Twenty-fifth AR*, 1903–04, xv–xvi; Smithsonian Institution, *AR*, June 30, 1904, 100; Frederick W. Putnam to MCS [no date], William H. Holmes to MCS, August 2, 1901, and F. W. Clarke to Chairman, Committee on Ethnology, Louisiana Purchase Exposition, August 5, 1901, MCS Papers, MS4689, NAA.
41. Parezo and Troutman, "The 'Shy' Cocopa Go to the Fair," 8; Fowler, *A Laboratory for Anthropology*, 215.
42. BAE, *Twenty-fifth AR*, 1903–04, xi–xvi, xxi–xxii.
43. MCS to Holmes, February 7, March 25, and April 5, 1904, BAE, LR, MCS, NAA.
44. MCS to Holmes, February 7 and 19, April 8, May 14, and June 10, 1904, ibid.
45. MCS to Holmes, February 19 and March 4 and 25, 1904, and MCS to J. B. Clayton, April 1 and 25, 1904, ibid.
46. MCS to Langley, March 2, 1904, and MCS to Holmes, April 5, 1904, ibid.
47. MCS to Holmes, April 3, 12, and 22, and May 14, 1904, ibid.
48. MCS to Holmes, April 5 and 8, 1904, ibid.; MCS to Charles W. Fuergerson, November 18, 1905, MCS Papers, MS4689, NAA.
49. MCS to Holmes, April 5, 8, and 12, 1904, BAE, LR, MCS, NAA.
50. MCS to Holmes, March 6 and April 5, 1904, ibid.; MCS, "The Zuni Indians," 564–66.
51. MCS to Holmes, May 25, 1904, BAE, LR, MCS, NAA.
52. MCS to Holmes, June 30, July 1, and August 30, 1904, ibid.
53. MCS to Holmes, February 19, March 4 and 11, April 5, 8, and 12, and May 25, 26, and 30, 1904, MCS to Langley, March 2, 1904, and MCS to Clayton, April 1, 1904, ibid.; McFeely, *Zuni and the American Imagination*, 111, 128–29, 132–36.
54. MCS to Holmes, April 8 and July 6, 1904 [two letters dated July 6], BAE, LR, MCS, NAA; Parezo, "The Formation of Ethnographic Collections," 40.
55. MCS to Holmes, March 4 and 25, and July 1 and 6, 1904, BAE, LR, MCS, NAA.
56. MCS to Holmes, May 26, 1904, ibid.
57. Ahlstrom and Parezo, eds., "Matilda Coxe Stevenson's 'Dress and Adornment of the Pueblo Indians,'" 299–304.
58. Ibid.; BAE, *Twenty-sixth AR*, 1904–1905, xvii.
59. MCS, "The Zuni Indians," 313.
60. Ibid.; MCS to Holmes, July 8, 1904, BAE, LR, MCS, NAA. Possibly Stevenson presented the gifts to President Roosevelt during her scheduled meeting with

him on January 23, 1904. Secretary to the President to MCS, January 20, 1904, MCS Papers, MS4689, NAA.

61. This description of Nai'uchi's death and attendant rituals is from MCS, "The Zuni Indians," 313–17.

62. MCS to Holmes, June 30 and July 6, 1904 [two letters of the latter date], BAE, LR, MCS, NAA.

63. MCS to Holmes, June 22, 1904, ibid.

64. MCS to Holmes, March 6 and April 12 and 22, 1904, and MCS to Clayton, April 1, 1904, ibid.

65. MCS to Holmes, March 11, 1904, ibid; James Switzer to MCS, January 21, 1906, and James N. Baldwin to MCS, February 2, 1906, MCS Papers, MS4689, NAA; Cottrell, *Roger Nash Baldwin and the American Civil Liberties Union*, 16–17.

66. MCS to Holmes, June 10, 1904, BAE, LR, MCS, NAA; Walcott to MCS, June 29, 1907, MCS Papers, MS4689, NAA.

67. MCS to Clayton, August 11, 1904, and MCS to Holmes, August 31 and [November 10], 1904, BAE, LR, MCS, NAA.

68. MCS to Holmes, [November 10], 1904, ibid.

69. MCS to Clayton, September 19, 1904, and MCS to Holmes, [November 10], 1904, ibid; Fowler, *A Laboratory for Anthropology*, 214–15; Parezo and Troutman, "The 'Shy' Cocopa Go to the Fair," 3–8. For an overview of the Louisiana Purchase Exposition, see Rydell, *All the World's a Fair*, 154–83.

70. BAE, *Twenty-fifth AR*, 1903–04, xi–xiii; MCS to Holmes, April 8, 1904, BAE, LR, MCS, NAA; David Francis to MCS, September 1, 1905, MCS Papers, MS4689, NAA; Parezo, personal communication.

71. BAE, *Twenty-third AR*, 1901–1902, xl; BAE, *Twenty-sixth AR*, 1904–1905, xvii–xviii; BAE, *Twenty-seventh AR*, 1905–1906, 7–8; MCS to Langley, October 11, 1905, MCS Papers, MS4689, NAA.

72. Roscoe, *The Zuni Man-Woman*, 9; Woodbury, "Zuni Prehistory and History to 1850," 473.

73. MCS, "The Zuni Indians," 14–15.

74. Ibid., 15–20.

75. Parezo, "Matilda Coxe Stevenson," 50; MCS, "The Zuni Indians," 19, 608.

76. MCS, "The Zuni Indians," 119–20. The extract is found on 119. Indigenous peoples have often perceived women ethnologists as having a masculine gender. Lavender, *Scientists and Storytellers*, 160–61.

77. MCS, "The Zuni Indians," 293.

78. Ibid., 384–85, 532. For an interesting account of the life of a Zuni woman, see Elsie Clews Parsons, "Waiyautitsa of Zuni, New Mexico," 443–57.

79. MCS, "The Zuni Indians," 295–96.

80. Ibid., 349–54, 361–69.

81. Ibid., 373–77.

82. Ibid., 392–406, 429–38.

83. Ibid., 379–83.

84. Ibid., 381–82.

85. Ibid., 608.

86. Walter Hough to MCS, December 18, 1905, P. C. Warman to MCS, January 27, 1906, George H. Pepper to MCS, February [no date], 1906, and Arnold Hague to MCS, June 5, 1906, MCS Papers, MS4689, NAA.

87. Sofie Nordhoff-Jung to MCS, November 27, 1908, and [date unclear], MCS Papers, MS4689, NAA; Moldow, *Women Doctors in Gilded-Age Washington,* 156.

88. Victoria Siddons to MCS, [December 1910], MCS Papers, MS4689, NAA; Lurie, "Women in Early American Anthropology," 58–59; Parezo, "Matilda Coxe Stevenson," 46.

89. MCS to May Clark, February 26, 1906, and MCS to Holmes, March 12, 1906, BAE, LR, MCS, NAA.

90. Graves, *Thomas Varker Keam,* 168; Zumwalt, *Wealth and Rebellion,* 245, 247.

91. MCS to Holmes, October 6, 1906, BAE, LR, MCS, NAA.

92. Parsons, *Pueblo Indian Religion;* Kroeber, "Zuni Kin and Clan," 39–204. Parsons rarely wrote of Stevenson in the text of *Pueblo Indian Religion,* yet in a single chapter (chapter 4), she cited Stevenson in nearly one hundred footnotes and endnotes. Kroeber, referring to Stevenson as an "indefatigable worker," stated, "I have no information to add to Mrs. Stevenson's truthful description and at some points very full account of the Zuni customs concerned with the house, marriage, and motherhood" (89, 93).

93. Eggan, "One Hundred Years of Ethnology and Social Anthropology," 119–52; Basso, "History of Ethnological Research," 14–21; Eggan and Pandey, "Zuni History, 1850–1970," 475; Brugge, "The Zuni Indians," 75–76; Hart, *Pedro Pino,* 123; Parezo, "Matilda Coxe Stevenson," 58.

94. Foote, *Women of the New Mexico Frontier,* 118, 145–46; Pandey, "Anthropologists at Zuni," 329; Fowler, *A Laboratory for Anthropology,* 116; Tedlock, *The Beautiful and the Dangerous,* 173, 175.

Chapter 6

1. Bodine, ed., "The Taos Blue Lake Ceremony," 91.

2. William H. Holmes to MCS, January 19, 1906, and MCS to Holmes, March 21, 1906, BAE, LR, MCS, NAA; *Santa Fe Daily New Mexican,* February 8, 1906.

3. MCS to Holmes, February 12 and March 21, 1906, BAE, LR, MCS, NAA.

4. For evidence that Stevenson met True in 1904 while visiting Santa Clara, see a three-page report by Matilda Coxe Stevenson (typed, but not by Stevenson), MCS, Miscellaneous ethnographic notes, MS2100, NAA. The "Miss Fuie" in this document is obviously Miss True.

5. MCS to Holmes, March 21, 1906, BAE, LR, MCS, NAA. For population figures, see *Thirteenth Census of the United States, 1910,* vol. 3, *Population,* 167.

6. Waters, *To Possess the Land,* 69–70, 89, 95, 146–47.

7. MCS to Holmes, May 2, 1906, BAE, LR, MCS, NAA.

8. MCS to Holmes, March 15 and May 29, 1906 (with attachment), ibid.; *Santa Fe Daily New Mexican,* February 8, 1906.

9. MCS to Holmes, March 12, 15, and 21, 1906, BAE, LR, MCS, NAA.

10. MCS to May Clark, February 26, 1906, and MCS to Holmes, March 12, 18, and 21 [two letters of this date], 1906, ibid.

11. Clinton J. Crandall to the Governor of Taos, February 27, 1906, Isaac W. Dwire to MCS, March 11, 1906, and MCS to Holmes, March 15, 1906, ibid.

12. MCS to Holmes, March 15 and 18, 1906, ibid.

13. Holmes to MCS, March 28, 1906, MCS Papers, MS4689, NAA.

14. MCS to Holmes, April 7 and 18 and May 2 [two letters of this date] and 29, 1906, BAE, LR, MCS, NAA.

15. MCS to Holmes, May 14 and 29, 1906, ibid.

16. MCS to Holmes, May 29, 1906, ibid.

17. Francis Leupp to MCS, May 30, 1906, and MCS to Holmes, June 12, 1906, ibid.

18. MCS to Holmes, May 14, June 12, and July 3, 1906, ibid.

19. MCS to Holmes, June 12, 1906, ibid.

20. MCS to Holmes, June 15 and 29 and July 12, 1906, ibid.

21. MCS to Holmes, June 12 and 30, 1906, ibid.

22. MCS to Holmes, June 12 and July 3, 1906, ibid.

23. MCS to Holmes, [July] 10, August 21, and September 19, 1906, ibid.

24. Parsons, *Taos Pueblo,* 14; Gordon-McCutchan, *The Taos Indians and the Battle for Blue Lake,* 13.

25. MCS to Holmes, July 12, 1906, BAE, LR, MCS, NAA; Parezo, "Matthews and the Discovery of Navajo Drypaintings," 64; Zumwalt, *Wealth and Rebellion,* 237.

26. MCS to Holmes, June 30, 1906, BAE, LR, MCS, NAA; MCS, "Notes on the Pueblo of Taos," MS4842, NAA. More-recent scholars who have worked at Taos Pueblo state that this tribe has no clans. See Parsons, *Taos Pueblo,* 5, and Bodine, "Taos Pueblo," 260.

27. MCS to Holmes, October 6 and 11, 1906, BAE, LR, MCS, NAA; *La Revista de Taos,* September 28 and October 5, 1906.

28. MCS to Holmes, June 15 and August 21, 1906, BAE, LR, MCS, NAA.

29. MCS to Holmes, June 29 and November 5, 1906, ibid.; Waters, *To Possess the Land,* 6–9, 70–78, 86, 91.

30. Waters, *To Possess the Land,* 91–92, 139; Memorandum of agreement signed by Manby and Hill, dated November 12, 1906, Arthur R. Manby to MCS, December 11, 1909, and undated document showing MCS had acquired twenty thousand shares, MCS Papers, MS4689, NAA; Stevenson to Holmes, April 7 and May 2, 1906, BAE, LR, MCS, NAA.

31. Waters, *To Possess the Land,* 1–4, 92–97, 135–41, 218–26; MCS to A. B. Renehan, April 25, 1910, MCS Papers, MS4689, NAA. For more on Manby and his strange death, see Jenkins, "Arthur Rochford Manby," and Peters, *Headless in Taos.*

32. MCS to Holmes, December 12, 1906, and July 4 and [undated letter, sent with July 4 letter], 1908, BAE, LR, MCS, NAA; Mrs. True to MCS, January 9, 1908, MCS to Mrs. True, [letter fragment, undated] and January 27, 1908, and Renehan to Mrs. True, July 13, 1908, Civil Case no. 6398, Santa Fe County, NMSRCA; Peacock, personal communication; Jacobs, "Clara True and Female Moral Authority," 99–100.

33. MCS to Holmes, November 16 and December 12, 1906, BAE, LR, MCS, NAA. Parsons says the origin of the split dates from at least a century before she did fieldwork in the 1920s. She also notes that in 1897, the progressives made "charges of human sacrifice," presumably against the conservatives, before a lawyer in Santa Fe. Parsons, *Pueblo Indian Religion*, 2:1137–38.

34. MCS to Holmes, November 16 and 19, 1906, BAE, LR, MCS, NAA; BAE, *Twenty-eighth AR*, 1906–1907, 11.

35. MCS to Holmes, October 6 and 17 and November 18, 1906, BAE, LR, MCS, NAA.

36. MCS to Holmes, November 26, 1906, ibid.

37. MCS to Holmes, October 6, November 19 and 26, and December 12, 1906, and January 2 and March 7, 1907, ibid.; BAE, *Twenty-eighth AR*, 1906–1907, 11.

38. MCS to Holmes, December 3 and 27, 1906, and January 2, 1907, BAE, LR, MCS, NAA.

39. MCS to Holmes, February 4, 1907, Holmes to MCS, February 12, 1907, and MCS to Clayton, February 20, 1907, ibid.

40. MCS to Holmes, November 26 and December 3 and 27, 1906, ibid.

41. MCS to Charles W. Fuergerson, November 18, 1905, MCS Papers, MS4689, NAA. For the lyceum movement, see Bode, *The American Lyceum.*

42. See letters by Francis Barnes, dated January 2, 1907, to Bible and Scorer, Redpath Bureau, George W. Britt, and Sue McClary, MCS Papers, MS4689, NAA.

43. Anselm Weber to Hodge, February 11, 1907, and Weber to William H. Ketcham, February 11, 1907, BAE, LR, NAA. For a published account of this controversy—one that sides with Father Weber—see Wilken, *Anselm Weber*, 160–69.

44. Weber to Hodge, February 11, 1907, and Weber to Ketcham, February 11, 1907, BAE, LR, NAA.

45. MCS to Holmes, February 25, 1907, BAE, LR, MCS, NAA.

46. MCS to Holmes, February 25 and 27, 1907, ibid.

47. Wilken, *Anselm Weber*, 168; Eggan and Pandey, "Zuni History, 1850–1970," 478.

48. MCS to Holmes, February 1 and 4 and March 7, 1907, and Holmes to MCS, February 8 and 12, 1907, BAE, LR, MCS, NAA; BAE, *Twenty-eighth AR*, 1906–1907, 11.

49. BAE, *Twenty-eighth AR*, 1906–1907, 11; BAE, *Twenty-ninth AR*, 1907–1908, 11; Curtis to MCS, February 21, 1906, and May 5, 1907, MCS Papers, MS4689, NAA; MCS to Curtis, March 15, 1905, in "Some letters and extracts regarding Mr. Edward S. Curtis and his work," James Stevenson Scrapbook, Museum of

Indian Arts and Culture/Laboratory of Anthropology; Fowler, *A Laboratory for Anthropology*, 323–25.

50. MCS to Charles D. Walcott, November 17, 1908, BAE, LR, MCS, NAA; Curtis, *The North American Indian*; Fowler, *A Laboratory for Anthropology*, 324–25; Sandweiss, *Print the Legend*, 270–71; Lyman, *The Vanishing Race and Other Illusions*. For a balanced account of Curtis and his project, see Gidley, *Edward S. Curtis.*

51. Holmes to MCS, August 15, 1907, MCS to Holmes, August 13 and September 9 and 23, 1907, and July 4, 1908, and MCS to Leupp, December 23, 1908, BAE, LR, MCS, NAA; MCS to F. True, [1908], Civil Case no. 6398, Santa Fe County, NMSRCA; James Stevenson, Pension Application Files, RG 15, NA.

52. *MCS vs. C. True et al.*, August 24, 1908, and C. True to MCS, November 6, 1907, Civil Case no. 6398, Santa Fe County, NMSRCA; MCS to Leupp, December 23, 1908, BAE, LR, MCS, NAA.

53. Receipt signed by C. True, September 25, 1907, and MCS to F. True, November 15, 1907, and January 27, 1908, Civil Case no. 6398, Santa Fe County, NMSRCA; MCS to Holmes, July 4, 1908, and MCS to Leupp, December 23, 1908, BAE, LR, MCS, NAA.

54. C. True to MCS, November 6, 1907, MCS to F. True, January 27, 1908, and MCS to C. True, February 20, 1908, Civil Case no. 6398, Santa Fe County, NMSRCA; MCS to Holmes, July 4, 1908, BAE, LR, MCS, NAA.

55. C. True to MCS, November 6, 1907, Civil Case no. 6398, Santa Fe County, NMSRCA.

56. MCS to C. True, February 20 and March 13, 1908, segment of letter to F. True [no date], and MCS to Charles E. Dagenett, April 20, 1908, Civil Case no. 6398, Santa Fe County, NMSRCA; MCS to Clark, October 27, 1907, BAE, LR, MCS, NAA.

57. Jacobs, "Clara True and Female Moral Authority," 99–100; MCS to C. True, February 20 and March 13, 1908, and MCS to Dagenett, April 30, 1908, Civil Case no. 6398, Santa Fe County, NMSRCA.

58. MCS to C. True, November 15, 1907, and MCS to F. True, January 6, 15, and 27 and [March] 1908, Civil Case no. 6398, Santa Fe County, NMSRCA.

59. F. True to MCS, April 10, 1908, F. True to Mr. Bryan, May 16, 1908, MCS to Lizzie Randall, May 20, 1908, and Randall to MCS, May 26, 1908, Civil Case no. 6398, ibid.

60. MCS to Randall, May 20, 1908, Civil Case no. 6398, ibid; MCS to C. True, May 20, 1908, Civil Case no. 8003, Santa Fe County, NMFJD; BAE, *Twenty-ninth AR*, 1907–1908, 11; Holmes to Stevenson, May 28, 1908, BAE, LR, MCS, NAA.

61. *Santa Fe Daily New Mexican*, June 1 and 3, 1908; Randall to Stevenson, May 26, 1908, Civil Case no. 6398, Santa Fe County, NMSRCA; Renehan to MCS, June 5, 1908, MCS Papers, MS4689, NAA; MCS to Holmes, July 4, 1908, BAE, LR, MCS, NAA.

62. MCS to Holmes, June 15, July 2, and July 4, 1908, BAE, LR, MCS, NAA.

63. MCS to Holmes, July 9 and 31 and September 25, 1908, and November 23, 1909, and Holmes to MCS, July 29, 1908, ibid. Holmes made sure the photographs were sent to Tilly.

64. MCS to Holmes, July 31, October 8, and November 17, 1908, and March 30, 1909, and MCS to Walcott, November 17, 1908, BAE, LR, MCS, NAA.

65. MCS to Holmes, September 5 and November 5, 1908, ibid.

66. MCS to Walcott, November 17, 1908, ibid.

67. MCS to Holmes, January 6 and February 5, 1909, ibid. For the Buffalo Dance, see Sweet, *Dances of the Tewa Pueblo Indians*, 79.

68. MCS to Walcott, November 17, 1908, and February 6, 1909, BAE, LR, MCS, NAA; MCS to Walcott, December 1, 1908, MCS Papers, MS4689, NAA.

69. The quotation by Kroeber is from Deacon, *Elsie Clews Parsons*, 162. See also Zumwalt, *Wealth and Rebellion*, 152, 215–16, 229.

70. C. R. Layton to W. I. Adams, January 9, 1909, Adams to MCS, January 11, 1909, and MCS to Walcott, [no date, 1909], MCS Papers, MS4689, NAA.

71. MCS to Walcott, February 6, 1909, and MCS to Holmes, February 15, March 16 and 30, and December 6, 1909, BAE, LR, MCS, NAA; Mitchell Carroll to MCS, February 3, 1909, Anthropological Society of Washington to MCS, February 18, 1909, and MCS to Holmes, July 14, 1909, MCS Papers, MS4689, NAA.

72. MCS to Walcott, December 21, 1908, BAE, LR, MCS, NAA; Sofie Nordhoff-Jung to MCS, January 31, 1909, MCS Papers, MS4689, NAA.

73. MCS to Holmes, July 14, 1909, MCS Papers, MS4689, NAA; MCS to Walcott, May 21, 1909, and MCS to Holmes, March 30, 1909, BAE, LR, MCS, NAA.

74. MCS to Holmes, February 5 and November 23, 1909, MCS to Walcott, February 6, 1909, and MCS to Clayton, November 24, 1909, BAE, LR, MCS, NAA

75. MCS to Holmes, November 23 and December 23, 1909, and January 24, 1910, and MCS to Hodge, January 3, 1910, ibid.

76. BAE, *Fortieth AR*, 1918–1919, 10; Bodine, "The Taos Blue Lake Ceremony," 91–92, 100.

77. Bodine, "The Taos Blue Lake Ceremony," 92, 100–104; MCS to Holmes, August 21 and October 11, 1906, BAE, LR, MCS, NAA. Stevenson recorded Venturo Romero's name as Ventura.

78. Laird, *Encounter with an Angry God*, xv–xxii; Fowler, *A Laboratory for Anthropology*, 270; MCS to Holmes, July 31, 1908, BAE, LR, MCS, NAA.

79. Fowler, *A Laboratory for Anthropology*, 261–67; *Santa Fe Daily New Mexican*, July 27 and 29, August 11, and December 5, 1908.

80. MCS to Holmes, September 14, 1908, and MCS to Walcott, November 17, 1908, BAE, LR, MCS, NAA; *Santa Fe Daily New Mexican*, November 7, 1908; Fowler, *A Laboratory for Anthropology*, 261–69.

81. MCS to Walcott, December 1, 1908, MCS Papers, MS4689, NAA; MCS to Holmes, November 23, 1909, and January 24, 1910, BAE, LR, MCS, NAA. Nancy

Parezo identifies the person sent out by the American Museum of Natural History as Hermann K. Haeberlin. Parezo, "Matilda Coxe Stevenson," 60n6.

82. MCS to Renehan, June 20, 1908, and Renehan to MCS, June 22 and 27, 1908, MCS Papers, MS4689, NAA; C. True to MCS, [no date], Civil Case no. 8003, County of Santa Fe, NMFJD.

83. MCS to Holmes, July 4, 1908, BAE, LR, MCS, NAA.

84. *MCS vs. C. True et al.*, August 24, 1908, and Renehan to Randall, September 23, 1908, Civil Case no. 6398, Santa Fe County, NMSRCA.

85. Nordhoff-Jung to MCS, November 27, 1908, MCS Papers, MS4689, NAA.

86. C. True to Renehan, December 5, 1908, BAE, LR, MCS, NAA; Jacobs, "Clara True and Female Moral Authority," 107.

87. Jacobs, "Clara True and Female Moral Authority," 100–107. See also Jacobs, *Engendered Encounters*, 30–47. Discussions with anthropologist Terry Reynolds concerning power relations between Indians and Bureau of Indian Affairs personnel helped place True's battle with Stevenson in perspective.

88. Jacobs, "Clara True and Female Moral Authority," 104; MCS to Holmes, October 17, 1908, BAE, LR, MCS, NAA.

89. MCS to Leupp, December 23 and 29, 1908, BAE, LR, MCS, NAA; MCS to Walcott, May 8, 1909, MCS Papers, MS4689, NAA; *L. M. Randall vs. MCS*, Civil Case no. 6417, and *F. D. True vs. MCS*, Civil Case no. 6418, Santa Fe County, NMSRCA.

90. *Santa Fe Daily New Mexican*, March 13 and 15, 1909; MCS to Holmes, March 16, 1909, BAE, LR, MCS, NAA.

91. *Santa Fe Daily New Mexican*, April 20–30, 1909; MCS to Walcott, May 8, 1909, MCS Papers, MS4689, NAA.

92. *Santa Fe Daily New Mexican*, June 25 and July 20, 1909.

93. MCS to John R. McFie, September 15, 1909, and MCS to Renehan, September 21, 1909, MCS Papers, MS4689, NAA.

94. *Stevenson vs. True et al.*, February 18, 1910, Civil Case no. 6398, Santa Fe County, NMSRCA; Renehan to MCS, February 18, 1910, and MCS to Renehan, April 25, 1910, MCS Papers, MS4689, NAA; MCS to Hodge, February 12, 1910, BAE, LR, MCS, NAA; *Santa Fe Daily New Mexican*, February 18, 1910.

Chapter 7

1. MCS to Frederick W. Hodge, February 12, 1910, BAE, LR, MCS, NAA.

2. Hodge assumed the title of ethnologist-in-charge of the bureau. Woodbury and Woodbury, "The Rise and Fall of the Bureau of American Ethnology," 289–90. On the poor lighting, see BAE, *Thirty-fourth AR*, 1912–1913, 31.

3. MCS to Jean A. Jeancon, March 18, 1910, Sofie Nordhoff-Jung to MCS, March 15 and May 14, 1910, MCS to A. B. Renehan, March 21, 1910, and MCS to H. Pollard, [no date, 1910] and April 7, 1910, MCS Papers, MS4689, NAA.

4. MCS to H. Pollard, April 7, 1910, and MCS to Renehan, April 25, 1910, ibid.

5. BAE, *Thirty-second AR*, 1910–1911, 19; MCS to Hodge, November 24, 1910, and February 9, 1911, BAE, LR, MCS, NAA. For Stevenson's paper "Dress and Adornment," see Ahlstrom and Parezo, "Matilda Coxe Stevenson's 'Dress and Adornment of the Pueblo Indians.'"

6. MCS to H. Pollard, March 25, [no date, 1910], and April 7, 1910, MCS Papers, MS4689, NAA.

7. MCS to Hodge, May 26, 1910, BAE, LR, MCS, NAA.

8. Fowler, *A Laboratory for Anthropology*, 269. The BAE was to have "the privilege of the publication of all scientific results." BAE, *Thirty-second AR*, 1910–1911, 11. The Stevenson–Hewett conference was held on May 31. See note on MCS to Hodge, May 26, 1910, BAE, LR, MCS, NAA.

9. Chauvenet, *Hewett and Friends*, 70–80, 94, 119; Elliott, *The School of American Research*, 19–20; Fowler, *A Laboratory for Anthropology*, 267–68. For a detailed look at the Prince–Hewett controversy, see Stensvaag, "Clio on the Frontier," 293–308.

10. Aleš Hrdlička to MCS, October 20, 1910, MCS Papers, MS4689, NAA. On Tilly's reputation, see Woodbury, "Past is Present, Tilly's Trials," 3–4; Lurie, "Women in Early American Anthropology," 64; Fowler, *A Laboratory for Anthropology*, 114; Parezo, "Matilda Coxe Stevenson," 51–54.

11. MCS to Hodge, November 8 and 24, 1910, BAE, LR, MCS, NAA; MCS to the Andersons, January 5, 1911, MCS Papers, MS4689, NAA.

12. MCS to Hodge, November 24, 1910, and February 9, 1911, BAE, LR, MCS, NAA.

13. MCS to Hodge, May 31, 1911, ibid.; Ahlstrom and Parezo, "Matilda Coxe Stevenson's 'Dress and Adornment of the Pueblo Indians,'" 267. On the Smithsonian's publishing committee, see Noelke, "The Origin and Early History of the Bureau of American Ethnology," 232–33.

14. Ahlstrom and Parezo, "Matilda Coxe Stevenson's 'Dress and Adornment of the Pueblo Indians,'" 267.

15. MCS to Hodge, June 2, 1911, and Hodge to MCS, June 6, 1911, BAE, LR, MCS, NAA.

16. Ahlstrom and Parezo, "Matilda Coxe Stevenson's 'Dress and Adornment of the Pueblo Indians,'" 271–72.

17. Ibid., 292–312.

18. Clipping from the *Washington Star*, February 26, 1911, located in James Stevenson Scrapbook, Museum of Indian Arts and Culture/Laboratory of Anthropology; *Santa Fe Daily New Mexican*, March 4, 1911. John Ruskin's work is correctly titled "The Queen of the Air, Being a Study of the Greek Myths of Cloud and Storm." See Cook and Wedderburn, eds., *The Works of John Ruskin*.

19. MCS to Hodge, May 1 and 31, 1911, BAE, LR, MCS, NAA.

20. MCS to Hodge, May 1 and 20, 1911, ibid.

21. MCS to Hodge, May 1 and 20, 1911, and Hodge to MCS, June 2, 1911, ibid.

22. Fowler, *A Laboratory for Anthropology*, 301; Hodge to MCS, June 2, 1911, BAE, LR, MCS, NAA.

23. Report of Miss Barbara Freire-Marreco to Somerville College Research Fund Committee, April 17, 1911, Hewett Collection, Angélico Chávez History Library; Fowler, *A Laboratory for Anthropology*, 269, 322.

24. Barbara Freire-Marreco to Edgar Lee Hewett, November 5, 1911, Hewett Collection, Angélico Chávez History Library; MCS to Hodge, December 3, 1911, BAE, LR, MCS, NAA; *Santa Fe Daily New Mexican*, October 3, 5, and 12 and November 11, 1912.

25. MCS to Hodge, July 1, 1911, BAE, LR, MCS, NAA.

26. MCS to Hodge, July 1, August 3, October 30, and December 7, 1911, ibid. Hodge apparently made sure that Stevenson received the photographs. See Hodge to MCS, December 14, 1911, ibid.

27. MCS to Hodge, October 5 and 21, 1911, BAE, LR, MCS, NAA; *Santa Fe Daily New Mexican*, October 2–5, 1911.

28. MCS to Hodge, December 3 and 7, 1911, and January 4 and 15, [February], and July 22, 1912, BAE, LR, MCS, NAA; *Santa Fe Daily New Mexican*, November 24, 1911.

29. MCS, "Ethnobotany of the Zuni Indians," 35–38. See also Robbins, Harrington, and Freire-Marreco, *Ethnobotany of the Tewa Indians.*

30. MCS, "Ethnobotany of the Zuni Indians," 35–38.

31. Ibid., 39–64.

32. Ibid., 65–100. Anthropologist Barbara Tedlock describes Stevenson's Zuni ethnobotany as "one of the earliest, and most thorough, published works on Native American plant knowledge and use." Tedlock, *The Beautiful and the Dangerous*, 298n10.

33. MCS to Hodge, January 15, 1912, BAE, LR, MCS, NAA; *Santa Fe Daily New Mexican*, January 4 and 5, 1912; *New York Times*, January 4, 1912.

34. MCS, "Studies of the Tewa Indians of the Rio Grande Valley," 35–41; *Santa Fe Daily New Mexican*, January 22 and 23, 1912; MCS to Hodge, February [no date], 1912, BAE, LR, MCS, NAA.

35. MCS, "Studies of the Tewa Indians of the Rio Grande Valley," 37; MCS to Hodge, December 7, 1911, and March 12 and November 6, 1912, BAE, LR, MCS, NAA.

36. *Santa Fe Daily New Mexican*, March 25 and 26 and April 8, 1912; MCS to Hodge, April 8, 1912, BAE, LR, MCS, NAA; Betty Kellogg to MCS, December 14 [no year], MCS Papers, MS4689, NAA.

37. *Santa Fe Daily New Mexican*, May 25 and 28, 1912.

38. MCS to Hodge, March 12, April 15, and May 1, 1912, BAE, LR, MCS, NAA.

39. MCS to Hodge, May 13, 1912, ibid.

40. MCS to Hodge, August 10, 1912, ibid.

41. MCS to Hodge, August 10, 1912 [two letters of this date], ibid.; BAE, *Thirty-third AR*, 1911–1912, 19–23.

42. MCS to Hodge, May 13, 1912 [two letters of this date], BAE, LR, MCS, NAA.

43. MCS to Hodge, February 15, 1913, MCS Papers, MS4689, NAA; MCS to Hodge, February 23, 1913, and Hodge to MCS, March 1, 1913, BAE, LR, MCS, NAA; MCS, "Studies of the Tewa Indians of the Rio Grande Valley," 35–41; BAE, *Thirty-fourth AR*, 1912–13, 14–15.

44. MCS to Hodge, March 8, 1913, BAE, LR, MCS, NAA.

45. Hodge to Charles D. Walcott, May 8, 1913, and Hodge to MCS, November 13, 1913, ibid.

46. MCS to Hodge, November 21, 1913, and July 16, 1914, ibid.; MCS to Hodge, January 20 and February 3, 1914, MCS Papers, MS4689, NAA; *Santa Fe Daily New Mexican*, November 11 and 25, 1913.

47. James Stevenson, Pension Application Files, RG 15, NA; Mortgage between Matilda Coxe Stevenson and A. B. Renehan, March 23, 1912, Renehan-Gilbert Papers, NMSRCA.

48. *Santa Fe Daily New Mexican*, July 19, 1912; MCS to Hodge, July 22, 1912, BAE, LR, MCS, NAA.

49. Jacobs, "Clara True and Female Moral Authority," 103; Renehan to MCS, September 11, 1909, MCS to Renehan, September 21 and 27, 1909, MCS to H. Pollard, April 7, 1910, and H. Pollard to MCS, July 6, 1910, MCS Papers, MS4689, NAA.

50. *Santa Fe Daily New Mexican*, February 6, 7, and 8 and June 20, 1911, and May 11, 1912; Zumwalt, *Wealth and Rebellion*, 147; C. True to Freire-Marreco, [July 1911], Hewett Collection, Angélico Chávez History Library; C. True to Parsons, April 6 and June 15, 1911, ECP Papers, American Philosophical Society Library.

51. *Santa Fe Daily New Mexican*, August 19, 1912.

52. C. True to Hewett, August 7, 1912, Hewett to C. True, August 8, 1912, and John R. McFie to Hewett, December 10, 1912, Hewett Collection, Angélico Chávez History Library; C. True to ECP, January 22, 1914, ECP Papers, American Philosophical Society Library; *Santa Fe Daily New Mexican*, October 29, 1913, and January 26, 1914. According to the press, the International Congress of Americanists fostered the "scientific study of the two Americas and their inhabitants" (*Santa Fe Daily New Mexican*, October 29, 1913).

53. *Santa Fe Daily New Mexican*, August 23, 1912, and January 29–31, 1913.

54. Ibid., May 28, 1913.

55. See documents and C. True to MCS, April 14, 1913, and C. True to Manager Smithsonian Institute Farm, May 1, 1913, Civil Case no. 8003, Santa Fe County, NMFJD; *Santa Fe Daily New Mexican*, May 10, 12, 26, and 28, 1913; Hodge to MCS, April 21, 1913, BAE, LR, MCS, NAA.

56. *Santa Fe Daily New Mexican*, May 7, 10, and 12, 1913.

57. Ibid., May 21 and 22, 1913.

58. Ibid., May 24 and 28 and June 21, 1913; see documents in Civil Case no. 8003, Santa Fe County, NMFJD.

59. Renehan to Hodge, April 30, 1914, BAE, LR, MCS, NAA; documents in Civil Case no. 8183, Santa Fe County, NMFJD.

60. Hodge to F. H. Abbott, October 1, 1913, MCS Papers, MS4689, NAA; MCS to George W. James, October 14, 1914, MCS Correspondence, P-E 211, Bancroft Library; James, *New Mexico*, 71, 358.

61. *Santa Fe Daily New Mexican*, July 5 and August 13–September 13, 1913; MCS to Hodge, June 21, 1913, MCS Papers, MS4689, NAA; MCS to James, October 14, 1914, MCS Correspondence, P-E 211, Bancroft Library; *Matilda Coxe Stevenson vs. Mary F. Bryan and Clara D. True*, Civil Case no. 1454, Docket Book, Rio Arriba County, NMFJD.

62. MCS to Hodge, December 16, 1913, BAE, LR, MCS, NAA; Hodge to MCS, January [date missing], 1914, MCS Papers, MS4689, NAA.

63. *Santa Fe Daily New Mexican*, August 4, 1913.

64. F. Bryant to MCS, [December 1913], and June 16, 1914, MCS Papers, MS4689, NAA.

65. *Santa Fe Daily New Mexican*, May 30, 1914; MCS to Hodge, May 28, 1914, BAE, LR, MCS, NAA.

66. Lease agreement, March 25, 1914, between MCS and J. Douglass Walker, MCS Papers, MS4689, NAA; see documents in Civil Case no. 8183, Santa Fe County, NMFJD.

67. See documents in Civil Case no. 8183, Santa Fe County, NMFJD; Renehan to Hodge, April 30, 1914, BAE, LR, MCS, NAA; *Santa Fe Daily New Mexican*, April 28, 1914.

68. Renehan to Hodge, May 12, 1914, BAE, LR, MCS, NAA.

69. Renehan to Hodge, May 12, 1914, BAE, LR, MCS, NAA. On Stevenson's alleged problems with alcohol, see Lurie, "Women in Early American Anthropology," 64; Woodbury, "Past is Present, Tilly's Trials," 3–4; Foote, *Women of the New Mexico Frontier*, 141; Parezo, "Matilda Coxe Stevenson," 52. I have found no documentary evidence to support the charge that Stevenson was an alcoholic. Possibly her struggle with heart disease, which led to fainting and falling spells, contributed to suggestions that she was an alcoholic.

70. Hodge to Renehan, June 3, 1914, BAE, LR, MCS, NAA.

71. MCS to Mrs. Scott, September 15, 1914, and MCS to Herman Schweizer, September 16, 1914, MCS Papers, MS4689, NAA. Hewett had been named director of exhibits for the San Diego exposition in 1911. Among his Santa Fe associates who helped with the exhibits were John P. Harrington, Jesse Nusbaum, Kenneth Chapman, and Sylvanus Morley. See Fowler, *A Laboratory for Anthropology*, 272–74.

72. Fowler, *A Laboratory for Anthropology*, 272–73; Chauvenet, *Hewett and Friends*, 109–20; Lowitt, *Bronson M. Cutting*, 45–50; *Santa Fe Daily New Mexican*, October 3,

16, and 23–29, 1913; MCS to Hodge, October 27, 1913, and January 12, 1915, BAE, LR, MCS, NAA.

73. MCS to Hodge, January 14, 1914, BAE, LR, MCS, NAA; *Santa Fe Daily New Mexican,* July 30, September 21, and November 10 and 19, 1914.

74. MCS to Hodge, August 26, 1914, BAE, LR, MCS, NAA; MCS to Scott, September 15, 1914, and MCS to Hodge, February 3, October 23, and November 11, 1914, MCS Papers, MS4689, NAA.

75. *Santa Fe Daily New Mexican,* August 7, 1914; MCS to Hodge, August 26, 1914, BAE, LR, MCS, NAA.

76. MCS to G. H. Van Stone, June 15, 1914, and MCS to John E. Watkins, June 15, 1914, MCS Papers, MS4689, NAA; *Santa Fe Daily New Mexican,* July 15, 1914; Altherr, "The Pajarito or Cliff Dwellers' National Park Proposal," 271.

77. MCS to Scott, September 15, 1914, MCS Papers, MS4689, NAA.

78. Renehan to Hodge, April 9, 1915, BAE, LR, MCS, NAA.

79. *Santa Fe Daily New Mexican,* March 13, 1915; *Santa Fe State Recorder,* March 19, 1915.

80. *Santa Fe Daily New Mexican,* March 29, 1915. The Southwestern Anthropological Society apparently was short-lived, leaving few records of its meetings or activities.

81. MCS to Hodge, March 24, April 2, and May 11, 1915, BAE, LR, MCS, NAA.

82. MCS to Hodge, May 30, 1915, ibid.; MCS to Herman E. Gasch, May 31, 1915, Testamentary Paper of MCS, Superior Court of the District of Columbia.

83. MCS to Hodge, April 5, 1913, BAE, LR, MCS, NAA; MCS to Hodge, May 9, 1914, MCS Papers, MS4689, NAA; MCS, "Strange Rites of the Tewa Indians," 73–80; Foote, *Women of the New Mexico Frontier,* 142–44.

84. MCS to Hodge, September 30 and December 22, 1914, and January 1, 12, and 22, 1915, and Hodge to MCS, December 17, 1914, and January 27, 1915, BAE, LR, MCS, NAA.

85. [Name unclear] to Mr. Dorsey, April 17, 1915 (containing clipping from the *Washington Post*), Hodge to MCS, April 19, 1915, and MCS to Hodge, April 21, 1915, ibid.; Jacobs, *Engendered Encounters,* 110.

86. *Santa Fe Daily New Mexican,* April 19–May 25, 1915; Foote, *Women of the New Mexico Frontier,* 142–44, 176n47; Simmons, *Witchcraft in the Southwest,* 127–34; Gray, ed., *Tonita Peña: Quah Ah,* 42–44.

87. MCS to Hodge, May 11 and 30, 1915, and Gasch to Charles D. Walcott, June 24, 1915, BAE, LR, MCS, NAA; MCS to Gasch, May 31, 1915, Testamentary Paper of MCS, Superior Court of the District of Columbia.

88. *Washington Evening Star,* June 24, 1915; *New York Times,* June 25, 1915; *Santa Fe Daily New Mexican,* June 28, 1915.

89. Hodge to Gasch and American Security and Trust Company, December 24, 1915, Hodge to Bolitha Laws, January 3 and November 6, 1917, Hodge to C. G. Sloane [*sic*] & Co., January 16, 1918, Walcott to Attorney General, May 29,

1916, and Gasch to Hodge, December 26, 1916, and November 5, 1917, BAE, LR, MCS, NAA; Catalogue of C. G. Sloan & Co., "The Stevenson Sale," Manuscript and Pamphlet File, no. 865, NAA.

90. BAE, *Thirty-sixth AR*, 1914–1915, 16–17.

91. John P. Harrington to J. Walter Fewkes, April 2 and May 9, 1918, December 24, 1921, and April 3, 1922, BAE, LR from John P. Harrington, NAA.

92. ECP to Fewkes, October 31, 1918, April 24 and December 3, 1922, and January 27, 1924, and Fewkes to ECP, April 27 and December 23, 1922, BAE, LR from ECP, NAA; ECP, *The Social Organization of the Tewa of New Mexico*, 7. See also Deacon, *Elsie Clews Parsons*, 291, 463n14. In 1922, at Parson's request, John R. Swanton of the Bureau of American Ethnology located some of Stevenson's papers in the bureau's vault. This included 423 pages of Tewa material, which he described as "a disjointed body of field notes, partly typewritten, but not arranged and treating of all sorts of things"—clans, ceremonials, names, medicines, and so on. Clearly he had not located Tilly's Tewa ethnography. Nor did he find any of Stevenson's Taos material, which four years earlier Harrington had said amounted to 469 pages. John R. Swanton to ECP, March 16, 1922, Parsons Family Papers, Rye Historical Society; Harrington to Fewkes, April 2, 1918, BAE, LR, John P. Harrington, NAA.

93. Stevenson's incomplete ninety-page draft of a manuscript on "the ceremonies and beliefs of the Tewa" is listed in an old card catalogue of the Harrington papers at the NAA. My thanks to Paula Fleming for reproducing the catalogue cards, numbered 4709–4711 Tewa. On a recent trip to the NAA, however, this manuscript could not be located.

Chapter 8

1. Parezo, "Matilda Coxe Stevenson," 46. I am indebted to Desley Deacon for the phrase "omniscient scientist." Deacon, "The Republic of the Spirit," 30.

2. My thanks to Louis A. Hieb for help in clarifying my thinking about Stevenson's pioneering ethnographic reporting.

3. Holmes, "In Memoriam, Matilda Coxe Stevenson," 552–59.

4. On a younger generation's critical assessment of Stevenson, see Lurie, "Women in Early American Anthropology," 64, 234n53; Parezo, "Matilda Coxe Stevenson," 51–58. See also Nusbaum, *Tierra Dulce*, 52; Lambert, "Bits and Pieces from the Past," 161–63.

5. MCS to Frederick W. Hodge, January 4, 1912, BAE, LR, MCS, NAA.

Bibliography

Manuscript Collections

American Philosophical Society Library, Philadelphia
  Elsie Clews Parsons Papers
Angélico Chávez History Library, Santa Fe
  Edgar Lee Hewett Collection
The Bancroft Library, Berkeley
  Matilda Coxe Stevenson Correspondence, P-E 211
Georgetown University Library, Washington, D.C.
  "The Sofie Nordhoff-Jung Papers"
Museum of Indian Arts and Culture/Laboratory of Anthropology, Santa Fe
  James Stevenson Scrapbook
National Anthropological Archives, Suitland, Maryland
  Bureau of American Ethnology Records, Letters Received (from)
    Elsie Clews Parsons
    James Stevenson
    John P. Harrington
    Matilda Coxe Stevenson
  Catalogue of C. G. Sloan & Co., Auctioneers, "The Stevenson Sale," Manuscript and Pamphlet File, no. 865
  Catalogue of Ethnological and Archaeological Collections from Hopi Pueblos, October–November 1885, MS775

James Stevenson, "Annual Report" [1886–87], MS4734
James Stevenson, "Annual Report" [1887–88], in John P. Harrington Papers
John P. Harrington Papers
Joy McPherson, "Matilda Coxe Stevenson Papers"
Matilda Coxe Stevenson, Miscellaneous ethnographic notes, MS2100
Matilda Coxe Stevenson, Notes on the Pueblo of Taos, MS4842
Matilda Coxe Stevenson Papers, MS4689
A Petition Signed by Twenty Hopi Indians, MS3967
Records Relating to the Investigation of the Bureau of American Ethnology, 1903
William H. Holmes, Letters Received, MS4745
National Archives, Washington, D.C.
Records of the Adjutant General's Office, RG 94, Compiled Military Service Records, Civil War
Records of the Bureau of the Census, RG 29
Population Schedules of the Seventh Census of the U.S., 1850, Texas, microfilm M432, roll 914
Population Schedules of the Eighth Census of the U.S., 1860, District of Columbia, microfilm M653, roll 103
Population Schedules of the Ninth Census of the U.S., 1870, District of Columbia, microfilm M593, roll 124
Population Schedules of the Tenth Census of the U.S., 1880, District of Columbia and Pennsylvania, microfilm T9, rolls 122, 1171
Records of the Geological Survey, RG 57
Hayden Survey, Letters Received, microfilm M623
Records of the Veterans Administration, RG 15, Pension Application Files, Civil War Series
New Mexico First Judicial District, Judicial Complex, Santa Fe
Rio Arriba County District Court Records, Civil Case no. 1454
Santa Fe County District Court Records, Civil Cases nos. 8003, 8183
New Mexico State Records Center and Archive, Santa Fe
Records of U.S. Territorial and New Mexico District Courts for Santa Fe County, Civil Cases nos. 6398, 6417, 6418
Renehan-Gilbert Papers
Territorial Archives of New Mexico, L. Bradford Prince, Letters Received, microfilm, rolls 112–113
Rye Historical Society, Rye, New York
Parsons Family Papers
Smithsonian Institution Archives, Washington, D.C.
Charles D. Walcott Collection
Samuel P. Langley, Incoming Correspondence
U.S. National Museum, Accession Records

Superior Court of the District of Columbia, Washington, D.C.
Office of the Register of Wills, Testamentary Paper of Matilda Coxe Stevenson

Government Documents

Bureau of American Ethnology. *Annual Reports of the Bureau of American Ethnology.* Washington, D.C.: GPO, 1894–1932.

Bureau of Ethnology. *Annual Reports of the Bureau of Ethnology.* Washington, D.C.: GPO, 1879–1893.

Compendium of the Tenth Census, Part 1 (June 1880). Washington, D.C.: GPO, 1885.

Congressional Directory for the First Session of the Thirty-sixth Congress. Washington, D.C.: Postmaster, House of Representatives, 1860.

Congressional Directory for the Second Session of the Thirty-fifth Congress. Washington, D.C.: Postmaster, House of Representatives, 1859.

Historical Statistics of the United States, Colonial Times to 1970. Part 1. Washington, D.C.: Bureau of the Census, 1975.

Smithsonian Institution. *Annual Reports of the Smithsonian Institution.* Washington, D.C.: GPO, 1879–1915.

Thirteenth Census of the United States, 1910. Vol. 3, *Population.* Washington, D.C.: GPO, 1913.

U.S. Geological and Geographical Survey of the Territories. *Annual Reports of the U.S. Geological and Geographical Survey of the Territories.* Washington, D.C.: GPO, 1873–1878.

U.S. Geological Survey of the Territories. *Annual Reports of the U.S. Geological Survey of the Territories.* Washington, D.C.: GPO, 1869–1872.

U.S. National Museum. *Annual Reports of the U.S. National Museum.* Washington, D.C.: GPO, 1885–1917.

Newspapers

Albuquerque Morning Journal
Cheyenne Daily Leader
Denver Rocky Mountain News
Eureka Herald (Kansas)
New York Times
La Revista de Taos (New Mexico)
Santa Fe Daily New Mexican
Santa Fe New Mexican
Santa Fe State Recorder
Washington Evening Star
Washington National Tribune
Washington Post

Books and Articles

Ahlstrom, Richard V. N., and Nancy J. Parezo, eds. "Matilda Coxe Stevenson's 'Dress and Adornment of the Pueblo Indians.'" *The Kiva* 52 (summer 1987): 267–312.

Alleman, Tillie Pierce. *At Gettysburg: Or, What a Girl Saw and Heard of the Battle.* New York: W. L. Borland, 1889.

Altherr, Thomas L. "The Pajarito or Cliff Dwellers' National Park Proposal, 1900–1920." *New Mexico Historical Review* 60 (July 1985): 271–94.

Babcock, Barbara A., and Nancy J. Parezo. *Daughters of the Desert: Women Anthropologists and the Native American Southwest, 1880–1980.* Albuquerque: University of New Mexico Press, 1988.

Bandelier, Adolph F. *The Southwestern Journals of Adolph F. Bandelier, 1880–1882.* Edited by Charles H. Lange and Carroll L. Riley. Albuquerque: University of New Mexico Press, 1966.

———. *The Southwestern Journals of Adolph F. Bandelier, 1883–1884.* Edited by Charles H. Lange and Carroll L. Riley. Albuquerque: University of New Mexico Press, 1970.

———. *The Southwestern Journals of Adolph F. Bandelier, 1889–1892.* Edited by Charles H. Lange, Carroll L. Riley, and Elizabeth M. Lange. Albuquerque: University of New Mexico Press, 1984.

Bartlett, Richard A. *Great Surveys of the American West.* Norman: University of Oklahoma Press, 1962.

Bassford, Amy O., and Fritiof M. Fryxell, eds. *Home-Thoughts, From Afar: Letters of Thomas Moran to Mary Nimmo Moran.* East Hampton, N.Y.: East Hampton Free Library, 1967.

Basso, Keith H. "History of Ethnological Research." In *Handbook of North American Indians,* vol. 9, *Southwest,* ed. Alfonso Ortiz, 14–21. Washington, D.C.: Smithsonian Institution, 1979.

Batkin, Jonathan. "Tourism is Overrated: Pueblo Pottery and the Early Curio Trade, 1880–1916." In *Unpacking Culture: Art and Commodity in Colonial and Postcolonial Worlds,* ed. Ruth B. Phillips and Christopher B. Steiner, 282–97. Berkeley: University of California Press, 1999.

Bender, Norman J., ed. *Missionaries, Outlaws, and Indians: Taylor F. Ealy at Lincoln and Zuni, 1878–1881.* Albuquerque: University of New Mexico Press, 1984.

Bird, Isabella L. *A Lady's Life in the Rocky Mountains.* Norman: University of Oklahoma Press, 1960.

Blessing, Arthur R. "Robley Dunglison Evans." In *Dictionary of American Biography,* ed. Allen Johnson and Dumas Malone. Vol. 6:210. New York: Charles Scribner's Sons, 1931.

Bode, Carl. *The American Lyceum, Town Meeting of the Mind.* Carbondale: Southern Illinois University Press, 1968.

Bodine, John J., ed. "The Taos Blue Lake Ceremony." *American Indian Quarterly* 12 (spring 1988): 91–105.

———. "Taos Pueblo." In *Handbook of North American Indians*, vol. 9, *Southwest*, ed. Alfonso Ortiz, 255–67. Washington, D.C.: Smithsonian Institution, 1979.

Bonney, Orrin H. (with Lorraine G. Bonney). *The Grand Controversy: The Pioneer Climbs in the Teton Range and the Controversial First Ascent of the Grand Teton.* New York: AAC Press, 1992.

Boyd, William H. *Boyd's Directory of Washington.* Washington, D.C.: Wm. H. Boyd, 1870 and subs. eds.

Brayer, Herbert Oliver, ed. "Exploring the Yellowstone with Hayden, 1872, Diary of Sidford Hamp." *Annals of Wyoming* 14 (October 1942): 252–98.

Brugge, David M. "The Zuni Indians." *Arizona and the West* 16 (spring 1974): 75–76.

Bryant, Keith L., Jr. *History of the Atchison, Topeka and Santa Fe Railway.* Lincoln: University of Nebraska Press, 1974.

Camp, Charles L., ed. *George C. Yount and His Chronicles of the West.* Denver: Old West Publishing Co., 1966.

Cassidy, James G. *Ferdinand V. Hayden: Entrepreneur of Science.* Lincoln: University of Nebraska Press, 2000.

Chauvenet, Beatrice. *Hewett and Friends: A Biography of Santa Fe's Vibrant Era.* Santa Fe: Museum of New Mexico Press, 1983.

Chittenden, Hiram Martin. *The Yellowstone National Park.* Cincinnati: Robert Clarke Co., 1895.

Clay-Clopton, Virginia. *A Belle of the Fifties; Memoirs of Mrs. Clay of Alabama, Covering Social and Political Life in Washington and the South, 1853–66.* New York: Doubleday, Page, and Co., 1904.

Cook, E. T., and Alexander Wedderburn, eds. *The Works of John Ruskin.* Vol. 19. New York: Logmans, Green, and Co., 1905.

Cottrell, Robert C. *Roger Nash Baldwin and the American Civil Liberties Union.* New York: Columbia University Press, 2000.

Crampton, C. Gregory. *The Zunis of Cibola.* Salt Lake City: University of Utah Press, 1977.

Crocket, George L. *Two Centuries in East Texas; A History of San Augustine County and Surrounding Territory from 1685 to the Present Time.* Dallas: Southwest Press, 1932.

Culin, Stewart. "Games of North American Indians." In *Twenty-fourth Annual Report of the Bureau of American Ethnology, 1902–1903*, 3–809. Washington, D.C.: GPO, 1907.

Curtis, Edward S. *The North American Indian; Being a Series of Volumes Picturing and Describing the Indians of the United States, and Alaska.* 20 vols. Cambridge, Mass.: University Press, 1907–30.

Cushing, Frank Hamilton. "Outlines of Zuni Creation Myths." In *Thirteenth Annual Report of the Bureau of Ethnology, 1891–92*, 321–447. Washington, D.C.: GPO, 1896.

Cushing, Frank Hamilton, J. Walter Fewkes, and Elsie Clews Parsons. "Contributions to Hopi History." *American Anthropologist* 24 (July–September 1922): 253–98.

Deacon, Desley. *Elsie Clews Parsons: Inventing Modern Life.* Chicago: University of Chicago Press, 1997.

———. "The Republic of the Spirit: Fieldwork in Elsie Clews Parsons's Turn to Anthropology." *Frontiers* 12, no. 3 (1992): 12–38.

Degler, Carl N. *At Odds: Women and the Family in America from the Revolution to the Present.* New York: Oxford University Press, 1980.

Dorchester, Daniel. "Report of Superintendent of Indian Schools." *Sixty-first Annual Report of the Commissioner of Indian Affairs, 1892,* 526–99. Washington, D.C.: GPO, 1892.

Ealy, Ruth R. *Water in a Thirsty Land.* Privately printed, 1955.

Eggan, Fred. "One Hundred Years of Ethnology and Social Anthropology." In *One Hundred Years of Anthropology,* ed. J. O. Brew, 119–52. Cambridge: Harvard University Press, 1968.

Eggan, Fred, and T. N. Pandey. "Zuni History, 1850–1970." In *Handbook of North American Indians,* vol. 9, *Southwest,* ed. Alfonso Ortiz, 474–81. Washington, D.C.: Smithsonian Institution, 1979.

Elliott, Malinda. *The School of American Research, A History.* Santa Fe, N.Mex.: School of American Research, 1987.

Evans, Robley D. *A Sailor's Log: Recollections of Forty Years of Naval Life.* New York: D. Appleton and Co., 1901.

Faris, James C. *The Nightway: A History and a History of Documentation of a Navajo Ceremonial.* Albuquerque: University of New Mexico Press, 1990.

Fay, George E. *Treaties, Land Cessions, and Other U.S. Congressional Documents Relative to American Indian Tribes; Zuni Indian Pueblo, New Mexico.* 2 Parts. Greeley, Colo.: Museum of Anthropology, University of Northern Colorado, 1971, 1981.

Ferguson, T. J., and Barbara J. Mills. "Settlement and Growth of Zuni Pueblo: An Architectural History." *The Kiva* 52 (summer 1987): 243–66.

Fernlund, Kevin J. *William Henry Holmes and the Rediscovery of the American West.* Albuquerque: University of New Mexico Press, 2000.

Fewkes, Jesse Walter. "A Comparison of Sia and Tusayan Snake Ceremonials." *American Anthropologist* 8 (o.s.) (April 1895): 118–41.

———. "Tusayan Snake Ceremonies." In *Sixteenth Annual Report of the Bureau of American Ethnology, 1894–95,* 273–311. Washington, D.C.: GPO, 1897.

Field, Cynthia R., Richard E. Stamm, and Heather P. Ewing. *The Castle: An Illustrated History of the Smithsonian Building.* Washington, D.C.: Smithsonian Institution Press, 1993.

Flack, J. Kirkpatrick. *Desideratum in Washington: The Intellectual Community in the Capital City, 1870–1900.* Cambridge, Mass.: Schenkman Publishing Co., 1975.

Fletcher, Alice C. "On the Preservation of Archaeologic Monuments." In *Proceedings of the American Association for the Advancement of Science* 36 (1888): 317.

Fletcher, Alice C., and T. E. Stevenson. "Report of the Committee on the Preservation of Archaeologic Remains on the Public Lands." In *Proceedings of the American Association for the Advancement of Science* 37 (1889): 35–37.

Foote, Cheryl J. *Women of the New Mexico Frontier, 1846–1912.* Niwot, Colo.: University Press of Colorado, 1990.

Foster, Mike. *Strange Genius: The Life of Ferdinand Vandeveer Hayden.* Niwot, Colo.: Roberts Rinehart Publishers, 1994.

Fowler, Don D. *A Laboratory for Anthropology: Science and Romanticism in the American Southwest, 1846–1930.* Albuquerque: University of New Mexico Press, 2000.

Gallman, J. Matthew. *Mastering Wartime: A Social History of Philadelphia During the Civil War.* New York: Cambridge University Press, 1990.

Gidley, Mick. *Edward S. Curtis and the North American Indian, Incorporated.* New York: Cambridge University Press, 1998.

Goode, G. Brown. "Biographical Notice of James Stevenson." In *Annual Report of the National Museum, 1889,* 187–90. Washington, D.C.: GPO, 1891.

Gordon-McCutchan, R. C. *The Taos Indians and the Battle for Blue Lake.* Santa Fe, N.Mex.: Red Crane Books, 1991.

Graves, Laura. *Thomas Varker Keam, Indian Trader.* Norman: University of Oklahoma Press, 1998.

Gray, Samuel L., ed. *Tonita Peña: Quah Ah, 1893–1949.* Albuquerque, N.Mex.: Avanyu Publishing, 1990.

Green, Constance McLaughlin. *Washington, Village and Capital, 1800–1878.* Princeton, N.J.: Princeton University Press, 1962.

Green, Jesse, ed. *Cushing at Zuni: The Correspondence and Journals of Frank Hamilton Cushing, 1879–1884.* Albuquerque: University of New Mexico Press, 1990.

———, ed. *Zuni: Selected Writings of Frank Hamilton Cushing.* Lincoln: University of Nebraska Press, 1979.

Hafen, LeRoy R., and Ann W. Hafen, eds. *The Diaries of William Henry Jackson, Frontier Photographer.* Glendale, Calif.: Arthur H. Clark Co., 1959.

Haines, Aubrey L. *The Yellowstone Story: A History of Our First National Park.* 2 vols. Rev. ed. Niwot, Colo.: University Press of Colorado, 1996.

Haller, John S., Jr., and Robin M. Haller. *The Physician and Sexuality in Victorian America.* Urbana: University of Illinois Press, 1974.

Hart, E. Richard. "Historic Zuni Land Use." In *Zuni and the Courts: A Struggle for Sovereign Land Rights,* ed. E. Richard Hart, 8–14. Lawrence: University Press of Kansas, 1995.

———. *Pedro Pino: Governor of Zuni Pueblo, 1830–1878.* Logan: Utah State University Press, 2003.

———. "Protection of Kolhu/wala:wa ('Zuni Heaven'): Litigation and Legislation." In *Zuni and the Courts: A Struggle for Sovereign Land Rights,* ed. E. Richard Hart, 199–207. Lawrence: University Press of Kansas, 1995.

Hieb, Louis A. "Alexander M. Stephen and the Navajos." *New Mexico Historical Review* 79 (summer 2004): 353–95.

————. "'The Flavor of Adventure Now Rare': H. C. Rizer's Account of James Stevenson's 1882 Bureau of Ethnology Expedition to Canyon de Chelly." *Journal of Arizona History* 46 (autumn 2005): 205–48.

————. "A Question of Authorship: A. M. Stephen's Catalogue of the Keam Collection [1884]." *Kiva* 69 (summer 2004): 401–23.

Hinman, Ida. *The Washington Sketch Book: A Society Souvenir.* Washington, D.C.: Hartman and Cadick, 1895.

Hinsley, Curtis M. *Savages and Scientists: The Smithsonian Institution and the Development of American Anthropology, 1846–1910.* Washington, D.C.: Smithsonian Institution Press, 1981.

Hogan, William Ransom. *The Texas Republic; A Social and Economic History.* 1946. Reprint, Austin: University of Texas Press, 1969.

Holmes, W. H. "In Memoriam, Matilda Coxe Stevenson." *American Anthropologist* 18 (October–December 1916): 552–59.

————. "James Stevenson." *American Anthropologist* 18 (October–December 1916): 557–58.

Hough, Walter. "Erminnie Adelle Platt Smith." In *Dictionary of American Biography,* ed. Dumas Malone. Vol. 17:262. New York: Charles Scribner's Sons, 1935.

————. "James Stevenson." In *Dictionary of American Biography,* ed. Dumas Malone. Vol. 17:631–32. New York: Charles Scribner's Sons, 1935.

Hughes, J. Donald. *American Indians in Colorado.* Boulder, Colo.: Pruett Publishing Co., 1977.

Hurd, Charles. *Washington Cavalcade.* New York: E. P. Dutton and Co., 1948.

Isaac, Gwyneira. "Re-Observation and the Recognition of Change: The Photographs of Matilda Coxe Stevenson (1879–1915)." *Journal of the Southwest* 47 (autumn 2005): 411–55.

Jackson, William Henry. *Time Exposure: The Autobiography of William Henry Jackson.* Albuquerque: University of New Mexico Press, 1986.

Jacobs, Margaret D. "Clara True and Female Moral Authority." In *The Human Tradition in the American West,* ed. Benson Tong and Regan A. Lutz, 99–115. Wilmington, Del.: Scholarly Resources Inc., 2002.

————. *Engendered Encounters: Feminism and Pueblo Cultures, 1879–1934.* Lincoln: University of Nebraska Press, 1999.

James, George Wharton. *New Mexico, The Land of the Delight Makers; The History of its Ancient Cliff Dwellings and Pueblos, Conquest by the Spaniards, Franciscan Missions.* Boston: Page Co., 1920.

"James Stevenson." *National Cyclopaedia of American Biography.* Vol. 12:556–57. New York: James T. White and Co., 1904.

Jayanti, Vimala. "Erminnie Adelle Platt Smith (1836–1886)." In *Women Anthropologists: A Biographical Dictionary,* ed. Ute Gacs, et al., 327–30. New York: Greenwood Press, 1988.

Jenkins, Myra Ellen. "Arthur Rochford Manby." *Westerners Brand Book.* Vol. 22. Denver, 1966.

Jones, James Pickett. *John A. Logan, Stalwart Republican from Illinois.* Tallahassee: University Press of Florida, 1982.

Judd, Neil M. *The Bureau of American Ethnology, A Partial History.* Norman: University of Oklahoma Press, 1967.

Keim, De B. Randolph. *Keim's Illustrated Hand-Book: Washington and Its Environs: A Descriptive and Historical Hand-book to the Capital of the United States of America.* Washington, D.C.: De B. Randolph Keim, 1887.

Kohlstedt, Sally Gregory. "In from the Periphery: American Women in Science, 1830–1880." *Signs* 4 (autumn 1978): 81–96.

Kroeber, Alfred L. "Zuni Kin and Clan." *Anthropological Papers of the American Museum of Natural History* 18, no. 2 (1917): 39–204.

Laird, Carobeth. *Encounter with an Angry God: Recollections of My Life with John Peabody Harrington.* Banning, Calif.: Malki Museum Press, 1975.

Lamb, Daniel S. "The Story of the Anthropological Society of Washington." *American Anthropologist* 8 (July–September 1906): 564–79.

———. "William Manuel Mew, 1835–1902." *Proceedings of the Washington Academy of Sciences* 5 (1903–1904): 401–402.

Lambert, Marjorie F. "Bits and Pieces from the Past." In *Clues to the Past: Papers in Honor of William M. Sundt,* eds. Meliha S. Duran and David T. Kirkpatrick, 155–71. Papers of the Archaeological Society of New Mexico, vol. 16. Albuquerque: Archaeological Society of New Mexico, 1990.

Lamphere, Louise. "Gladys Reichard Among the Navajo." *Frontiers* 12, no. 3 (1992): 98–115.

———, ed. "Women, Anthropology, Tourism, and the Southwest." *Frontiers* 12, no. 3 (1992): 5–150.

Langford, Nathaniel P. "The Ascent of Mount Hayden, A New Chapter of Western History." *Scribner's Monthly* 6 (June 1873): 129–57.

Larson, T. A. *History of Wyoming.* Lincoln: University of Nebraska Press, 1965.

Lavender, Catherine J. *Scientists and Storytellers: Feminist Anthropologists and the Construction of the American Southwest.* Albuquerque: University of New Mexico Press, 2006.

Lincoln, Charles H. "Robert Adams." In *Dictionary of American Biography,* ed. Allen Johnson. Vol. 1:94–95. New York: Charles Scribner's Sons, 1928.

Logan, Mrs. John A. *Reminiscences of a Soldier's Wife: An Autobiography.* New York: Charles Scribner's Sons, 1913.

Lowitt, Richard. *Bronson M. Cutting: Progressive Politician.* Albuquerque: University of New Mexico Press, 1992.

Lurie, Nancy O. "Relations Between Indians and Anthropologists." In *Handbook of North American Indians,* vol. 4, *History of Indian–White Relations,* ed. Wilcomb E. Washburn, 548–56. Washington, D.C.: Smithsonian Institution, 1988.

———. "Women in Early American Anthropology." In *Pioneers of American Anthropology: The Uses of Biography*, ed. June Helm, 29–81. Seattle: University of Washington Press, 1966.

Lyman, Christopher M. *The Vanishing Race and Other Illusions: Photographs of Indians by Edward S. Curtis*. Washington, D.C.: Smithsonian Institution Press, 1982.

Lystra, Karen. *Searching the Heart: Women, Men, and Romantic Love in Nineteenth-Century America*. New York: Oxford University Press, 1989.

Mark, Joan. *A Stranger in Her Native Land: Alice Fletcher and the American Indians*. Lincoln: University of Nebraska Press, 1988.

Mason, Otis T. "The Planting and Exhuming of a Prayer." *Science* 8 (July 9, 1886): 24–25.

———. "Report on the Department of Ethnology in the U.S. National Museum, 1889." In *Annual Report of the U.S. National Museum for the Year Ending June 30, 1889*, 281–88. Washington, D.C.: GPO, 1891.

McElroy's Philadelphia City Directory for 1863. Philadelphia: A. McElroy and Co., 1863.

McFeely, Eliza. *Zuni and the American Imagination*. New York: Hill and Wang, 2001.

McGee, Anita Newcomb. "The Women's Anthropological Society of America." *Science* 13 (March 29, 1889): 240–42.

McNitt, Frank. *The Indian Traders*. Norman: University of Oklahoma Press, 1962.

Mead, Margaret, and Ruth L. Bunzel, eds. *The Golden Age of American Anthropology*. New York: George Braziller, 1960.

Merrill, Marlene Deahl, ed. *Yellowstone and the Great West: Journals, Letters, and Images from the 1871 Hayden Expedition*. Lincoln: University of Nebraska Press, 1999.

Merrill, William L., and Richard E. Ahlborn. "Zuni Archangels and Ahayu:da, A Sculpted Chronicle of Power and Identity." In *Exhibiting Dilemmas: Issues of Representation at the Smithsonian*, eds. Amy Henderson and Adrienne L. Kaeppler, 176–205. Washington, D.C.: Smithsonian Institution Press, 1997.

Moldow, Gloria. *Women Doctors in Gilded-Age Washington: Race, Gender, and Professionalization*. Urbana: University of Illinois Press, 1987.

Moore, Joseph West. *Picturesque Washington: Pen and Pencil Sketches*. Providence, R.I.: J. A. and R. A. Reid, 1884.

Morand, Sheila. *Santa Fe, Then and Now*. Santa Fe, N.Mex.: Sunstone Press, 1998.

Morgan, Lewis Henry. *Houses and House-Life of the American Aborigines*. Contributions to North American Ethnology, vol. 4. Washington, D.C.: GPO, 1881.

Moss, Carolyn J., ed. *Kate Field: Selected Letters*. Carbondale: Southern Illinois University Press, 1996.

Mulhern, James. *A History of Secondary Education in Pennsylvania*. 1933. Reprint, New York: Arno Press, 1969.

Nash, Gary B. *First City: Philadelphia and the Forging of Historical Memory*. Philadelphia: University of Pennsylvania Press, 2002.

Noble, David Grant, ed. *Santa Fe: History of an Ancient City*. Santa Fe, N.Mex.: School of American Research Press, 1989.

Nusbaum, Rosemary. *Tierra Dulce: Reminiscences from the Jesse Nusbaum Papers.* Santa Fe, N.Mex.: Sunstone Press, 1980.

Organization and Historical Sketch of the Women's Anthropological Society of America. Washington, D.C.: Women's Anthropological Society, 1889.

Osborn, Henry Fairfield. *Cope: Master Naturalist, The Life and Letters of Edward Drinker Cope, With a Bibliography of His Writings Classified by Subject.* Princeton, N.J.: Princeton University Press, 1931.

Pandey, Triloki N. "Anthropologists at Zuni." *Proceedings of the American Philosophical Society* 116 (August 15, 1972): 321–37.

Parezo, Nancy J. "Cushing as Part of the Team: The Collecting Activities of the Smithsonian Institution." *American Ethnologist* 12 (November 1985): 763–74.

———. "The Formation of Ethnographic Collections: The Smithsonian Institution in the American Southwest." In *Advances in Archaeological Method and Theory*, vol. 10, ed. Michael B. Schiffer, 1–47. New York: Academic Press, 1987.

———. "Matilda Coxe Stevenson: Pioneer Ethnologist." In *Hidden Scholars: Women Anthropologists and the Native American Southwest*, ed. Nancy J. Parezo, 38–62. Albuquerque: University of New Mexico Press, 1993.

———. "Matthews and the Discovery of Navajo Drypaintings." In *Washington Matthews: Studies of Navajo Culture, 1880–1894*, eds. Katherine Spencer Halpern and Susan Brown McGreevy, 53–73. Albuquerque: University of New Mexico Press, 1997.

———. "Now Is the Time to Collect." *Masterkey* 59 (winter 1986):11–18.

———, ed. *Hidden Scholars: Women Anthropologists and the Native American Southwest.* Albuquerque: University of New Mexico Press, 1993.

Parezo, Nancy J., and John W. Troutman. "The 'Shy' Cocopa Go to the Fair." In *Selling the Indian: Commercializing and Appropriating American Indian Cultures*, eds. Carter Jones Meyer and Diana Royer, 3–43. Tucson: University of Arizona Press, 2001.

Parezo, Nancy J., and Margaret A. Hardin. "In the Realm of the Muses." In *Hidden Scholars: Women Anthropologists and the Native American Southwest*, ed. Nancy J. Parezo, 270–93. Albuquerque: University of New Mexico Press, 1993.

Parsons, Elsie Clews. *Pueblo Indian Religion.* 2 vols. Bison Books Edition. Lincoln: University of Nebraska Press, 1996.

———. *The Social Organization of the Tewa of New Mexico.* 1929. Reprint, New York: Kraus Reprint Corporation, 1964.

———. *Taos Pueblo.* Menasha, Wisc.: George Banta Publishing Co., 1936.

———. *Tewa Tales.* 1926. Reprint, Tucson: University of Arizona Press, 1994.

———. "Waiyautitsa of Zuni, New Mexico." *Scientific Monthly* 9 (November 1919): 443–57.

Paul, Rodman Wilson. *Mining Frontiers of the Far West, 1848–1880.* New York: Holt, Rinehart and Winston, 1963.

Peters, Steve. *Headless in Taos: Arthur Rochford Manby.* Santa Fe, N.Mex.: Self-published, 1972.

Pettit, Jan. *The Utes, The Mountain People.* Colorado Springs, Colo.: Century One Press, 1982.

Porter, Joseph C. *Paper Medicine Man: John Gregory Bourke and His American West.* Norman: University of Oklahoma Press, 1986.

Powell, John W. "James Stevenson." In *Ninth Annual Report of the U.S. Geological Survey, 1887–1888,* 42–44. Washington, D.C.: GPO, 1889.

Robbins, Wilfred W., John P. Harrington, and Barbara Freire-Marreco. *Ethnobotany of the Tewa Indians.* Bureau of American Ethnology Bulletin, no. 55. Washington, D.C.: GPO, 1916.

Rockwell, Wilson. *The Utes; A Forgotten People.* Ouray, Colo.: Western Reflections, 1956.

Rodgers, Andrew Denny. *John Merle Coulter: Missionary in Science.* Princeton, N.J.: Princeton University Press, 1944.

Rohde, Joy Elizabeth. "It was No 'Pink Tea,' Gender and American Anthropology, 1885–1903." In *Significant Others: Interpersonal and Professional Commitments in Anthropology,* ed. Richard Handler, 261–90. Madison: University of Wisconsin Press, 2004.

Rohner, Ronald P. "Franz Boas, Ethnographer on the Northwest Coast." In *Pioneers of American Anthropology: The Uses of Biography,* ed. June Helm, 149–222. Seattle: University of Washington Press, 1966.

Roscoe, Will. *The Zuni Man-Woman.* Albuquerque: University of New Mexico Press, 1991.

Rossiter, Margaret W. *Women Scientists in America: Struggles and Strategies to 1940.* Baltimore, Md.: The Johns Hopkins University Press, 1982.

Rothman, Ellen K. *Hands and Hearts: A History of Courtship in America.* New York: Basic Books, 1984.

Russell, Frank. "The Pima Indians." In *Twenty-sixth Annual Report of the Bureau of American Ethnology, 1904–1905,* 3–389. Washington, D.C.: GPO, 1908.

Rydell, Robert W. *All the World's a Fair: Visions of Empire at American International Expositions, 1876–1916.* Chicago: University of Chicago Press, 1984.

Sandweiss, Martha A. *Print the Legend: Photography and the American West.* New Haven, Conn.: Yale University Press, 2002.

Scott, Clifford H. *Lester Frank Ward.* Boston: Twayne Publishers, 1976.

Sewall, May Wright, ed. *The World's Congress of Representative Women.* Chicago: Rand McNally, and Co., 1894.

Shankman, Arnold M. *The Pennsylvania Antiwar Movement, 1861–1865.* Rutherford, N.J.: Fairleigh Dickinson University Press, 1980.

Showalter, Elaine. *The Female Malady: Women, Madness, and English Culture, 1830–1980.* New York: Penguin Books, 1987.

Simmons, Marc. *Albuquerque: A Narrative History.* Albuquerque: University of New Mexico Press, 1982.

———. *Witchcraft in the Southwest: Spanish and Indian Supernaturalism on the Rio Grande.* Flagstaff, Ariz.: Northland Press, 1974.

Stensvaag, James T. "Clio on the Frontier: The Intellectual Evolution of the Historical Society of New Mexico, 1859–1925." *New Mexico Historical Review* 55 (October 1980): 293–308.

Stevenson, James. "Ancient Habitations of the Southwest." *Journal of the American Geographical Society of New York* 18 (1886): 329–42.

———. "Ceremonial of Hasjelti Dailjis and Mythical Sand Painting of the Navajo Indians." In *Eighth Annual Report of the Bureau of Ethnology, 1886–87,* 229–85. Washington, D.C.: GPO, 1891.

———. "Illustrated Catalogue of the Collections Obtained from the Indians of New Mexico and Arizona in 1879." In *Second Annual Report of the Bureau of Ethnology, 1880–81,* 307–422. Washington, D.C.: GPO, 1883.

———. "Illustrated Catalogue of the Collections Obtained from the Indians of New Mexico in 1880." In *Second Annual Report of the Bureau of Ethnology, 1880–81,* 423–65. Washington, D.C.: GPO, 1883.

———. "Illustrated Catalogue of the Collections Obtained from the Pueblos of Zuni, New Mexico, and Wolpi, Arizona, in 1881." In *Third Annual Report of the Bureau of Ethnology, 1881–82,* 511–94. Washington, D.C.: GPO, 1884.

———. "Report of Explorations in New Mexico and Arizona." In *Annual Report of the Smithsonian Institution, 1880,* 136–38. Washington, D.C.: GPO, 1881.

Stevenson, Matilda Coxe. "A Chapter of Zuni Mythology." In *Memoirs of the International Congress of Anthropology,* ed. C. Staniland Wake, 312–19. Chicago: Schulte Publishing Co., 1894.

———. "Ethnobotany of the Zuni Indians." In *Thirtieth Annual Report of the Bureau of American Ethnology, 1908–1909,* 31–102. Washington, D.C.: GPO, 1915.

——— [Tilly E.]. "The Religious Life of the Zuni Child." In *Fifth Annual Report of the Bureau of Ethnology, 1883–84,* 533–55. Washington, D.C.: GPO, 1887.

———. "The Sia." In *Eleventh Annual Report of the Bureau of Ethnology, 1889–90,* 3–157. Washington, D.C.: GPO, 1894.

———. "Strange Rites of the Tewa Indians." *Smithsonian Miscellaneous Collections* 63, no. 8 (1914): 73–80.

———. "Studies of the Late Washington Matthews." *American Anthropologist* 12 (April–June 1910): 345.

———. "Studies of the Tewa Indians of the Rio Grande Valley." *Smithsonian Miscellaneous Collections* 60, no. 30 (1913): 35–41.

————. "The Sun and the Ice People Among the Tewa Indians of New Mexico." *Smithsonian Miscellaneous Collections* 65, no. 6 (1915): 73–78.

————. "Tusayan Legends of the Snake and Flute People." *Proceedings of the American Association for the Advancement of Science* 41 (1893): 258–70.

————. "Zuni Ancestral Gods and Masks." *American Anthropologist* 11 (o.s.) (February 1898): 33–40.

———— [T. E.]. "Zuni and the Zunians." Washington, D.C.: Privately printed, 1881.

————. "Zuni Games." *American Anthropologist* 5 (July–September 1903): 468–97.

————. "The Zuni Indians: Their Mythology, Esoteric Fraternities, and Ceremonies." In *Twenty-third Annual Report of the Bureau of American Ethnology, 1901–1902*, 3–608. Washington, D.C.: GPO, 1904.

————. "Zuni Religion." *Science* 11 (March 23, 1888): 136–37.

————. "The Zuni Scalp Ceremonial." In *The Congress of Women*, ed. Mary K. O. Eagle, 484–87. 1894. Reprint, New York: Arno Press, 1974.

Sweet, Jill D. *Dances of the Tewa Pueblo Indians: Expressions of New Life.* 2nd ed. Santa Fe, N.Mex.: School of American Research Press, 2004.

Tedlock, Barbara. *The Beautiful and the Dangerous: Encounters with the Zuni Indians.* New York: Penguin, 1992.

Temkin, Andrea S. "Alice Cunningham Fletcher (1838–1923)." In *Women Anthropologists: A Biographical Dictionary*, ed. Ute Gacs, et al., 95–101. New York: Greenwood Press, 1988.

Ten Kate, Herman. *Travels and Researches in Native North America, 1882–1883.* Edited by Pieter Hovens, William J. Orr, and Louis A. Hieb. Albuquerque: University of New Mexico Press, 2004.

Thompson, Edith M. Schultz, and William Leigh Thompson. *Beaver Dick, The Honor and the Heartbreak: An Historical Biography of Richard Leigh.* Laramie, Wyo.: Jelm Mountain Press, 1982.

Thompson, Raymond Harris. "Edgar Lee Hewett and the Political Process." *Journal of the Southwest* 42 (summer 2000): 273–318.

Tobias, Henry J., and Charles E. Woodhouse. *Santa Fe: A Modern History, 1880–1990.* Albuquerque: University of New Mexico Press, 2001.

Transactions of the Anthropological Society of Washington. Washington, D.C.: Printed for the Society, 1882.

Trenholm, Virginia Cole. *The Arapahoes, Our People.* Norman: University of Oklahoma Press, 1970.

Trigger, Bruce G. *A History of Archaeological Thought.* Cambridge: Cambridge University Press, 1989.

Truettner, William H., ed. *The West as America: Reinterpreting Images of the Frontier, 1820–1920.* Washington, D.C.: Smithsonian Institution Press, 1991.

Tylor, Edward B. "How the Problems of American Anthropology Present Themselves to the English Mind." *Science* 4 (December 19, 1884): 545–51.

Vedder, Sarah E. *Reminiscences of the District of Columbia: Or, Washington City Seventy-Nine Years Ago, 1830–1909.* St. Louis: A. R. Fleming Printing Co., 1909.

Wake, C. Staniland, ed. *Memoirs of the International Congress of Anthropology.* Chicago: Schulte Publishing Co., 1894.

Waters, Frank. *To Possess the Land: A Biography of Arthur Rochford Manby.* Chicago: Swallow Press, 1973.

Weimann, Jeanne Madeline. *The Fair Women.* Chicago: Academy Press, 1981.

White, Leslie A. *Zia—The Sun Symbol Pueblo.* 1962. Reprint, Albuquerque: Calvin Horn Publisher, 1974.

White, Richard. *"It's Your Misfortune and None of My Own": A New History of the American West.* Norman: University of Oklahoma Press, 1991.

Whiteley, Peter M. *Deliberate Acts: Changing Hopi Culture Through the Oraibi Split.* Tucson: University of Arizona Press, 1988.

Whyte, James H. *The Uncivil War: Washington During the Reconstruction, 1865–1878.* New York: Twayne Publishers, 1958.

Wickersham, James P. *A History of Education in Pennsylvania.* 1886. Reprint, New York: Arno Press, 1969.

Wilken, Robert L. *Anselm Weber, O.F.M., Missionary to the Navaho, 1898–1921.* Milwaukee: Bruce Publishing Co., 1955.

Wilkins, Thurman. *Thomas Moran: Artist of the Mountains.* 2nd ed. Norman: University of Oklahoma Press, 1998.

Wilson, Chris. *The Myth of Santa Fe: Creating a Modern Regional Tradition.* Albuquerque: University of New Mexico Press, 1997.

Wilson, John P. "Cushing at Zuni: Another View." *The Archaeological Society of New Mexico* 28 (2002): 141–46.

Wilson, Margaret Gibbons. *The American Woman in Transition: The Urban Influence, 1870–1920.* Westport, Conn.: Greenwood Press, 1979.

Winchester, Robert Glenn. *James Pinckney Henderson, Texas' First Governor.* San Antonio, Tex.: The Naylor Co., 1971.

Woloch, Nancy. *Women and the American Experience.* 2nd ed. New York: McGraw-Hill, Inc., 1994.

Woodbury, Nathalie F. S. "Past is Present, Tilly's Trials." *Anthropology Newsletter* 27 (March 1986): 3–4.

Woodbury, Richard B. "Zuni Prehistory and History to 1850." In *Handbook of North American Indians,* vol. 9, *Southwest,* ed. Alfonso Ortiz, 467–73. Washington, D.C.: Smithsonian Institution, 1979.

Woodbury, Richard B., and Nathalie F. S. Woodbury. "The Rise and Fall of the Bureau of American Ethnology." *Journal of the Southwest* 41 (autumn 1999): 283–96.

Woody, Thomas. *A History of Women's Education in the United States.* 2 vols. New York: Science Press, 1929.

Worster, Donald. *A River Running West: The Life of John Wesley Powell.* New York: Oxford University Press, 2001.

Zumwalt, Rosemary Levy. *Wealth and Rebellion: Elsie Clews Parsons, Anthropologist and Folklorist.* Urbana: University of Illinois Press, 1992.

Unpublished Theses and Dissertations

Cain, Ellen Marie. "God, Grace, and Government: Taylor and Mary Ealy in the American Southwest, 1874–1881." Ph.D. diss., University of New Mexico, 2001.

Lawson, Michael J. "Baskets, Pots, and Prayer Plumes: The Southwest Ethnographic Collections of the Smithsonian Institution." Ph.D. diss., Arizona State University, 2003.

May, Laurie D. "The Women's Anthropological Society, 1885–1899: 'Earnest in the Search for Truth.'" M.A. thesis, George Washington University, 1988.

Noelke, Virginia. "The Origin and Early History of the Bureau of American Ethnology, 1879–1910." Ph.D. diss., University of Texas at Austin, 1974.

Online Sources

"The Battle of Gettysburg, 1863." <http://www.eyewitnesstohistory.com/gtburg.htm>. (September 3, 2003).

Henry, Mary. Diary. <http://www.si.edu/archives/documents/mary.htm>. (September 3, 2003).

Seitter, John Reid. "Union City: Philadelphia and the Battle of Gettysburg." <http://www.gdg.org/seiter.htm>. (September 4, 2003).

Personal Communications

Fernlund, Kevin. February 25, 2004.

Hart, E. Richard. June 12, 2005.

Hieb, Louis A. November 2004–March 2006.

Parezo, Nancy J. January 3, 2005.

Peacock, Ronnie. April 17, 2003.

Index